DROPPERS

DROPPERS

America's First Hippie Commune, Drop City

MARK MATTHEWS

UNIVERSITY OF OKLAHOMA PRESS : NORMAN

Also by Mark Matthews

Smoke Jumping on the Western Fire Line: Conscientious Objectors during World War II (Norman, 2006)

A Great Day to Fight Fire: Mann Gulch, 1949 (Norman, 2007)

Unless otherwise noted, all photographs are from the private collection of Eugene Debs Bernofsky.

Library of Congress Cataloging-in-Publication Data

Matthews, Mark, 1951–
  Droppers : America's first hippie commune, Drop City / Mark Matthews.
      p.   cm.
  ISBN 978-0-8061-4058-2 (pbk. : alk. paper)
  1. Drop City (Colo. : Commune) 2. Communal living—Colorado—
History. 3. Hippies—Colorado—History. 4. Counterculture—Colorado—
History. I. Title.
  HQ971.5.C6M38 2010
  307.77'40869—dc22

                                                        2008053776

The paper in this book meets the guidelines for permanence and durability of the Committee on Production Guidelines for Book Longevity of the Council on Library Resources, Inc. ∞

1 2 3 4 5 6 7 8 9 10

To Juan A. Llado and the kind, generous people of the Dominican Republic

LBJ's Vision of America

This nation . . . has man's first chance to create a Great Society: a society of success without squalor, beauty without barrenness, of genius without the wretchedness of poverty. We can open the doors of learning. We can open the doors of opportunity and closed community—not just to the privileged few, but, thank God, we can open doors to everyone. . . . For half a century we called upon unbridled invention and untiring industry to create an order of plenty for all. The challenge of the next half-century is whether we have the wisdom to use that wealth to enrich and elevate our national life, and to advance the quality of our American civilization.

—*Lyndon B. Johnson*
Ann Arbor, Michigan, 1965

Bernofsky's Vision of America

In 1965, our idea was to let humanity evolve through a process of satisfying wholesome creative drives. Then we would have a world of peace and fulfillment. It was all done in the context of the ugly Vietnam War where blood was being shed on both sides for no reason. . . . I wanted to try to make something positive and wholesome based on the idealism of my youth. We wanted to counterbalance all the chaos around us and demonstrate that we could build another type of life. . . . The war had grown to be a constant background noise, a disturbing STATIC across American society.

—*E. V. D. Bernofsky*
Missoula, Montana, 2004

DROPPERS

STATIC. . . . *A well-timed bomb presumably planted by the Viet Cong blasted the Brink Hotel in downtown Saigon which serves as a U.S. officers quarters, injuring 63 Americans and killing two Americans.* . . . *Purchasing power is increasing most rapidly for two disparate groups: the oldsters and the youngsters.* . . . *After seven days ended the battle of Binhgia—longest and bloodiest of the South Viet Nam War. The final score: 195 government troops, 182 wounded, 62 missing, five Americans killed, 9 wounded, three captured; an estimated 140 Viet Cong dead, two captured.* . . . *the U.S. may be willing to carry on the war for another decade—its financial cost of $2 million a day is tolerable.* . . . *While one white woman stood on a chair screaming "Get him, get him, get him!" Robinson landed two punches on Martin Luther King's head, and two kicks to his groin.* . . . *Massed in the street before the embassy was a cursing fist-shaking throng led by some 300 yellow-robed Buddhist monks.* . . . *The U.S. government to give $5.5 million to support clinics where birth control information and supplies are given.* . . .
(January 1965)[1]

Film Premier

The first time I heard Eugene Victor Debs Bernofsky talk about Drop City, this nation's first hippie commune, I was attending a small gathering in Missoula, Montana, during the fall of 2002.[2] A score of people connected with the local environmental community had congregated at the house of an activist to celebrate the premiere of Bernofsky's latest film, *Trembling Waters*. Before screening the unconventional video on a conventional television set in a conventional middle-class living room, Bernofsky described the piece as an environmental advocacy film. Over the last twenty years he had already produced a dozen such works, including *Undermining Yellowstone*, which had been instrumental in drawing public attention to a proposed gold-mining operation on the border of Yellowstone National Park during the years of the Clinton administration. In *Trembling Waters* Bernofsky attempted to turn public opinion against the Dupont

3

Chemical Corporation, which wanted to develop a titanium mine along the border of Georgia's Okeefenokee Swamp. In the film a dozen or so local "crackers," scientists, and environmentalists expressed their concerns that the mine would alter the water table within the wetlands, leading to the death of the swamp and its myriad wildlife species as well as the destruction of the local tourist and outdoor recreation industry.

As usual, there was nothing slick about a Bernofsky World Wide Films production. The voices of the participants sometimes cracked with emotion; the presentation avoided most hard science and statistics in order to concentrate on the human interest and wildlife angles. Bernofsky had already copied the film onto hundreds of videocassettes and had mailed them to media outlets across the Southeast and to politicians in Washington, D.C. DuPont would later abandon the project because of rising public opposition.

After the modest premiere that evening, many guests lingered around a large dining-room table in hopes that the filmmaker would tell some vintage Bernofsky tales. He didn't disappoint. Bernofsky was an impresario, a master at delivering interesting context with ironic twists and perfect comedic timing. I swallowed his stories hook, line, and sinker—until I noticed, at times, the rapscallion gleam in his eye, which left me questioning my naivety. I noticed others looking about, making eye contact, attempting to corroborate the truth or identify a prevarication. But Bernofsky never broke the spell. He kept us bewitched, never once admitting he might be pulling our legs. He was a deft storyteller. I left, that evening, a believer of everything he told us—even though I knew better. That evening, he told the following tale about the nation's first hippie commune.

"A bunch of us were driving back from Pueblo, Colorado, where we had spent the day chopping the tops off of junked cars to use as construction material for a geodesic dome we were building. It was getting dark, and we saw this glitzy gold

The mailman cinematographer (Photo by Mark Matthews)

Cadillac parked in front of this backwoods country saloon. We knew we needed one more car top and we all started fantasizing about how wonderful a golden panel would look at the top of the dome, so I told the boys that I'd go into the bar and make sure that everything was cool while they chopped off the top. I stayed in the bar for about five minutes and ordered some beers to go, and in the meantime, I distracted the bar patrons with some shucking and jiving. Meanwhile, the boys were out there in the dark, quietly and quickly chopping that car's roof off. And when I went back out there, we all zipped into the truck and stormed on out of there. And I remember, a tense moment when the sheriff followed us for a block or so and Steve Baer, who was driving, was kind of sweating it a little—but we got back on the highway and bombed along to Trinidad."

| Audubon Article |

Bernofsky had made some vague mention of Drop City, located about ten miles outside Trinidad, Colorado, when I first interviewed him for an *Audubon* magazine assignment earlier that year. He told me he had founded the commune with two fellow graduates from the University of Kansas in the spring of 1965. I mentioned the fact in the article, but at the time I didn't think to indulge in any fact-checking. During the same interview he also informed me he had majored at KU in a scientific field called radiation biology or radiation biophysics—I don't remember exactly. I never bothered to fact-check that bit of information either.

A few months after the *Audubon* piece appeared, I ran into Bernofsky on the street in Missoula. He was chuckling to himself, and I asked him what was up. He then confessed that he had *laid a dropping* on me only once during our interview. I asked what a "dropping" was. "Well, it's something like this. There is no such field of study at KU that I told you I had majored in."

When I pressed him as to why he had lied to me, he answered: "People put too much emphasis on degrees and titles. I knew you would be more impressed if I told you I had majored in some esoteric scientific field than if I told you I had studied early childhood education. Interestingly enough, the alumni magazine at the University of Kansas phoned me for an interview after your article appeared in *Audubon*. They also wanted to write a story on me. They asked me the same question about my major, and I laid the same dropping on them. They mentioned the exact same imaginary field of study. Now that was a major dropping, considering they were writing about their own institution."

I ran into Bernofsky from time to time—something not hard to do in a small university town like Missoula, home to many outdoor enthusiasts and a glut of locally owned coffee shops. Bernofsky rode his bicycle everywhere—a hybrid street-and-mountain bike with a heavy durable frame and skinny tires. After retiring from the postal service, he had begun to make movies virtually from the seat of this bike, pedaling from Missoula to far-flung realms such as North Dakota and Utah in order to track down the possible exploitation of public lands by corporate America—mostly mining companies. (He had flown to Georgia to film the Okeefenokee.) In many respects, he was a low-budget Michael Moore, but not as ego driven, nor as physically big. He did, however, dress as casually as Moore—usually donning jeans, a white canvas shirt with frayed cuffs, and a ball cap that featured the World Wide Films logo. Whenever outdoors, he slipped on a pair of shades with thick black frames that somehow or other he had managed to keep from breaking or misplacing for more than forty years. You can see him wearing the same sunglasses in photos taken at the commune in 1965. By the time I met him, Bernofsky had already turned sixty. His curly dark hair had thinned on top to form a thick bird's nest around a goose egg–sized bald spot, and any grandmother would have enjoyed taking a stab at pinching his chubby cheeks. I never would have considered supplementing the thousand words I had already written about Bernofsky for *Audubon* had it not been for the novelist T. C. Boyle.

| T. C. Boyle |

One Sunday morning during the winter of 2003, I came upon a review of Boyle's newest novel, *Drop City*, in the *Missoulian*. The reviewer described the work as a satirical look at a hippie commune. The next time I ran into Bernofsky I mentioned the review, and he told me he'd already contacted the publisher to request a free copy, since "I was the one who founded the real Drop City." The publisher complied, and Bernofsky later lent the novel to me.

The plot of Boyle's book alternates between two parallel story lines. One line follows the paths of a young hippie couple, Star and Marco, and their cohorts who live at a commune in Sonoma County, California; the other keeps track of a handful of survivalist homesteaders in Alaska, including Sess Harder and his mail-order bride, Pamela. The young residents of the commune frequently walk about naked, have sex with multiple partners, get high on various drugs such as pot and LSD or get drunk on wine and beer, argue, fight, seemingly defecate behind every bush, and beg and bully money from visitors. They work as little as possible and show little artistic talent or initiative. At one point a bunch of young men rape a teenage girl, but no one takes action against them. Eventually, when local law and health authorities threaten to bulldoze the property, the commune's leader decides to relocate rather than fight city hall. The two plots intertwine by mid-book, when a busload of hippies from the commune drive to Alaska to develop a new community in the wilderness—the ultimate back-to-the-land statement. At one point in the novel, when the commune leader announces he is relocating to Alaska, I actually laughed out loud—which I seldom do when reading. Overall I found the novel amusing, but I soon forgot the characters and situations; nor could I wring any deep message out of the text (probably the reason for its popularity).

But there was one thing I couldn't get out of my mind—I kept picturing Bernofsky in the role of the commune leader, named Sender. I could imagine him *shucking and jiving* the immigration officials at the Canadian border, to distract them from searching the bus for drugs by telling them that the hippies were connected with the Grateful Dead rock band—just as the Sender character does. And I could imagine Bernofsky suggesting something just as romantic and ridiculous as relocating to Alaska.

Even though Boyle named his novel *Drop City*, the author seemed to know nothing about Bernofsky. Instead, Boyle allegedly based his commune leader, Norm Sender, on a certain Ramon Sender, the first resident of an early commune located just outside Sebastapol, California, called the Morning Star Ranch. Boyle's Sender character promotes the original Morning Star philosophy of "LATWIDNO"—Land Access to Which Is Denied No One.

Reaction to Boyle's Novel

Timothy Miller, a historian of American religion and a commune expert at the University of Kansas, pointed out in a review that Boyle also makes direct allusions to other intentional communities of that period. Boyle writes of a child drowning in a murky swimming pool, an incident that occurred at Olompali Ranch in Marin County. Outside Boyle's Drop City, a car hits and kills a loose horse, another incident that happened at Olompali Ranch. Boyle also distorts the open-marriage policy of the Kerista commune in San Francisco, into "making it with anybody who asked, no matter their race or creed or color or whether they were fat or old or retarded or smelled like the underside of somebody's shoe."[3]

Boyle's depiction of communes angered some former intentional community residents. Pam Hanna, a writer who once lived at Morning Star, described Boyle's characterization of her community as a condemnatory cartoon from hell, the *Zap Comix* version. She complained that he "takes snippets of actual lifestyles and happenings of the period, and weaves [them] into a complete fabrication and caricature, not readily apparent to anyone who has not lived through and participated of the communal life of the era. Nowhere is there mention of the new social order attempted or the continuation of that social order in hundreds of communes that survive to the present time." Ramon Sender also accused Boyle of misrepresenting the residents of Morning Star as "humorless, unrelentingly wasted and sad, with no redeeming qualities."[4]

Bernofsky's critique of the novel was more terse: "It's total bullshit. It was nothing like that." I sensed a challenge in Bernofsky's tone of voice. When I remarked that people might be interested in reading about the real Drop City, Bernofsky looked at me and said: "It's about time you recognized that. What do you think I've been hinting at for the last year? I'm surprised it took you so long to suggest it."

In reality I had loftier ambitions than just writing about a commune. I had recently gotten interested in the literary concept of writing biographies about seemingly normal, un-famous people who had led fascinating lives that remained far below the media radar. During our casual conversations, Bernofsky had already told me about his lifetime complicity in subversive but still legal actions to keep the political and financial establishments from riding roughshod over his fellow citizens. Besides taking on international mining companies, he had championed union causes during the Reagan years, when most Americans turned to worshipping management and denigrating labor. He had exposed the hypocrisy and mismanagement within the postal service, for which he had worked for thirty years. He had been an underground avant-garde film director during the seventies and eighties. I envisioned a full-blown biography of the man—*The Bernofsky Files*—in three parts, covering his youth, the commune era, and the environmental-advocacy film-making anti-career.

When I suggested this slant to Bernofsky, he balked. "I don't want you turning me into some posturing buffoon." Feeling that he might react this way, I had prepared the perfect argument to convince him to cooperate: I told him he was right, that the world should be content with reading books about truly inspiring people like Dick Cheney, George W. Bush, Donald Trump, and Paris Hilton. By the look on Bernofsky's face I knew I'd struck home. "Why do you want to waste all your time writing about me?" he asked. After I explained why I thought it was important, he shrugged and agreed to do it.

I would not classify myself as a James Boswell, who flattered and fawned over the subject of the first modern biography, Samuel Johnson, but Bernofsky certainly did show signs of brilliant sarcasm and insightful wisdom equal to those of the eighteenth-century essayist, critic, and father of the English dictionary. I dived into the project, certain that a story of Bernofsky's life would amuse as well as inspire—and maybe even more than Boswell's *Life of Johnson.*

The Interviews Begin

On February 25, 2004, I drove across town to Bernofsky's home, a modest cottage standing next to one of the town's fire stations. A series of government and industrial signs warning the public to stay out of certain places and to refrain from certain activities—no bicycle riding, no trespassing, private property, which Bernofsky had *collected* from various sources over the years—lined a wooden fence surrounding a big backyard. He called the signs his Wall of Bureaucratic Negativity. After a short tour of his small and thoroughly frozen vegetable garden, Bernofsky escorted me into a tidy office in the house, where he edited his films on a computer that one of his two sons had built for him. When he asked me where he should start, I indicated that the beginning would be a good place. He took me literally.

"I was born in 1941. I went to Public School 132 in Brooklyn." He stopped to show me his junior high school diploma dated June 29, 1956, as if, after the radiation biology prevarication I would demand documented evidence to verify every aspect of his life. But my eyes strayed to a pastel drawing dated 1943, which hung on the wall above the desk. The handsome man

with spectacles, wavy hair, and mustache had an intense expression on his face. Bernofsky identified the man as his father,
David Bernosfky.

"He was a developed intellectual," Bernofsky said. "He was
born in Riga, Latvia, in 1903. His father, my grandfather Bernard
Bernofsky, had been an active socialist-Marxist revolutionary
in Latvia and Eastern Europe. His family were secular Jews.
Bernard was selected by his cell (the title capitalists gave the
organizations) to go to Philadelphia to organize socialist groups.
The capitalists accused Bernard and his associates of fomenting
revolution, but they never talked about themselves as violent
revolutionaries. They wanted to achieve humanitarian ideals.
They saw that the wealth of nations was derived from its workers and they thought it should belong to the workers as well.

"In Philadelphia, my father's parents moved into a house
on Orchard Street in a very poor section of town. My grandmother Rose supported the family by selling buttons, ribbons,
latches, and trimmings from a pushcart on Market Street, while
Bernard was out organizing. My dad grew up in that kind of
environment. He was gifted intellectually and musically, and
he became a very proficient violinist and supported himself
by giving music lessons. That's also how he put himself through
Temple University, where he was one of the few immigrant
children to be accepted into a graduate program at the time.
He majored in philosophy in graduate school and was offered
a teaching assistantship. As he taught an introductory course
in philosophy, it became apparent to the administration that
he was a Marxist and they fired him. That action only inspired
my father to become more active in the neighborhood socialist
groups, and the Party soon assigned him to educate new recruits.
He was in his early twenties at the time, a tough little street-
savvy bugger," is how Bernofsky described him.

While at Temple, David Bernofsky played the mando-cello
in the Philadelphia Mandolin Orchestra, where he met Maria
Adele Stipleman.

"My mother," Bernofsky continued, "was born in 1907 in
Chernovitz, Bukovina, Rumania, a town surrounded by mountains,
just like here in western Montana. She came from a middle-
class family; her mother was a teacher, and her father was a
Jewish Marxist like David's father. Her dad was a wonderful,
jovial, tough son-of-a-bitch who, like a lot of Jews from small
villages, had been drafted into the czar's army. He had to serve
for twenty years. During one battle—maybe it was during the
Russo-Japanese War—he lost a leg. For the rest of his life he
stomped around on a wooden or iron peg, but his spirits were
always high. After the amputation, my grandfather moved the
family from Russia to Austria, where they stayed in Vienna for
a couple of years so he could avoid any further military commitment. Then they sailed to America and settled in Philadelphia. My mom was thirteen or fourteen at the time and spoke
no English. She liked to tell us the story about when she was
being processed at Ellis Island and some kind person handed
her a banana to eat. She'd never seen a banana before and she
ate it skin and all. 'The skin was so bitter,' she'd tell us, 'but
the person was so kind I just had to smile and thank him.' My
mother's family lived in a better neighborhood than my father's
family because they had a little money. After my mother and
father met in the orchestra, Dad would visit Mary's home, but
my grandmother didn't want Dad coming around. When she
saw him coming she would step outside and throw rocks at him.

David and Mary Bernofsky

"So they found some other ways to meet,
and they soon moved in together in a Communist commitment that didn't require any
official capitalistic marriage documents, which they considered
phony. During World War II, Dad decided to join the army to
fight Hitler, but he needed to show a marriage certificate so
that my mother could receive any benefits—and so they got
married, by a judge. My brother was born in 1933 and my parents

David and Mary
Bernofsky

named him after Karl Marx. He later dropped the Marx, and
changed his first name to Carl. My parents weren't officially
married until 1943. When I was older, I was going through my
father's papers one day and I found the marriage certificate. I
showed it to Carl and said: 'Look at this Carl, you're a bastard.'
He was absolutely blown away and thereupon confronted my
parents, and they finally told him the truth. When my father
had gone to sign up for the service, they wouldn't take him
anyway because he was as blind as a bat. So he had gotten
married for nothing.

"My parents named me after the socialist leader Eugene Victor Debs. Both of them loved Debs because he spoke out so articulately for the working people and opposed the ruling classes. He was thrown in jail during World War I. He was a fiery speaker and, personally, a man of deep, straightforward compassion and gentleness. He was hated by those in power because he exposed their constant hypocrisy to their faces. My parents may have heard Debs talk. I'm not sure if they ever met him. Unlike Debs, my father had a well-thought-out rationalization for bloody revolution—to storm the bastions and take over. If it had to be violent, it would be. Debs felt it could be done in a more organized, more diplomatic way by using the force of public opinion. Both men believed in the inevitability of the establishment of socialism. Debs believed in an evolutionary movement while Dad thought, 'why wait and suffer and bleed for a hundred years? Let's take over now.'

"Soon after shacking up in Philadelphia, my parents moved to New York City," Bernofsky continued. "The Party sent my dad there to organize revolutionary groups. Since he was one of the main socialist educators on the East Coast they wanted him in New York. Before they moved, my grandmother Rose called some of her suppliers on New York's East Side and asked them to extend wholesale credit to my father so he could purchase a pushcart. All the wholesalers on the East Side were Jewish. When I was older, I would go with my dad on Sundays to the wholesalers and I would see nothing on the shelves in one place but zippers—from small delicate zippers for women's skirts to some with great big teeth for men's jackets; another wholesaler would carry nothing but ribbons, and another something else. They got my father started and eventually he developed a business. Wherever he went he would talk about socialist ideology, and after a while it became known that David Bernofsky was a left-wing activist. People always seemed happy to see him and they respected his work. Eventually, everyone knew about his ideas."

I found Bernofsky's tale fascinating, but I couldn't help thinking about the imaginary college major of radiation biology. I knew that World War II marked the high point of socialism in the United States, especially after Russia joined the fight against fascism. But after the war, especially during the fifties, U.S. politicians had done their best to obliterate American communism. So I asked Bernofsky if the FBI had ever harassed his father. He assured me that the agency had a thick file on David Bernofsky, adding that there was probably a file on himself as well. I asked him if there was any chance he might send in a Freedom of Information Act request to obtain a copy of the files. "I don't think I want to get involved in digging up those ghosts," he said. But in the end Bernofsky came through and hand delivered a copy of an extensive file to me.

. . . The economy's health is also nourished by the fact that the economic effects of World War Two's high birth rate are being fully felt. Onetime war babies are having children of their own. . . . There has been increased activity by Moslem fanatics; who are particularly opposed to the shah of Iran selling mosque-owned estates to land-hungry peasants and his grants of social and political equality to women. . . . One reason why homosexuals are so rarely cured is that they rarely try treatment. Too many of them actually believe that they are happy and satisfied the way they are. . . . Devising major modern weapons has become such an expensive business that few nations can afford to get into it alone. Result: many of them in the free world are coming shopping in the U.S. . . . as each Negro turned away, he merely went to the end of the line. This enraged Sheriff James Clark, who started whacking about with his billy club and crying: "You are making a mockery of justice." . . . What McNamara did not say was that the present U.S. policy of advising but not fighting in Viet Nam is hardly a winning strategy. . . .
(February 1965)[5]

FBI Files

Everything Bernofsky told me about his father checked out in the FBI file. The feds noted that David Bernofsky of 202 Avenue F, Brooklyn, New York, registered with the American Labor Party in 1943. The next year, he joined the Boro Park Club of the C(ommunist) P(arty) of the Ninth Assembly District (AD), Brooklyn New York. On February 27, 1950, the file noted, the elder Bernofsky became the education director for the Waterfront Region. The bureau also stated that he subscribed to communist publications such as *The Worker* and the *National Guardian*. After interviewing David Bernofsky on August 19, 1953, a special agent filed this report: "He admitted his identity and stated that he did not care to cooperate with the FBI. He said that he did not consider the CP to be a group which desires to overcome/throw the Government of the United States by force and violence and added: I do not care to discuss this topic further now or at any further time with the FBI."[6]

Bernofsky then told me, "My father set up his pushcart on Thirteenth Avenue in Brooklyn. Mostly Jews and Italians shopped in that area. Pushcart vendors spread along the sidewalks for several blocks offering various items; one would sell carrots and cabbage, another bananas, another pickles. They stood out there all winter long in the freezing cold. After the war my father went to see Mayor LaGuardia and told him that he had organized the pushcart vendors and that they wanted the city to provide them an indoor market. A year later, the city built City Market on Thirteenth Avenue. My dad's prestige grew after that. Now the vendors set up stands lining the aisles inside the building. At night they would pull down the shutters and lock up. I was really proud when I saw the place packed with people. It was like a mall. On the exterior wall, they mounted a brass plaque stating its history with my dad's name included in a list of people who helped in the project. That was the

kind of work he wanted to do in conjunction with the Communist Party. I remember walking around the market as a little
kid, visiting the stalls, and the vendors were always so happy to
give me something to eat. I didn't have to buy anything.

"When I was in the third grade, my father opened up a store
a block from the market on Thirteenth Avenue. He called it
Dave's Notions and Trimmings, and he made covered buttons
and buckles for Italian women who wanted them to match the
material of dresses they designed and sewed. Dad had a button-
making machine with molds for ball, flat, half-round, and other
types of buttons. He set me up in the back of the store and I
worked there. After a while I got to be pretty good at it, and
my father paid me small amounts of money. I think I started
doing that in the fourth grade. Before that, in the City Market,
I was one of the kids who took care of the rat traps in the
basement. I cleaned out the trapped rats and set fresh traps.
It was a grim and scary job. Sometimes my mother helped me
with an allowance, and my brother was always generous."

The Second Interview

My next interview with Bernofsky took place
on March 2, 2004. This time I rode my bicycle
downtown to a small coffee shop, The Cata-
lyst, on Higgins Avenue in Missoula. After crossing the bridge
over the Clark Fork River, I passed under the shadows of the
Wilma building, a handsome buff-colored brick building constructed in a subtle rhomboid shape. The eight-story structure,
the tallest downtown, housed a grand theater and apartments
at the time. The rest of the main drag, which dead-ended at the
old Northern Pacific Railroad depot about half a mile away,
sported buildings of brick and stone two to four stories tall.
The architectural designs dated from the turn of the twentieth
century to the fifties. Over the last decade, most of the shops
and stores had transformed from utilitarian enterprises such as
pharmacies and low-budget clothing stores to upscale boutiques

and coffee shops. I locked my bike to a stand near The Catalyst, at the alley corner of an Art Deco building across the street from the turn-of-the-century brick mercantile, which at the time housed The Bon department store. That winter had been mild, with moderate temperatures and little snow (as had been the trend a number of years), which made for good biking weather. A few minutes later I spotted my interviewee coming up Higgins, pedaling at his slow methodical pace.

Bernofsky dismounted on the far side of the avenue and pushed his bike across at the pedestrian crossing. He wore a woolen watch cap under his bike helmet. Inside, we ordered drip coffee. When the barrista turned her back to fill our cups, Bernofsky snatched a fifty-cent muffin from the "day-old plate" on the counter and slipped it into his jacket pocket. He countered my astonished stare with the grin of a Cheshire cat. "What?" his sparkling eyes asked. I said nothing. I followed him up a set of stairs to a small balcony where there were a half dozen tables, each big enough for two. From our perch we looked down on about two-thirds of the main floor. Bernofsky took out the muffin and said, "I only took it to shock you. I put the money in the tip jar. Besides, the coffee is overpriced." He didn't add sugar or cream. After taking a sip, he began to tell me the story of his life, from the beginning again.

"I was born at the Brooklyn Doctors Hospital. The only home I remember was at 202 Avenue F. It was a six-story tenement at the corner of East Second Street. We lived in a ground floor apartment whose windows looked out on the street and the courtyard. It was a corner apartment. My mom loved it. The hallway and stairway were very dark. The foyer was about twenty feet long and led to the kitchen, which had a window looking out on the courtyard. The living room lay straight ahead. My parents slept there on a fold-away bed. To the right was a bedroom that I shared with my brother.

"My brother's desk sat in the foyer. Books spilled off of shelves everywhere. We had a great number of books that had

Red diaper
babies Eugene
Victor Debs and
Karl Marx

been published by International Publishers—left-wing, radical
material. There was the complete works of Lenin, and of Marx,
Engels, and Ricardo—alternative literature. And the naturalists
like Balzac and Zola—stories about ordinary people and their
struggles. There was also Henry Miller and Arthur Miller. The
conversations around the table were often heated and intense
and sometimes got out of hand. I rebelled against both my
father's Stalinism and my mother's Trotskyism. My brother stayed

out of the fray because he wanted to become a scientist. There was also tons of music, too. Other musicians would come over to play trios and quartets with my parents. And people on the FBI's black list constantly came through the underground to spend the night, sleeping on another pullout bed."

Red Diaper Babies Eugene Victor Debs and Karl Marx

Bernofsky explained that many of his childhood friends were also "red diaper" babies, like Fred Papele from Montauk Junior High School whose mother, Annie Papele, was sympathetic to the American Labor Party and had participated in the progressive movement for a while. "She was an intelligent, compassionate woman who really cared about human rights issues. I think Fred's dad was in the construction business."

Bernofsky later lent me a book about red diaper babies.[7] Apparently, Communist Party members first used the term as a derogative expression aimed at comrades who had risen through Party ranks because of their birthright rather than through hard work and commitment. The John Birch Society co-opted the phrase in 1964 when it published the names of children from communist families who attended the University of California at Berkeley, where students were becoming involved in political activism. Instead of being intimidated, those red diaper students who were already politically active merely used the list to recruit others.

The two Bernofsky boys discovered many other red diaper babies like Fred Papele among their playmates. In some neighborhoods, especially in the Red Belt of the Bronx, politics had tipped so far to the left that most inhabitants considered Socialists to be extreme right-wingers. In 1944 the Special Committee of the Un-American Activities reported that communists were running for office in New York under the auspices of the American Labor Party: "The communists are thus enabled to present their candidates for elective office under other than a straight communist label."[8]

The committee also reported that the APL had aggressively targeted the entire state of New York. "Although they fell short of their goal, APL succeeded in capturing the Manhattan and Brooklyn sections of the American Labor Party but outside of New York City they have been unable to win control."[9] Moreover, the Bernofsky boys' politically inspired first and middle names weren't unusual. During the thirties and forties, many left-leaning parents gave their children names associated with the Leftist parties or their famous leaders. One set of twins bore the first names Marx and Engel; another boy was named Lesta, a combination of Lenin and Stalin. In the girl's name Commilda, the "C-o-m-m" stood for Communist, and the "i-l-d" for the International Labor Defense. Lenin spelled backward produced the name Ninel. There were also instances of Stalina and Proletaria.

Bicycle Boy

"East Second Street was six blocks down from Ocean Parkway, which traverses Brooklyn from Prospect Park to Coney Island," Bernofsky explained. "It's a four-lane street. On one side was an old horse path, on the other side a pedestrian walkway and a bicycle path. Along the pedestrian path stood benches where the tenement residents hung out. I did a lot of bike riding on a three-speed English racer that I had gotten for my sixth grade graduation at Montague Junior High.

"In the other direction, a block west, ran the elevated train— the Culver Line, which came out of Manhattan from under the East River and ran above McDonald Avenue to Coney Island. The trains were a constant presence, really loud day and night. Along McDonald Avenue ran trolley cars, electrified with booms reaching up to the wires. The trolleys whizzed by around the clock. There was a car barn nearby where the trains turned around

Bicycle boy

or were repaired. For some reason there was an element in my emotional makeup that would say to me, 'there's got to be something else than all this cement, traffic, trains, and trolley cars.' And so I went looking for it. I cut school and went on long bike rides and walks—as far as I could go. But I could never get beyond the concrete and the noise of people. I often rode the ferry that went to Staten Island. It cost a nickel. I believe that my obsession to get out originated from my gazing out at the ocean from Brighton Beach. The parkway and trolleys ended at the ocean, and I would end my rides there. I could see nothing but endless water. And this fascinated me and gave me an emotional conception that something lay beyond.

I wanted out of the city prison. Everything was closing in on me.
I always felt like a little shadow in the big canyon of buildings.
I experienced nightmares. I spent years walking and riding
my bicycle, wondering if I could even get across the George
Washington Bridge. When I finally did, the world opened up
for me—in New Jersey, of all places. When I finally pedaled
across the bridge and crossed it into New Jersey, I could see
the mountains at New York's Bear Mountain State Park. That was
a major transformation for me. I had started my wanderings
about age twelve or thirteen.

Public Education

"The only thing I ever loved about public
education was kindergarten—the singing,
dancing, painting, and birthday parties,"
Bernofsky said. "We had wonderful teachers who loved the kids,
and we played with building blocks on the floor in this big
room with tables scattered about. It was a warm, wonderful
deal. On my first day of first grade, my mom walked me to
P[ublic] S[chool] 132, which was a gigantic building—like a
stone mausoleum. I remember walking down the hallway until
we came up to the door of the classroom. I looked into the
room and saw all the desks lined up in perfect rows. I'm looking
in, but I don't go in. I say to my mother: 'What is this? I'm not
going in there.' She explains to me that first grade is different
from kindergarten and that everyone has their own seat. I turn
around and run down the hall with my mom chasing after
me. I run out the school and down a block before she catches
up with me and we walk home, but only after she promised I
didn't have to go back. When we got home she told me she
would introduce me to Mrs. Tully so that I could talk to her
about how I felt. If I decided I liked Mrs. Tully, then I could sit
in a seat and see what it was like. If not, I didn't have to go to
school. Mrs. Tully really knew about child psychology. Somehow she praised me. 'I can teach you how to become a very

skilled reader,' she told me. I really wanted to learn how to read. Later, she used me in the classroom to help the other children learn to read, and I didn't feel so locked up in those rows and files of seats. That grid thing really upset me. It took me a long time to feel comfortable. Mrs. Tully kept me busy learning and she opened up my mind.

"When I was twelve I inherited a camera. For the first time I realized I could make my own world. Up until then I felt as if I had been forced into a mold, to sit in this desk, read this book, walk down this street—but when I started looking through the lens of the camera and developing the photographs I started getting a feeling of building a soul that was uniquely mine. My brother, Carl, who had many interests and abilities, had constructed a mobile darkroom in our bathroom—with a red light, a yellow, and a blue, an enlarger, chemical trap, developer, stopper, fixer, printer, and tank for developing negatives. It was organized in units that he could move in and out out of the bathroom. I was in the fifth or sixth grade at the time and Carl showed me how the things worked. When he got a 35 mm camera he gave me the old Kodak bellows camera. It was rectangular in shape, and the bellows would click open. For the first time I felt as if I had a tool and a weapon. On the bicycle I went on expeditions whenever I was able to get away. Many days I skipped school in junior high and pedaled down Thirteenth Avenue West to the Hudson River with my camera. Then I would cruise along the walkway to the Staten Island Ferry Terminal. Many days I only had a nickel to cover the fare, and I stayed on for several trips across the river. The opportunities for photography were amazing. I was able to turn the camera outward to the scenery as well as inward toward the passengers. At that time I was never harassed by the police or any truant officer.

An Old Bellows Camera

"People left me alone. The only time I was accosted was by a cop in Prospect Park who wanted to know why I wasn't in

school. I never told my parents about my trips. The teachers
never complained. They were happy when I didn't show up
since I did everything I could to make their lives miserable—
because they made my life miserable. I always loved going out
on solo adventures. I didn't need other people, not even a
friend. It was self-reinforcing, though I never knew that at the
time. Things were always going on. The bike and the camera
gave me my peculiar idea of normalcy and sanity. Everything
else seemed an anomalous mass of gelatinous misery.

"I had hundreds of boxes full of black-and-white photographs. They were small with a white border around them.
The development process gave me a feeling of self-worth, control, purpose, and meaning. I wanted to play with the negatives
under the enlarger. My brother taught me the standard way,
but I would take a negative and hold it at an angle under the
enlarger to get a great distorted image. I thought that was
terrific. I would also experiment by putting negatives on top
of each other, or I would curl them and bend them. I ended
up with many images that had no commercial value and were
very chaotic looking. All of a sudden I'm riding my bike all
over Staten Island, taking funny-looking pictures of the Statue
of Liberty and the infamous Brooklyn Asylum, tugboats and
freighters. I was unaware of art, I was just having fun and
playing with the stuff. It was an investigation. People would say
'Study this, learn this, take the negative and put it in this slot.'
I was always saying there must be more. I was driven to prove
it and demonstrate it to myself—for my own satisfaction.

"And I haven't quit. It's an element of my personality that's
always been there. It all started when I ran away from that first
grade classroom. Until then everything was open, free, and
available. Suddenly, everything was slotted into a rigid defini-
tion of life and reality. But for me, life was going to go on as a
fun experiment of discovery. Since then, I have always thought
of art as really phony, that is, to sit down and deliberately create

a work of art for profit and ego. I'm not hanging anything of mine up on the walls of the Museum of Modern Art—not that anyone's ever asked.

"Despite my trouble in school, I loved to read. I often went to the little public library under the El, next to Smith's Candy Store. I read parts of every book in that library, beginning with the As. It was a quiet and peaceful place. And the librarians were kind. It was a major escape from the insanity of the streets, school, and home—where my parents were constantly busy with Party activity. I remember reading a kids' book, *The Eyes of the Woods*. It was a frontiersman story set during the colonial period and the hero was involved with the Indians. That book also planted in me the idea that there was something else out there. I didn't read every book in that library, but I looked at every one—maybe two thousand in all. As I got older I earned a reputation as a troublemaker in the classroom. I believed from junior high on that I had more knowledge and intelligence than any teacher. I wanted to learn, but I couldn't learn in school.

Erasmus High School

"I attended Erasmus High School, a disaster area crammed with thousands of students, in the hallways, in the classrooms, and in a meaningless dictatorship of education. The building—a Gothic stone structure, three or four stories high with a square courtyard in the center—stood on Flatbush Avenue across the street from the First Dutch Reformed Church in which Peter Stuyvesant was buried. The school was named after Desiderius Erasmus, a progressive philosopher of the Enlightenment. As soon as you walked through the main gate, you were in the courtyard facing a statue of Erasmus holding one of his heavy tomes. When it came time to take the regents' exams, students would go up to the statue and throw money up into his book for good luck. I considered it my job to climb up there and help myself to some of that good luck once in a while. Erasmus was, and may still be, the halls of yearning, in the sense that it served to deaden and stifle all youthful enthusiasm. It reminded me of images I had conjured up of the Bastille Prison in eighteenth-century Paris. It seemed as if the youth, when not chained to the walls of the classrooms, were dragging chains with them down the hallways. The adults, by insisting on quiet and regiment, seemed like prison wardens—with very few exceptions.

"The environment was just the opposite of what I found on the street. We were oppressed by this big physical structure, and by adults whose only responsibility seemed to be to put in their eight hours of work. They had very limited ideas about anything significant in life, or for the young idealists in their classrooms. I soon discovered that the oligarchic principles of the school would not hold up if I flaunted them back at the teachers. If I ridiculed the instructors, they'd do nothing except try to enforce stricter discipline upon me. I survived by being the loudest and most disruptive wise guy I could be. In the middle of a lesson I'd blurt out some question, which the teacher would answer, and I'd say something irreverent and the class would break into hysterics. One of the benefits was that the teachers stopped calling on me to give answers. And they'd never test me in class. So then I had to initiate the disruptions myself. My classmates provided plenty of reinforcement. They'd come up to me and say stuff like 'I wish I had the nerve to stand up and give the teacher that kind of shit.' I was trying to establish my presence as a human being instead of a number in a row and file. The pressure from the adults to conform was intense, but I wasn't going to kowtow to them. I found encouragement at home because my parents did not fit into the mainstream either. They never condemned me when the authorities told them I was a discipline problem."

. . . For the first time, U.S. pilots and crewmen in U.S. B-57s and
F-100s swept out in repeated sorties against Viet Cong emplacements in
South Viet Nam. This time there was no talk of Americans being in South
Viet Nam on a mere "advisory" basis. . . . As Malcolm X spoke, three
men rushed down the aisle toward him. Eight feet away they opened fire.
. . . Smoking marijuana seems to be this year's way among students of
preserving the perennial illusion that the younger generation is going to
hell. . . . Suddenly the clubs started swinging. From the sidelines white
townspeople raised their voices in cheers and whoops. . . . according to
a Gallup poll, 67 percent of the U.S. population supports the air strikes.
. . . somewhere between 20 percent and 30 percent of college women are
not virgins by the time they graduate. . . . Since 1940 the crime rate
in this country has doubled. . . . the effect of six months of tumult at
Berkeley has been to show that "students have become somebody in being
able to act together." . . . From all over the U.S., bearded boys, girls in
boots, and a surprising assortment of clergymen flocked to Selma and
Montgomery by the busload. . . . continuous reports of record corporate
earnings have whetted their appetites for a larger share of the profits. . . .
Congress had before it a bill that would make gun-toting tougher. . . .
(March/April 1965) [10]

During our next interview, Bernofsky covered the remainder of his years at Erasmus High. "In the middle of the school
year when I was in the eleventh grade, I packed up a suitcase
and ran away from home. I took what cash I found in my
dad's sock drawer and took the typewriter. It was winter, and
there were about three months left to school. I went to a hotel
on 34th Street—a big, huge, grimy place with little rooms that

Pipe Dreams

they rented by the week. I slapped down the
rent and they gave me a key. The room had
a small window that looked out onto a brick
wall, and a beat-up bureau, and a bed. It was very cheap and
sleazy. I started pecking away on the typewriter. I wanted to

write the novel that would straighten everything out once and for all. The main character was a man who was stuck in a big pipe, deep underground. I called it *Pipe Dreams* or *Man in a Pipe*, or something like that. After two months, I had written forty to fifty pages of earth-shaking new material.

"When I ran away to write, I wanted to make stuff up. I had limited experience, but I had passion, feeling, and imagination. Nowadays, when I make stuff up, everyone thinks I'm a liar. They don't realize it's a challenge to make stuff up and make people believe it. If you're really going to tell lies and have people believe you, then it's good to practice it first. One day my parents, after receiving a tip from some friends, finally tracked me down. My mother begged me to come home and return to school. I did. The next year I earned a D or F average, but I passed all the regents' exams and graduated despite my poor grades. That would have been 1959."

I asked how the University of Kansas had ever accepted him into their program. Bernofsky explained that his brother, Carl, had gotten his bachelor degree from KU and still lived in Lawrence, Kansas, working toward a graduate degree.

"I sent Carl my high school transcript and asked him to get me into the school. Carl admitted to the admissions director that my grades sucked, but he explained that I had some ability and talent in writing. They asked to see some writing examples, so I sent them *Pipe Dreams*. Someone there read it and decided that I could at least read and write, and they accepted me on probation, providing I maintain a C average throughout my freshman year.

Lawrence, Kansas

"Before I moved to Lawrence, Kansas, I thought it would be a backward hick place full of dirt farmers and pig eaters, but I soon found the whole society of Lawrence to be open, trustful, and friendly. People would smile at me on the street and say hello. Making eye contact like that in New York was considered a challenge, and it probably still is. In the Midwest, though, people naturally wanted to get your attention. I was floored by that. Initially I was really excited to have the opportunity to go to college. I naively thought I'd be able to learn and study there, hang around with scholars, and open myself up to wisdom and personal development. But before the first semester was over, I'd realized that college was just a glorified extension of high school. The classes were huge. The campus was packed with kids. The University of Kansas was a factory—much bigger than Erasmus. It offered no opportunity for personal contact with the professors, and they herded us from class to class like cattle. I became disillusioned early on. That first semester I lived with Carl and his wife on Ohio Street, near the campus. They set me up in a private space in the attic where I could carry on. When it got dark outside, I liked to walk around the streets and look for cars in which people had left the keys in the ignition. I would borrow a car, to teach myself how to drive, and then return the car after about half an hour. As time went by, I began driving farther and farther out into the countryside—getting stoned on pot. I kept it discreet and never got into trouble. But I'm sorry now that I never replaced any of the gasoline I used up. To do that type of thing in the city would have been real dangerous.

"When I first arrived at KU, the student body seemed to have no knowledge of marijuana. I think I was the one who brought it to that school. After a while I couldn't go to class without getting stoned in the bathroom beforehand. I would laugh hysterically all the time and no one ever figured I was stoned. They didn't know pot from marmalade. I remember sitting at a table in the cafeteria and going on a laughing trip and the soda started spritzing out of my nose. People came over and asked if I was okay. Nobody understood I was zonked. During my second semester I rented my own apartment on

Massachusetts Avenue for sixteen dollars a month. I worked at different part-time jobs to pay the rent. One was in a university cafeteria—so I had some access to bags of food. I was maintaining a C average. And they kept telling me that school would get more interesting."

Around this time Bernofsky ran into his old high school classmate, Fred Pappele. "In high school, Fred had been a quiet smart kid with good grades, well behaved, and very sensitive and observant of every little nuance in the classes. But he kept quiet about his opinions. I think he thought I was funny and that some of my wise-guy charisma would rub off on him. But he never got the charisma—just the wise-guy part. In a sense, he was fearless in his ability to nail the truth down and tell it. When you finally got to talk to him, it was a worthwhile experience. On the surface he seemed like the classic nerd. In high school I had only hung out with him peripherally. We knew there was some kind of connection but didn't become close until we met in Lawrence. One of the reasons we started hanging out with each other was that we were alone and friendless in a strange place. It was a mutual case of disbelief when we met. In mid-semester of our sophomore year, Fred and I drove back to New York City in his yellow 1957 Chevy. Our plan was to take off the second semester and tour Eastern Europe. We had our passports, had done some planning, alerted the school to our intentions, and got the required medical shots. We were going to sail on a freighter to Yugoslavia."

For the most part, Bernofsky's FBI file corroborates this part of his story. The KU files examined by the FBI identified Bernofsky as Student #32700, who had enrolled at KU for the fall term of 1959 and majored in psychology. At this point, the FBI provided some different details. According to the school record, Bernofsky received passing grades that first year, but in fall of 1960 he failed Composition and Literature. Bernofsky also informed school officials that he was transferring to another institution, not embarking on a sea voyage to Europe. The FBI files did confirm that on November 8, 1960, Bernofsky received a one-year student travel passport that was good for Europe, Egypt, and India.[11]

"Three days before our departure," Bernofsky continued, "Fred was going to say good-bye to his girlfriend, Ellie. 'Do you want me to see if Ellie has a friend for a blind date?' he asked me. It turned out Ellie did have a friend, and we all got into Fred's car and drove upstate to Clinton, New York, where Fred's dad owned some cabins and land. The next day, I told Fred I didn't need to go on the trip. 'I've already found my Europe,' I told him. I think I fell so hard for my date because she didn't seem afraid of me and just accepted the freak I obviously was. There was also a Jewish connection. We couldn't get enough of each other." A month later, on Christmas Eve 1960, the FBI file reported that Bernofsky got married.[12]

Over our next few sessions in Missoula, Bernofsky shared with me some intimate details of the early years of his marriage. The couple returned to Lawrence, Kansas, where they both attended KU. The following summer they traveled to San Francisco, where Bernofsky landed his first postal job at the massive Rincom Annex, which handled all the mail going overseas to Asia, including letters posted to U.S. soldiers fighting in Vietnam. During that summer the couple parted temporarily, and Bernofsky returned alone to the campus of KU in the fall of 1961.

By this time, I had begun to type up transcripts of our interviews, which I later asked Bernofsky to fact-check. I was also eager to begin interviewing his wife for the project. I hoped she could add further texture to Bernofsky's stories, so I suggested

**All Change!
Shift of Focus**

that he let her read the transcripts as well. The next time we met, Bernofsky gave me some bad news. "My wife doesn't want to have anything to do with this project," he said. "She's a very private person and doesn't want people reading about her. Plus, she doesn't want other people co-opting her experiences. In fact, she told me that she wants to talk with you about it."

A few days later, during a phone conversation, his wife made three things perfectly clear. She didn't want me to publish any personal information about her mother or father, she didn't want me to write any personal facts about her, and she didn't want me to use her name. I was crestfallen. How could I write a biography about a man who'd been married for more than forty-seven years and not even mention his wife's name, or any personal facts about her, or about them as a couple? I tried to cajole her into allowing the biography to go ahead. I promised I'd let her read the finished manuscript and that I'd delete any sections she found embarrassing or untrue. She remained adamant. "Why do you want to write about my husband, anyway?" she demanded. Trying not to sound sentimental, I simply told her that I found her husband somewhat inspirational and very entertaining. She remained unimpressed.

For a while, Bernofsky and I thought it might be better to abandon the project, but I was loathe to drop the enterprise altogether. As an alternative I offered to amend the parameters of the story—back to Bernofsky's original suggestion that I write a social history about Drop City. As for his wife, we agreed I would simply ignore her existence—as much as possible—and never mention her name. To fill the void, Bernofsky suggested I contact some of the other people who lived at the commune. "At least this way, that asshole T. C. Boyle won't have the last word on Drop City," he concluded.

. . . the one job I want them to do is to find Viet Cong and kill them. We got one today, and we're going to get more. Sure, we're suffering casualties, but we're going to be dealing out more. We're fighting a war here now. . . . U.S. Marines rolled across the red dust of a once trim polo field on the

western outskirts of Santo Domingo and moved cautiously into the war-torn
capital of the Dominican Republic. . . . there is a new look in bicycles for
boys and girls: shoulder-high "monkey bars." . . . with 69,200 Americans
committed on land, at sea and in the air to the conflict in Viet Nam and
another 31,600 enforcing a precarious peace in the Dominican Republic,
the U.S. is a nation at war. . . . Peking's second nuclear explosion. . . .
the U.S. had already blasted just about every worthwhile military target
south of the populous Hanoi-Haiphong complex. . . . Cassius Clay
fought a fight that did not seem to be a fight. . . . the U.S. intervention
marks a return to "gunboat diplomacy." . . . finally did agree to squeeze
himself back into his Gemini 4 ship, he still had not had enough of space
walking. . . . singer Joan Baez, 24, strummed and sang to 1,000 British
pacifists. . . . announced publicly for the first time that U.S. troops have
been authorized to fight, in combat units, alongside their South Vietnamese
allies. . . . at a university, "getting off" means dropping all studies
without taking up a job—and U.S. campuses have thousands of such
nonstudents. . . . (May/June 1965)[13]

Bernofsky and I continued our weekly meetings over coffee. Throughout that winter we met at a couple of other java spots in Missoula but, in the end, kept returning to the little balcony loft within The Catalyst, which we typically had to ourselves on those Tuesday or Wednesday mornings. I decided to tell the real story of Drop City—from the point at which Bernofsky returned from San Francisco alone to begin his junior year at KU.

"I moved into a studio loft on Massachusetts Avenue with Clark Richert, an art student at KU. Clark got me involved in stretching canvases and guided me into making paintings so that I actually became productive. He enabled me to see that I perhaps had some worthwhile creative impulses, and he taught me how to express them. We became close friends and we were making a lot of neat things."

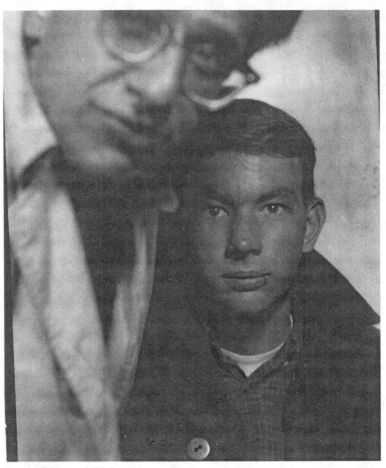

Bernofsky and Richert

Bernofsky and Richert

As Bernofsky and I had discussed, I contacted Richert and Richard Kallweit, another early commune member, to get their sides of the story.[14] "It is probably impossible to put actual and exact chronology on events pertaining to Drop City," Kallweit warned me. "Part of Drop City is actually the myth created. Sometimes, people who were never involved in an episode or who came to Drop City long after an event had allegedly happened, would

eventually claim a story as their own." At the time I had no idea
as to what he meant, but eventually his words proved prophetic.

Kallweit expressed only lukewarm interest in the project, but
Richert seemed genuinely excited, and he immediately answered
a list of questions I emailed him. He wrote that he had grown
up in a middle-class, mostly white, Protestant neighborhood
in Wichita, Kansas. In photos Bernofsky showed me, Richert
appeared tall, lanky, and ash-blonde. He was raised in the
Mennonite faith, steeped in the Anabaptist tradition. He never

| The Mennonite Religion |

realized how his church differed from other
protestant sects until he reached high school.
Then slowly, the early lessons of how the
Mennonite church was baptized in blood in sixteenth-century
Germany, Switzerland, and the Netherlands began to surface
in his consciousness. Having researched the sect for a previous
book, I knew a bit about the astounding history of his religion.

Dissatisfied with Martin Luther's rebellion against Catholicism in the early 1500s, claiming it did not go far enough, the
first Mennonites demanded that the reformists condemn child
baptism and replace it with adult baptism. ("Anabaptist" means
"re-baptizers.") Their demands earned them only the label of
"heretic" from both the state-sanctioned protestant churches
and the Catholics. These two powerful organizations burned
Mennonites alive and practiced the fine arts of quartering,
impaling, disemboweling, hanging, and drowning on them. The
Mennonites eventually published the *Martyrs Mirror*, a 1,582-
page tome measuring ten inches wide, fifteen inches long, and
five inches thick that contained many names of the murdered
Mennonites. In the 1700s some of the sect immigrated to the
Quaker colony of Pennsylvania where William Penn had guaran-
teed them freedom of worship. They eventually spread throughout the colonies. Later, many Russian Anabaptists, who lived
communally and called themselves Hutterites, immigrated to
the United States to settle in communities in the Midwest and

the northern plains of Montana, the Dakotas, and Canada.
The most significant aspect of the Mennonite sect, which today
continues to set them apart from most other Christian churches,
is their devotion to Christ's ideals of nonresistance. That is,
Mennonites read in the Sermon on the Mount that they should
do no harm to their neighbor or to their enemies, and they
actually try to act that way, despite how badly people may treat
them. Furthermore, they believe it better to let a human being
kill them than to kill a human being themselves, no matter
how despicable that person might be.

Richert paid little attention to his nonresistant heritage until
the Vietnam War stared him in the face. "As my consciousness
of the impending threat of the military draft increased," he
said, "the church's anti-war position became important to me.
By all accounts, I should have become a doctor or scientist.
My father worked as a mathematics teacher, while one of my
brothers became a physicist, and the other a mathematician;
my sister studied medicine. When I entered high school, I
assumed I would follow my siblings' path and study math or
science, but during my senior year I got involved with a group of
artists and decided to take the art route. Still, my early interest
in mathematics would influence my style of painting throughout my life. After high school, I enrolled at the University of
Kansas and fell under the influence of the Abstract Expres-
sionists, especially Willem DeKooning and Mark Rothko. I also
discovered the *happenings* of Allan Kaprow and the experimental performance work of Robert Rauschenberg and John
Cage, who were at the time based at Black Mountain College
in the Appalachian Mountains of North Carolina.

"In Lawrence, a friend and I rented a loft along Massachusetts Street, a downtown thoroughfare, where we staged several
chaotic happenings involving electronic music, vast amounts
of shredded newsprint, and strobe light–illuminated spinning
geometric paintings. Philosophically, at that time, I embraced

the experimental. I often described my artistic philosophy by quoting the West Coast artist Jay DeFeo: 'Only by chancing the absurd, may one hope to achieve the sublime.'"

Richert added that he had first gotten interested in the idea of forming an artists' community after his mother told him about her college experiences at a colony in Taos, New Mexico: "When in high school I drove to Taos to check out the scene there for myself, but I was disappointed to discover that Taos was not the small community of intense interaction between artists that I had envisioned. Still, I remained excited about the idea. Back home in Wichita, I hatched a grand scheme to turn my grandparents' abandoned farm into an ideal art community. My friends got behind the idea, but my family was against it." The vision lingered in the back of Richert's mind as he pursued his educational career at the University of Kansas.

Richert first caught sight of Bernofsky at the KU art department when the denim-dressed Bernofsky carrying a guitar came around after class to pick up his wife. The Mennonite and the Jew finally got to talk at a folk-music party at Bernofsky's apartment. Those present included several art students and some folk-nik types, including folksinger Karen Dalton, a Greenwich Village folk and blues singer. In the fall of 1962, when Bernofsky returned alone to Lawrence, Richert invited him to move into the loft.

"There was a certain notoriety to our loft," Bernofsky said. "We decided that, if we were going to make things, we wouldn't copy anything. One of the outcomes of this philosophy was that I made a painting on a huge canvas about six feet tall by nine feet wide. It was nonrepresentational—a series of very precise vertical stripes. I called it, *Dorian*, based on the idea of the classic Roman Doric column. I had studied the columns for a long time, and on the canvas I painted vertical stripes of different colors—dark in the middle, lighter as I went out. In the end, the painting took on the appearance of an optical illusion and actually looked liked a curved three-dimensional column. Clark convinced me to enter it in the Mid-American Art Show at the Nelson Art Gallery in Kansas City. He said the style of the piece was right up the judges' alley. 'If you get any recognition it would drive the Art Department nuts,' he told me. My painting took first place, and all of a sudden I had one thousand dollars. And just as Clark had said, everybody in the Art Department hated me. They thought it was a fluke.

"My paintings were expressionistic with lots of precision, hard-edged stuff. I loved everything about painting—building the frames, stretching the canvas, planning the piece. Clark had a handle on the seduction of the art world. He had put on a lot of one-man shows and already had a reputation as an artist. I was naive about it. I just had fun making stuff and fooling around. Clark and I defined our art as "droppings." We weren't artists, we were "droppers." A lot of times we would tie a rope to stuff

Droppings

and drop it down to the street and sit up there and watch the reactions of passersby. We thought we had invented a whole new approach to making things. It was a way to cope with the disgusting elitism of art. Our pieces were just droppings, others called them collages. It was funny.

"Once we set up an ironing board with an iron and a shirt on the street and then stuck the plug into the slots of a parking meter. People would come by, and some would stop, and try to iron the shirt, and laugh, and have a good time. Another time we cooked up a breakfast of bacon, eggs, toast, juice, and coffee, and set it out on the sidewalk in front of the hotel across the street from us. No one removed it all day long—not even the hotel people. People would walk up to it and look to see what was going on. Finally, someone rode their bicycle right through it and smashed it. Later that day, we went and cleaned it up.

"It was those kinds of thing that demonstrated to Clark and me that we could have fun infusing different visual realities in everyday life. This was the way of real art and a way to really involve people. Not make images for elite people to buy, sell, and trade."

Richert saw it in a similar light but added, "For me, we were performing art, a new kind of happening; for Gene, we were conducting psychological experimentation."

"I also turned Clark on to pot," Bernofsky said, "and he started playing chess the same way I did, taking hours to make a move. Sometimes we would break into the Stokley–Van Camp warehouse at night and steal food. It was about five blocks from the loft. We'd go in through a door on the roof and pile the stuff out on the ground by the loading dock. Then we'd go back and borrow a car and pick it up. The big cans and boxes of food would last us several months. One time there was a big semi truck sitting in the lot and we got into that. It was a bonanza of canned tuna and salmon. Because we lived downtown by the river, there were many old, poor, retired people living nearby. We became kind of a food bank and loved giving food away to elderly people. Chet, in particular, was an old hustler with one arm. He would visit us with his .22 and stand at the back window and shoot pigeons. Then he'd cook them on our stove. He called it scrapple. We would eat pigeon and wash it down with Pi, Pong, and PiLay soft drinks that we had gotten at the warehouse."

. . . *what to do about Medicare—or more precisely, how to oppose it— was the main issue facing the American Medical Association's governing body. . . . too many children are not emotionally, psychologically or physically ready to bridge the gap between crowded, repressive homes, where they are told to shut up, and the public school, where they are asked to open up and learn. . . . In the past decade, about 5,000 new million- aires have been added to the federal tax rolls. . . . 6 percent would continue present policy in Viet Nam, 35.4 percent would increase military action, while 38.4 percent would stop it. . . . the U.S. has created the*

world's first middle-class society, which enjoys not only spectacular luxury
but unprecedented leisure. Yet the U.S. has also created what can logically
be called the world's first servantless society. . . . Since the monsoon
began, the Viet Cong have lost some 4,500 dead to about 1,900 on the
government side. . . . Americans don't like long, inconclusive wars.
This is going to be a long, inconclusive war. . . . I suggest to you there
is no left or right, only an up or down. Up to the maximum of individual
freedom consistent with law and order, or down to the ant heap of totali-
tarianism. . . . (July 1965) [15]

Bernofsky's wife returned to KU the following fall, and they
both graduated in June 1964. During the second semester of
their senior year, Bernofsky said, they moved out of town onto
"a farm about fifteen miles southwest of Lawrence that had an
old barn and farmhouse, out in the direction of Lone Star Lake.
I was looking for a spot where I could grow marijuana without
too much paranoia. I was hoping to raise enough to pack it
up and sell it in the city and make a few thousand dollars so
we'd have a little cushion to find our way after graduation. I had
a bunch of seeds from some good marijuana

> **Capitalistic**
> **Free Enterprise**

stock—Panama Red, I think. In the spring, I
dug up the old garden near the house and
planted a large patch of seeds. In a couple of weeks they
started coming up and they looked like marijuana plants. The
suckers grew like weeds, up to five or six feet by mid-summer.

"One day, in the middle of the growing season, a farmer
stopped by and wanted to know why we were growing all those
weeds. He said: 'There're plenty of those plants growing along
the roadside.' I told him we were growing a plant that would
have a little better domestic use. He later showed us the plants
along the road. It was hemp. He said his dad had grown it
commercially during World War II and it had just spread like
crazy across the country. Some people would roll joints the

size of cigars with hemp and get dizzy smoking it and think they were high.

"In my plot, I had one hundred plants, four to five inches in diameter and eight feet high. I didn't know what I was doing. I harvested them and hung them upside down in the barn. After a week or so I asked a few friends to help shred the leaves off and pack it into plastic bags. Our idea was to sell it for one hundred dollars a bag. We could wind up with ten thousand dollars. A bunch of friends came out and we had fun bagging the plants and each person walked off with a pound. We tested the stuff and we thought we were getting high. It was a mixture of buds and leaves."

Bernofsky then returned to New York with his wife. "We bought a cheap car—a 1947 Dodge that was painted bright orange. It was a perfect car to drive cross-country to New York City with our one hundred bags of marijuana locked up in a big steamer trunk. We drove at around forty-five to fifty miles per hour. In New York we found an apartment on the Lower East Side on Avenue C and Second Avenue, where most of the population was either recently immigrated Puerto Ricans or very poor beatniks who were refugees from middle-class families. The Puerto Ricans seemed real tough, street savvy, and hard-working. We lived in an old slum that had housed original immigrants from Europe. I wanted to work out of that area because I knew the hippies and beatniks would want to score pot for the long winter months. At the time a pound was selling for six to seven hundred bucks. My plan was to unload our crop quickly and get out of there. One day there was a knock on the door of our apartment. It was Allen Ginsberg and his poet-lover, Peter Orlovsky. They wanted to welcome us into the rat-infested slum, and they both had brooms with them and began to sweep out our apartment. They were complete strangers but seemed kind and welcoming."

Allen Ginsberg and the Beat Generation

Ginsberg and Orlovsky shared a top-floor apartment in the building on the Lower East Side. The bard's pad contained furniture he had mostly salvaged from curbsides and alleyways. Chinese scrolls and Tibetan tankas decorated the freshly painted white walls, and he wrote at a table of wooden planks balanced on top of sawhorses. Biographer Barry Miles mentioned that Ginsburg would often write through the night and "would finish up watching the dawn break over the city, the saffron-colored drapes blowing out of the window in the summer breeze, as the first gruff Puerto Rican voices of the day drifted up to him from the street below."[16] According to Miles, friends of the poets— including two women who lived across the hall, an English poet called Harry Fainlight, a local poet named Szabo, and many others—often gathered at Ginsberg's pad for sexual orgies and drug extravagances. Gregory Corso and his wife, Sally, and their baby girl had permanently moved in, and Robert LaVigne was a frequent visitor. Half the people hanging around the apartment frequently got high on methedrine. One of the girls next door would drag her mattress across the hall to Ginsburg's apartment when lovers began to disrobe.

Ginsberg, a close friend of writers Jack Kerouac and William Burroughs, would become a bridge between the beat generation and the evolving hippie scene. In many respects Ginsberg and Bernofsky shared common backgrounds. Their families had emigrated from Eastern Europe, and both men had been raised as red diaper babies (but fifteen years separated the two), and they both would visit Morocco. Ginsberg just missed participating in the glory of World War II, having reached draft age just as the conflict was winding down. After entering Columbia University, he interacted with a group of mostly young men looking beyond the glitter of peace and prosperity offered by the postwar culture, who flinched at the notion that victory confirmed America's belief in its own Manifest Destiny to control the world. Instead, they witnessed white America continue to oppress its own citizens of color. They observed the rich manipulating the poor. They resisted the growing culture of consumerism and the standardization of American life with its forty-hour workweek, self-service supermarkets, tract homes in the suburbs, and stylish automobiles. They understood that most assembly-line factory jobs provided little intellectual stimulation, and they had no desire to sit in vast offices amidst an armada of desks with other white-collar workers. They also noted that even many of those who had bought into the American dream seemed unsatisfied with the status quo.

Hollywood had already begun to document the growing rates of alcoholism and narcotics abuse with such movies as *Days of Wine and Roses,* which dissected the lives of alcoholics, and *The Snake Pit,* whose heroine attempted to recover from a nervous breakdown in a state mental institution. The divorce rate had also increased. Young women, who had gained some independence during the war working in munitions factories, now found themselves out of work and facing a future that usually involved vacuuming living rooms. "Ground that women had won in the Jazz Age and during the war years was suddenly gone," said writer Joyce Johnson, "as if society had deliberately contracted amnesia. Women who had worked were now relegated to the home, and girls were sent to college to get their M.R.S. [degree]. Sexual intercourse was reserved for married couples. It was unusual in the early Fifties for a young woman to get her own apartment, and if she did, it was a sign that she would be up to no good there. The only proper way for a girl to achieve independence from her family was to put herself under the protection of a husband."[17]

Many men also felt out of synch with the times. Writer John Tytell described the fifties as "times of extraordinary insecurity, of profound powerlessness as far as individual effort was concerned, when personal responsibility was being abdicated in favor of corporate largeness, when the catchwords were coordination and adjustment, as if we had defeated Germany only to become *good Germans* ourselves. The nuclear blasts in Japan had created new sources of terror, and the ideology of technology became paramount; science was seen as capable of totally dominating man and his environment. And the prospects of total an-nihilation through nuclear explosion, of mass conditioning through the media, only increased the awesome respect for scientific powers of the Fifties."[18]

On the world front, America went back to war in Korea after communist insurgents trespassed across the forty-second parallel, and American bombers eventually reduced North Korea to piles of rubble. About two million Koreans, both in the North and the South, died in the conflict. America also intervened in Guatemala in 1954, not against communism but to protect United Fruit Company and American oil interests. In Lebanon in 1958, America used the communist-oriented arguments to protect U.S. oil interests there too. In the meantime, the government fought communism on the home front, and with a vengeance. The legendary House Un-American Activities Committee, led by Senator Joseph McCarthy, ruined the professional lives of hundreds of Americans and successfully asphyxiated the American Communist Party politically. Meanwhile the rich got richer, and the poor made babies. "The resources of the richest nation on earth were still irrationally allocated to the production of war goods and luxury goods," said historian Howard Zinn. "Urgent social needs, like housing, health care, schools, were considered secondary in importance. The distribution of income was still so badly distorted that the upper fifth of the population lived on twenty to thirty thousand dollars a year and the bottom fifth tried to get by on two to three thousand dollars a year. At the top of the economic scale was enormous wealth, at the bottom, poverty—and hunger."[19] While most white Americans exalted in newfound economic wealth and the affirmation of their social and political power, sensitive young men such as Ginsberg and Kerouac felt a chafing about the neck. Scratching only aggravated the hot spot until it turned into running sores. Self-diagnosis proved inefficient, as did professional analysis. Symbolically, they were in the pink of health and sitting on top of the world. Whatever worries they suffered, they had conjured up themselves. No white man in his right mind would have complained about the way things were going in the fifties.

Jack Kerouac

It was Kerouac, not Ginsberg, who became the most prominent star of the beat generation. People often confused the label "beat" with a state of being in a certain rhythm, manifesting a coolness epitomized by "bop" music, black saxophone players, and beatniks sporting goatees and sandals—images that mainstream America quickly co-opted and used as propaganda to malign or defame the beats. True, Kerouac and the beats loved bop, but they would not have described themselves as being in rhythm with anything. In fact, they might have professed to be out of rhythm, completely alienated from society. Rather than finger-popping cool, they viewed themselves as literally beaten. As the dictionary says: "pounded or stricken repeatedly; shaped and broken by repeated blows; punished by [figurative] hitting and whipping." And through this demoralizing spiritual and physical punishment they achieved beat-itude—supreme blessedness or happiness—only a step away from saintliness.

During the forties, Herbert Huncke, a male hustler and part of Kerouac's crowd of students, poets, artists, and hoodlums, had used the term "beat" to describe his usual physical and mental condition. He had most likely picked up the term from Swing Era blacks. In 1944 Cab Calloway defined the term in his *Hepster's Dictionary*. "Beat (adj.): (1) tired, exhausted. Ex., 'You look beat' or 'I feel beat.' (2) lacking anything. Ex, 'I am

beat for my cash'; 'I am beat to my socks' (lacking everything)."
Jack Kerouac and John Clellon Holmes picked up the term
and later coined the phrase the "beat generation" in 1949. "We
were talking about the Lost Generation and what this generation would be called," Kerouac said, "and we thought of various
names and I said—Ah, this is really a Beat Generation."[20]

Three years went by after the conversation between Kerouac
and Holmes before the term appeared in print. Holmes included
it in his book *Go*, which was published in 1952. "You know," he
said, "everyone I know is kind of furtive, kind of beat . . . a
sort of revolution of the soul, I guess you'd call it." Ginsberg,
whom Kerouac renamed Carlo Marx in *On the Road*, said the
beat generation was "a matter of seeing everybody lost in a
dream world of their own making. . . . That was the primary
perception. The idea of transience of phenomena—the poig-
nant Kewpie-doll dearness of personages vanishing in time.
Not a morbid interest in death but the realization of the mortal
turn. . . . It wasn't a political or social rebellion. Everybody
had some form of break in their consciousness or an experience
or a taste of a larger consciousness or satori."[21]

A dark brooding gloom marked the beats, even as they
groped like addicts for the transient pleasures inherent in
sex, drugs, and alcohol. Most beats were male, and many of
them were ex-GIs suddenly asked to assimilate quietly back
into society. According to Miles, the inner circle of early beats
who hung out at Times Square "had all read Spengler's *Decline
of the West* and believed that society was collapsing around
them and that the A-bomb would eventually do them all in."[22]
Ultimately, the beats went in search of community. Kerouac
made it clear that the road always led to a place where he felt
safe and welcomed. Kerouac's beat community embraced all—
drifters, hobos, prostitutes, migrant farmworkers, hitchhikers,
ex-cons, con artists, Negroes, Mexicans, boozers, and druggies—
all the unwanted, undesirable, so-called losers of society.

Throughout his career Ginsberg tirelessly publicized his fellow beat authors. By the late sixties he had become the elder spokesman for the hippie movement, encouraging society to shed its hang-ups by partaking in psychedelic drugs and enjoying personal sexuality. But that was a few years still down the road.

Bernofsky smiled smugly as he recalled his encounters with Ginsberg back in late 1964. "On the Lower East Side, Ginsberg was the head of the neighborhood tenants group, which was trying to get hot water in the building and the stairway fixed. He was a big, bearded, dirty bum and would sit stoned in the street and chant with cymbals on his fingers. He was the *gantza macher*—the big maker, the big shot. I called him the impresario of the Lower Eastside. The two of them, Ginsberg and Orlovsky, ended up buying five pounds of pot from us.

"While I was selling pot, it was a period of intense paranoia— I fantasized that I would be killed by street people or caught by authorities. I was always watching my back. How do you carry five pounds of marijuana through the Lower East Side without being afraid you'll be jumped by a Puerto Rican gang, arrested, or enticed by the chanting Ginsberg into some weird fantasy event?—because, Ginsberg and Orlovsky were obviously trying to entice us into their circle. But I focused on pulling this off. I felt no remorse. I figured, screw you society, you are amazingly degenerate to begin with. Look at all the money you are making from killing innocent people on both sides of the war in Vietnam. You warmongers are guilty. Not me. I'm innocent. Within a month we had our ten thousand dollars.

"Part of our idea for selling the pot was to have enough money to start our own civilization. We felt that the society about us had degenerated to such a point we couldn't live within it. But we felt people were good enough and under the right circumstances could live a good life. We wanted to build a society from the ground up—that would develop kind human beings. We felt we couldn't do it in the USA but needed a

really remote place that hadn't yet been impacted by human
beings. We chose the headwaters of the Nile in Central Africa."

*. . . To fulfill its new commitment, the U.S. must increase the size of its
armed forces, which numbered 2.6 million on July 1. They hoped that all
this could be accounted for by the boost in the monthly draft call. . . .
This summer the Nude Wave finally washed onto U.S. beaches, and
women from Los Angeles to Long Island have been wearing all manner
of suits of which brevity is the chief feature. . . . Last week President
Johnson signed into law a bill that will almost immediately add more
than 1 million American Negroes to the nation's voting rolls. . . . U.S.
automakers expect to build 9.1 million cars for the best year in history—
65 percent more than in 1961. . . . West Germany's Volkswagen is
gradually overtaking the Model T as the most produced single auto in
history. . . . One evening white Los Angelenos had nothing to worry
about but the humidity. The next—and for four nights after that—
marauding mobs in the Negro suburb of Watts pillaged, burned and
killed. . . . "Our Lake Erie is a wastebasket for factories. It is unfit for
fish to live in and for people to enjoy." . . . (August 1965)*[23]

At this point, I interrupted Bernofsky's narrative as I choked
on my coffee—one of the few times I ever interrupted him
during our sessions. I also laughed—about as hard as I laughed
when I read the part in Boyle's *Drop City* where he described
how the character Norm Sender announced to his followers
that he planned to move the commune up to the Yukon.

| A New Civilization in Africa |

Bernofsky remained unruffled. "We went down
to the docks," he continued, ignoring my
outburst, "and found a Yugoslavian freighter
that took twenty passengers on board. It left New York bound
for various ports in the Mediterranean. We decided to get off
in Morocco at Casablanca and walk across North Africa to
Egypt." This time he had to wait a moment, until my hoots of
laughter subsided. "My wife and I both obtained our visas to

be able to cross the borders," he calmly continued. "In Egypt we planned to follow the river. We could have gotten off in Cairo, but we wanted to walk across northern Africa."

Being a writer, I couldn't have imagined a more farfetched script: a white kid from Brooklyn traveling to the cradle of civilization, to create a new civilization. What irony. Ethnologists have long noted that, before the European colonization of the so-called Dark Continent, African native civilization promoted unity, balance, and harmony—the same characteristics Bernofsky seemed to crave. Leopold Sedar Senghor once wrote that African society was based both on the community and on the person. In this society, he said, "because it was founded on dialogue and reciprocity, the group had priority over the individual without crushing him, but allowing him to blossom as a person."[24]

It seemed Benofsky wanted to duplicate what Africans had already done. So, did he really go? According to the FBI file, Bernofsky did renew his passport on October 26, 1964, at New York City for six months' tourist travel to France, England, Morocco, Germany, Greece, and Italy. Bernofsky, the report said, "had taken a Yugoslav freighter to some place around Algiers from New York City December 29, 1964."[25]

Once in Africa, Bernofsky thought, he would "find some people who would have joined us. At the time we had plenty of faith in the cosmic forces—that what we were doing was positive and hopeful. And that if we were doing something worthwhile, we would be taken care of. At Casablanca, we met an individual working with the Peace Corps who had a residence in the French district and he invited us to stay with him. I decided to make an attempt to see if I could actually physically start to build, in an experimental way, some pieces of our supposed civilization in a foreign country. It was my first experience outside the USA, where everything was different— the food, clothing, and language. Would I be able to find a

hardware store, purchase tools and material to build a shelter?
I found a place in the Kasbah that supposedly sold nails. It
took me a day of talking to make them understand I wanted
to order fifty pounds of nails. A week later the nails arrived on
a boat from China. Then I got some wood. But the nails broke
in half when I gently tapped on them. It was then it dawned
on me that I would never be able to put together anything
with grass and sticks and mud. I just couldn't imagine how I was
ever going to be able to make any kind of structure. I realized
that if I was going to have any shot at doing this I'd have to
return to the USA—where I wouldn't have the language diffi-
culty and where I knew the nails would hold up. So after a
month of traveling around Morocco we decided it wasn't going
to work out for us in Africa.

"We wanted to come home through Spain because we knew
there was so much hard drug trade between Morocco and New
York. We flew to Malagua and took a train to Madrid. There we
went to El Prado Museum where we saw many of the paintings
of Goya. We returned home pretty much broke. I always believed
that the cosmic forces would take care of us in Africa. I no
longer believe that, of course. We were mistaken. But I didn't
learn this until later. The forces had bitter plans in store for us."

Enter Peter Rabbit | Through the years another version of Ber-
nofsky's African exploits surfaced. In 1971
writer Peter Rabbit, whose real name was Peter
Douthit, reported that Bernofsky was conned into a dope
caper while in Casablanca—to smuggle heroin into the States.
"The Bernofskys," Douthit wrote, "made contact with a dope
connection in New York and made plans to return to the U.S.
They flew to Spain and then to New York with the heroin
securely stashed up Mrs. Bernofsky's snatch. Customs in New
York did a thorough job of searching Bernofsky, up the ass

and everywhere, but for some reason ignored Mrs. Bernofsky."[26] According to Douthit's account, the heroin turned out to be a bag full of salt, and the New York dope dealer let Bernofsky off the hook because the Moroccans had fleeced him.

Douthit, aka Peter Rabbit, lived for a while with Bernofsky after he had founded Drop City. Bernofsky might have told him the truth or he might have spoon-fed the story to a writer he considered a naïve sap, just as he invented the radiation biology major for my benefit. The latter is probably the case. Another citizen of Drop City published yet another version of the smuggling story, only this time it involved big cakes of hash that the Bernofskys stuffed down their underwear. "When we finally opened up the bundles, they turned out to be camel shit," Bernofsky allegedly confessed to that writer.[27] Despite conflicting versions of his adventures, Bernofsky did indeed return to the Lower East Side and sold a few remaining bags of marijuana that he had stashed away in the old steamer trunk and stored in the basement of a relative's home.

When Clark Richert heard that his friend had returned stateside, he traveled to the Big Apple to hear firsthand about the great adventure. By then Richert had moved to Boulder, Colorado, after graduating from KU. He had also gotten married (mostly to escape the draft, he said), but he soon separated from his wife. While listening to Bernofsky's headwaters-of-the-Nile story, Richert recalled his old dream of forming a self-supporting artists' community. "Comparing our visions," Richert said, "we postulated synthesizing them and in a great moment of clarity agreed: Let's do it. We would own the property, build A-frame houses, pay no rent, make films and art and as Gene put it, *put our trust in dose Cosmic Forces*." But the cosmic forces did not indicate that the time was right, and the two friends again parted without formulating a concrete plan. "In the back of our minds," Richert continued, "we were all wondering: what do we do now? The only future I could see was graduation from the University of Colorado with an MFA degree—and then what?"

The Journey Begins

During the remainder of the spring of 1965, Bernofsky sold his few remaining bags of marijuana. "A few weeks later," he said, "we decided to get into our car and drive around the West to find a rural piece of land where we could build a meaningful civilization. I had raised a couple of thousand dollars selling the last of the marijuana crop, and we took off for Montana." By going rural, and especially in heading west, Bernofsky bucked a trend being set by his contemporaries. Ever since World War I, rural Americans had been migrating into the cities as technology wrought a sea change in farmer productivity. During the fifties, the nation lost more than 1.6 million farmers, and almost 1 million more during the sixties, thanks to mechanization. A few months before Bernofsky's departure, *Time* reported that the population drain was most pronounced in the West: "Fewer and fewer Americans, about one out of three, live in the great outdoors now celebrated almost entirely in never-ever television westerns. In a curious miracle of abandonment, Americans have become strangers in a landscape that they believe has built their national character."[28] Montana had one of the smallest populations in the Lower Forty-Eight at the time, and the state still boasts less than 1 million residents. Still, Bernofsky had little luck finding a home there.

"We drove all over the state and we found some land for sale, but we would have had to buy hundreds of acres at a time at twenty dollars an acre. We couldn't buy just five or ten acres. We tried because we really loved the state. Our next stop was Colorado, where we stopped off at Clark's house in Boulder. Clark and I again talked about finding a place where we could make things in peace and not be bothered. We again expressed our faith that the cosmic forces would generate enough income for us to survive on. Clark said he'd be happy to help me look.

El Moro

That was reassuring. I trusted Clark and thought he'd be a valuable asset to the endeavor. He was kind, generous, and thought-
ful; plus, he had a drive and fire to do something in life."

The two headed out on their search one sunny day in early
May 1965. "I believe the idea was that we would head north to
Missoula and buy land there," Richert said, "but following intui-
tion and half-baked leads, we gradually turned to the south."

The friends eventually drove almost to the border of New
Mexico where the landscape grew drier and supported little
vegetation beyond irrigated fields. They could see an occa-
sional cottonwood tree standing guard in a draw where water
ran periodically after a rain storm or after snow melted. After
a while they pulled off the highway and tooled around the
county gravel roads. Their circuitous route took them past the
poor Chicano laid-back town of Trinidad, Colorado.

"We went through Trinidad," Bernofsky said, "and were
driving around in a rural area about ten miles to the east, in

the El Moro area. There was nothing there but an old Depression-
era adobe schoolhouse—all dirt roads, semi-arid desert, and
rolling topography with some farmhouses. Where two dirt roads
intersected, we saw a 'For Sale' sign. The farmer, Mr. Anderson,
wanted to sell five acres where he used to run goats for two
hundred dollars an acre. I offered one hundred and fifty
an acre and told him I had the money right on me. I think
the Andersons saw we were O.K. young people. They were very
generous and offered to let us live in their farmhouse while we
built our own house. We closed the deal that day and I bought
the land."

The date was May 3, 1965. During my early research of
Drop City I had discovered a slender paper trail that continually

**Paper Trail
Drop City**

led back to this date. Sociologist Hugh Gardner designated that day's transaction as the
moment when more or less begins the "hippie"
era of modern communes. "In more ways than one the commune that was soon to sprout from the old goat pasture was
an integral part of the birth of the counterculture."[29] Other
social scientists agreed.

"Drop City brought together most of the themes that had
been developing in other recent communities—anarchy, paci-
fism, sexual freedom, rural isolation, interest in drugs, art—
and wrapped them flamboyantly into a commune not quite like
any that had gone before," wrote Timothy Miller. "Drop City
thus represents the point at which a new type of commune
building had definitively arrived. It was defiantly outrageous,
proclaiming itself a whole new civilization, its members
rejecting paid employment and creating wildly original funky
architecture. It pioneered what soon became a widespread
hippie love of integrated arts, creating multimedia extravagan-
zas, using color profusely, employing trash as source material,
blending art with everything else in life."[30]

Over the next decade, the back-to-the-land commune movement expanded to include at least five thousand—possibly ten
thousand—rural communal retreats. Thousands of others would
evolve in towns and cities, especially where colleges were located.
Sociologists estimate at least a half million young people would
become temporarily associated with a communal enterprise, a
scale that Gardner described as "unprecedented in our history,
involving more people and more organizations than all previous
commune movements in America combined."[31] Bernofsky
and Richert had no idea on that May day that they were
vanguards of a cultural revolution. They certainly didn't think
of themselves as hippies, since that term had yet to be coined.
They just knew they wanted to save society from the military-
industrial complex and the soul-deadening effects of capitalism
and its obsession with an unending accumulation of material
wealth. At that moment, the goat pasture symbolized a refuge
where they could dedicate their time to intellectual and artistic creation.

Even if the two friends personally did not inspire a generation, other young people at that time certainly experienced the
same emotions. "The new communes began to appear before
there was a clearly recognizable overall hippie culture, much
less a decaying one," Miller wrote. "Catalyzed by shifts in American culture in the late fifties and early sixties, the new generation of communes was not initially a product of hippiedom,
but rather a crucible that played a major role in shaping and
defining hip culture. In other words, the urban hippies did
not create the first sixties-era communes; it would be closer to
the truth to say that the earliest communes helped create the
hippies. Although communes were indeed founded by hippies
who fled the cities, they were johnnies-come-lately to the sixties
communal scene."[32]

. . . Nixon told newsmen in Tokyo that Washington's "constant repetition"
of its willingness to negotiate would only prolong the war. . . . The
Beatles open the 18th fall season of the Ed Sullivan show. . . . without
fanfare or even much reconciliation, ended the bloody civil war that began
April 24, took the lives of 3,000 Dominicans and 31 U.S. servicemen.
. . . the rumors have swirled around the mysterious disappearance of Che
Guevara. . . . only 2 1/4 percent of the 2.9 million Negro school children
in eleven Southern states actually sat in classrooms last year with whites.
. . . the U.S. will have more than 150,000 uniformed men in Viet Nam.
. . . every day, the average American disposes of four pounds of trash—
a total of 540 million lbs. throughout the nation. . . . abortions are on
the rise. . . . The resolution proclaimed the right of the U.S. or any other
American republic to intervene with "armed force" if need be, "to forestall
or combat" Communist subversion or aggression wherever it may occur in
the Western Hemisphere. . . . Poverty is the condition—and the aware-
ness—of being left behind while, economically, everyone else is marching
forward. . . . long hair has spread from hard-core rock 'n' roll fans to
the entire teen and postteen population. . . . A granny is not a grand-
mother but a garment. . . . Who are they? These Americans parading
about with placards and chanting: "Hey, hey, L.B.J.! How many kids
did you kill today?" They surely are not the U.S. majority. . . .
(September/October 1965)[33]

| Communes through-out U.S. History |

Bernofsky, with his African dreams, was not
the first person with hopes of developing a
new civilization in a land far from home, of
course. Nor were Bernofsky and Richert the first to try to
influence the direction of their fellow countrymen by setting
up an intentional community that deviated from mainstream
American society. The pair had little awareness of the long
history of communal activity that had already taken place in
the United States. If they had studied up on the subject, they
might have learned some valuable lessons, which could, perhaps,
have helped them smooth the bumpy road down which they

naively embarked. Ironically, Bernofsky's choice to first abandon his native country to fashion a communal way of life abroad, in the allegedly *primitive* and *undeveloped* setting of Africa (at least from a Westerner's viewpoint), mirrored the founding of this nation. The Pilgrims knew as little about Native American culture as Bernofsky, it seems, knew about African culture. It can also be argued that to some extent Plymouth Plantation started out as a commune.

The Pilgrims sailed from Holland with the idea of building a society based on a shared faith and moral structure. The participants pooled their resources to finance the voyage and later shared the crops they raised and the fish and wild game they harvested. But the Pilgrims had also accepted investment capital from English businessmen and had signed a contract stipulating that the joint stock and partnership would continue for seven years; after the seventh year the parties would dissolve the venture and split the capital and profits. From then on it would be every man for himself. The initial communal system did not last very long, however, as the colonists began arguing over individual workloads. In 1623, in order to escape the bickering, Governor William Bradford assigned private garden plots to individual families, rather than directing everyone to work a communal garden. When harvesttime came around Bradford heaved a sigh of relief. His faith in self-interest, he wrote, "had made all hands very industrious, so as much more corne was planted than other waise would have bene."[34]

Plymouth Plantation may have failed as a commune but this didn't stop others from trying to form alternative communities across the far reaches of this country over the next four hundred years. Some did it for religious purposes, others for social and philosophical reasons. Among the earliest American religious sects who voluntarily removed themselves from the mainstream in order to maintain their spiritual purity were the Labadists, whose congregation consisted of religious mystics.

They hoped to emulate the early Christian Church communism and set up segregated colonies in New York, Pennsylvania, and Maryland. Beginning in 1774 another group, the Shakers (who practiced celibacy), established fifty-eight communities in nine states. As early as 1874 the Hutterites, cousins to the Mennonites of the Anabaptist tradition, established communal dryland farms on the northern plains and in Alberta, Canada. In the mid-1800s newly immigrated Jews who had settled in the slums of New York City set up kibbutz-like farms in many states, including New Jersey, Kansas, Colorado, Wyoming, and Utah. Also in the 1800s the Mormons created some of the most successful cooperative communities, first in Illinois and later, when they were driven out by the locals, in Utah's Salt Lake Valley.

Others sought to live with like-minded people for more worldly reasons. One of the earliest secular communes in America fashioned itself after the Owenite Movement, inspired by English factory owner Robert Owen who wanted to provide his workers with a better life. The Owenites practiced absolute equality and held all goods in common, but the twenty-one communities they founded in the United States dissolved in less than four years. Another secular group, the New Harmony Community of Equality (or simply, New Harmony), was founded in Indiana in 1825 but dissolved after only two years because of dissension between the members and its leaders.

In the 1830s many Americans, disgruntled over the shift from an agrarian society to an industrial world, embraced the philosophy of early socialist Charles Fourier who introduced the idea of worker phalanxes to the world. Residents who bought shares in a Fourier community would theoretically prosper from dividends from agricultural, craft, and educational enterprises. They shared in the work, received equal wages, and lived communally. The most famous Fourier-inspired community was Brook Farm, founded in 1841 by George Ripley in West Roxbury,

Massachusetts, which writer Nathaniel Hawthorne immortalized in his book *The Blithedale Romance.* During the second half of the nineteenth century, about thirty-five phalanxes eventually developed, with eight thousand members from Michigan to New York to Texas. Most of these disbanded once the mortgage came due—including Brook Farm, shortly after a disastrous fire devastated a newly erected living center. Still, even more secular communities formed during the nineteenth century whose interests lay beyond economic security and social equality.

In 1876 a world-famous stage actress, Madame Modjeska, moved her colony from Poland to Anaheim, California, where thirty-three artists sank about fifty-four thousand dollars into erecting buildings and buying farming equipment for a highly developed cooperative. They then spent the next two years writing books, painting pictures, and producing plays while the crops withered and the stock died. When the barns burned down, they abandoned the colony. Also in 1876 a group of twenty-four Texas women who had initially met at a prayer meeting decided to leave their husbands to start a communal business in Belton. Two years later they moved the enterprise to Mount Pleasant, District of Columbia. The celibate community gradually shrank in size until it died out in 1906. In 1896 a community of people gathered at Commonwealth, Georgia, to live according to the teachings that Christ espoused in his Sermon on the Mount. They accepted anyone who asked for membership, no matter how poor, wicked, or sick. The three hundred residents shared the rewards of their volunteer labor in connection with a sawmill, printing plant, towel-weaving mill, a large nursery, and farming enterprises. They abandoned the nonresistant philosophy when certain members who had contributed nothing to the enterprise asked the courts to appoint a receiver and divide up the property. The community continued until 1900 as a democratic society until a typhoid epidemic decimated their numbers.

Other groups, like the German Colony of Anaheim, California, emulated the Massachusetts Pilgrims by setting up cooperative settlements. In 1857 fifty German families in Anaheim pooled their resources to purchase 1,165 acres of land and financed the tilling and planting for three years from a common fund. On an appointed date in 1860 they divvied up the profits and started farming individual plots.

In 1936 historian Ralph Albertson listed some of the reasons the majority of these early communes failed. He noted that communism always had a tough time competing with the general prosperity and unlimited opportunity found in America, and that the general lifestyle of American society quickly undermined any attempts at a quasi-monastic life of segregation and separation. He blamed dictatorial leadership at many of the communes for undermining the sense of fellowship and acknowledged that a high sense of idealism seldom translated into business acumen. Another interesting strain on many cooperative communities came in the form of self-published periodicals touting a commune's achievements long before it actually achieved anything. Many communities did not set any type of standard for selecting or accepting new members, who might eventually undermine the initial goodwill of the founders.[35]

Despite the many seeming setbacks, efforts at communal living continued well into the twentieth century. In 1906 author Upton Sinclair founded an experimental cooperative community called Helicon Hall at a defunct boys' school on the outskirts of Englewood, New Jersey, that attracted about forty intellectuals. In 1942 Clarence Jordan envisioned Koinonia Farm in South Georgia as an interracial commune. The idealists who joined began building homes for poor people, and their enterprise eventually evolved into Habitat for Humanity. In 1936 the School of Living founded by Ralph Borsodi promoted constructing clusters of homesteads whose occupants would cooperate with one another. When Mildred Loomis took over at Borsodi, she moved the School of Living to Brookville, Ohio, where the school's continuing education program focused on rural self-sufficiency. By 1965 the school had moved into new quarters at the Heathcote Center.

In 1962 an art gallery owner opened her land outside the town of Gorda, near Big Sur, California, to anyone who wanted to live there. The open-style community grew slowly until around 1967—when about two hundred people stayed there at one time or another, but not long enough to form a stable community. Tolstoy Farm first formed in 1963 about thirty miles west of Spokane, Washington. Its founder, Huw Williams, was a peace activist and invited some of his friends to join him at his grandparents' farm. About fifty people took him up on the offer that first summer. The community eventually devolved into a collection of scattered private households.

Other communities active in the early sixties included Cedar Grove, a Baha'i commune in New Mexico that featured a Shaker-like belief that work was spiritually important; the Amity Experimental Community, which came to life around 1959 seemingly as a group marriage; and a back-to-the-land movement outside Oxford, New York, called the Society for the Preservation of Early American Standards.[36] Neither Bernofsky nor Richert had studied the history of communes, so they could not learn from the mistakes or successes of the past. Moreover, they did not share a religious conviction nor had they developed any mutual well-defined philosophical principles. They only wanted to create art, and they were putting all their trust into the hands of the indefinable and wayward cosmic forces.

"While Clark and I were driving back to Boulder," Bernofsky continued, "we discussed the kind of dwelling we might make.

Geodesic Domes and Bucky Fuller

The only thing I could think of was a structure I had read about in John Steinbeck's *Grapes of Wrath*—made out of chicken wire, tar paper, and cement. If Tom Joad could live in it, it would be good enough for us. I figured I could get those materials, the only thing I needed was some kind of frame. Soon after that conversation, Clark spotted a small structure out in a farmer's field that was built out of one-by-two slats. 'Hey, this looks like a geodesic dome,' he said. 'Why don't we do something like this?' I thought: 'Perfect!' I didn't know at the time what an error that would be.

"Clark took all the measurements from the model and figured out how to expand it to make a fifteen-foot diameter dome. The one in the field had only about a four-foot diameter. The farmer told us he had gotten the plans from Buckminster Fuller. When we got back to Boulder, we saw a notice tacked to a telephone pole proclaiming that Bucky Fuller was going to lecture on the campus of the University of Colorado that night. We recognized that the cosmic forces were coming together, so we took our seats in the lecture hall that evening, and out walks this rectangular stump of a guy who seems to be half blind. When he starts speaking his eyes are closed, his head is up. We just knew that this guy was channeling the cosmic forces; he's telling us the good dome is the ultimate shelter for humans around the world; the simplest, strongest structure; the sphere itself is more natural than the rectangle. He says we need curved spaces around us for the fulfillment of our beings. All Clark and I needed to hear was the music of the cosmic vibrations coming from Bucky."

Fuller was seventy years old by that time. His intellectual career had gotten off to a dubious start before World War I when he dropped out of Harvard University—twice. But from the beginning he had proven a visionary. One of his first designs, conceived during World War I, envisioned a vertical take-off aircraft. After the war he joined corporate America, for a short stint, but soon quit his job to invest all his energy into figuring out ways to use advanced technology to design products and schemes that might enhance the quality of life for all on earth, without depleting the earth's natural resources. He apparently never gave a hoot about financial gain and conventional success. Fuller first investigated the world's housing crisis. Believing that modern home construction could never keep up with the expanding population, his initial projects focused on pre-fabricated housing that could be transported by helicopter or dirigible to any location around the world. His first home design, conceived in 1927, featured a forty-five-ton tower that supported twelve decks of apartments. If they had been mass-produced at that time, a single complex would have cost approximately twenty-three thousand dollars. Later designs of the dwelling called for wind-driven generators to provide electricity, heat, and air-conditioning. Fuller also designed single-family dwellings with as many as six rooms, which he dubbed the Dymaxion House.

Fuller derived the term "dymaxion" from some of his most oft-repeated words—"dynamism," "maximum," and "ions." His goal was to achieve maximum gain from minimal energy input. For Fuller the ultimate ideal home would function independent of power lines, waterlines, and sewers—like ships and aircraft. Fuller's first mass-produced products were the Dymaxion Deployment Units—twenty-foot-diameter converted corrugated metal grain-storage bins, which were used during World War II as radar stations, dormitories, and hospitals. The twelve-hundred-dollar package included a kerosene icebox and stove. Fuller also produced an aeronautically streamlined three-wheeled vehicle with two-front wheels (for drive) and a single rear-wheel (for steering). The eleven-passenger car could reach speeds of one hundred miles per hour and travel with ease across plowed fields. He later modified it to use three fifteen-to-twenty-horsepower engines. Once the vehicle was in motion, one engine could propel it for distances of up to fifty miles per gallon.

Fuller gained most fame, however, for promoting a form of engineering that he dubbed "tensegrity." This design used the triangulated spherical networks of the geodesic dome as a basic building block to separate compression and tension energies into their most advantageous form. Fuller discovered that the geodesic structure would maintain its entire network of compression and tension integrity even after removing whole segments. The dome officially arrived as an accepted architectural commodity in 1953 when the Ford Motor Company erected a Fuller-designed ninety-three-foot-diameter, eight-and-a-half-ton, aluminum-braced dome to cover its Rotunda Building. By the early sxities, two thousand industrial-sized domes had been erected around the world. Fuller also devised calculations for domes that would span two miles in diameter to enclose entire cities in a segregated and controlled environment space.

At the time of his speech at Boulder, Fuller was finishing up plans on a dome to house the U.S. exhibition hall for Expo 67, the Montreal World Fair. The 250-by-200-foot bubble of transparent plastic and steel would be spacious enough to hold the Statue of Liberty (without its pedestal). The sphere was to feature a computer system that directed 261 electric motors operating 4,700 metallic-fabric shades on the inside surface of the gigantic globe to regulate temperature. The shifting shades would also change the dome's color from silver to rainbow hues. At the lecture on the University of Colorado campus that May evening of 1965, Bernofsky and Richert surely would have found much inspiration and guidance from Fuller.

"Throughout the history of man," Fuller often said while promoting his *Grand Strategy for Solving Global Problems*, "there has never been enough to go around for everyone—there has always been scarcity. Therefore, the basic problem was: who gets what? Who survives and who doesn't? Every society has had a different system for deciding that question, and which group survived was usually decided by war! But just because it has always been that way doesn't mean that it always has to be that way in the future. Just because there was scarcity in the past, does that mean that there has to be scarcity in the future? No! Mankind now has enough knowledge to be able to invent our way into a future of plenty. We are just not aware of the fact that we now have that possibility."[37]

Fuller first confronted the energy issue in his talks: "By interconnecting all the world's electrical generating plants they could all swap power, especially between the light and dark sides of the earth, and therefore be run at almost peak capacity most of the time—without building any new generating plants. . . . We must also phase in all the various types of renewable energy as the fossil fuels start to run out. There are plenty of alternatives to choose from: solar, wind, hydroelectric, biomass, alcohol, geothermal, tides, photovoltaic, hydrogen, waves, etc. All these alternatives, when fully developed, would not only replace the non-renewable, polluting, and dangerous sources, but give us three times as much energy as we have now (not counting the gains through interconnecting).

"Now, what is the story for food? Much the same. We produce more than enough food for everyone, but much of it rots or is eaten by rodents because we don't have the means of storing, preserving, and transporting it. But, with adequate energy we could grow, preserve, and distribute plenty of food for everyone. In fact, if needed, we could probably grow two or three times as much as we do now. . . . And so, if we solve the energy and food problems, how do we provide good, inexpensive housing for everyone? Simple. Shelter people in mass-produced, self-contained, surplus-energy-producing, geodesic dome homes which would be helicopter-delivered to anywhere for a tenth the cost of conventional houses. . . . But most of all, if people no longer have to fight each other over limited resources, then the basic reason for war will be gone and war will become obsolete. The oldest dreams of mankind—peace, prosperity—will have come true."

About two thousand people sat in the audience that evening along with Bernofsky and Richert. After the lecture, Bernofsky said, "Clark and I ran down the aisle and told Bucky we were trying to build a dome in southern Colorado with chicken wire, tar paper, and cement. He said: 'Be sure to make it strong enough to withstand the snow.' Bucky also said it was great that we were using innovative materials. When he smiled benignly as he looked upward, we felt as if we were being lifted up to the celestial spheres, both figuratively and literally."

. . . *Morrison's self-immolation, his wife Anne soon explained, expressed "his concern over the great loss of life and human suffering caused by the war in Viet Nam." . . . estimates that U.S. industry will have to spend ten times its present $100 million annually for treating waste water if it hopes to end industrial pollution. . . . Roger LaPorte, 22, a student at Manhattan's Hunter College, doused his clothes with gasoline and set himself aflame on a street corner outside United Nations headquarters. . . . The work already given to U.S. companies by the Defense Department amounts to more than $300 million, and at least another $200 million in contracts is planned for coming months. The projects are being carried out by four private U.S. construction and engineering firms that have banded together in a giant venture called RMK-BRJ. . . . Boys look like girls, girls look like boys, and the songs they sing are not of love and laughter, but sour, self-pitying whines about how awful things are in a culture that supplies them with about $12 billion worth of such essential equipment as cars, clothes, acne lotions and hair sprays . . . the first manned rendezvous in space. . . .* (November/December 1965)[38]

"A couple of days later we packed up the '51 silver Chevrolet, drove down to El Moro, and moved into the Andersons' old "farm-

| Scrounging and Recycling |

house," Bernofsky said. "Next day Clark and I went scrounging around for two-by-fours so we could begin building something. We found a lumberyard in Trinidad that was throwing away three-foot-long pieces of cut-off ends and got permission to take them off

their hands for free. Exactly the kind of thing we were looking
for. We found the waste of our society—the detritus of society—
so extravagant that we thought we would be able to live off of
it. We needed five-and-a-half-foot pieces of two-by-fours, so we
scabbed pieces together. But we also needed nails, so we drove
around again, and sure enough, the cosmic forces smiled down
upon us. We came upon a team of Mexican laborers disman-
tling an old house and asked if we could pull the nails from
the timbers. They said, 'Sure, pull all the nails you want,' and
then they laughed. They were happy to get the clean wood
and we were happy to have nails. Clark had all the mathematics
worked out for the dome—the lengths of the segments and
the angles. We built the whole kit and were ready to put the
frame together, but we needed a foundation and had to figure
out where to place it. We also needed something to join the
hexagons and pentagons. Somewhere, we remembered seeing
piles of old creosoted railroad ties, and we thought we could
sink those into the ground vertically and make a round foundation. We loaded up the back of the silver Chevy with the ties
and drove them home. The bottom of the structure included
ten sides. We anchored each side to one of the railroad ties
that stuck out of the ground about a foot and a half. To hold
the sections together, we cut collars from a cast-iron sewer
pipe that we had found."

During the construction of the dome, the fledgling community began to expand. On weekends Richert's friends Bert and
Peggy Wadman often drove down from Boulder. "Bert, an
architecture student, was particularly interested in geodesic
domes. Meanwhile, Peggy, who had recently read *The Lord of
the Rings*, told tall tales of hobbits and trolls around the dinner
table," Bernofsky said. "'You guys read this,' Peggy told us,
'because you are just like hobbits.' The Wadmans were very
generous and contributed cash and groceries whenever they
showed up."

Around the same time Kallweit arrived at the former goat pasture. A good friend of Richert's, Kallweit had grown up in Buffalo, New York, and had also graduated from the University of Kansas art department. His parents had lived in a socialist commune in New Jersey for a while shortly after World War II. "We were happy to have him join our venture," Bernofsky said. "He was a hard-working, pleasant, neurotic young man who fit right in with the droppers. He was physically fit and a protégé of Clark's." Construction progressed more quickly with the additional sets of hands. "When we put together the frames of scabbed two-by-fours," Bernofsky said, "we wound up with a fifteen-foot-diameter structure. When we stepped back and looked at it we realized it wasn't a geodesic dome at all. In fact, what we had built was a dodecahedron—a hemisphere. Then, we got ready to apply sheathing to the structure. We went into town and bought a roll of cheap fifteen-gauge tar paper, cut the roll into triangles, and stapled them onto the structure. Next we bought a roll of hog wire and cut it into triangles with snippers, and used short roofing nails to attach the wire to the two-by-fours.

The First Dome

Next, we got a bag of cement and mixed up a batch, but as soon as we started smearing the cement onto the hog wire, the weight of the cement made the tar paper underneath bellow out to the point of bursting. We needed to figure out a way to hold the wire to the tar paper, so we retired to a bar in town. While we were there, I bought a bottle of pop and pried off the bottle top at the pop machine with the built-in church key. As the top tumbled down into a container, I looked down and saw that there were hundreds of bottle caps in the holder, and I asked the barkeeper if we could have the caps. He said: 'Sure, take all you want.'

"It was a gold mine of free caps—maybe seven or eight hundred a week. Back at the dome, we punched two holes through each cap and put one cap on the outside of the tar

The first dome

paper against the wire and another on the inside. Then we wove a short piece of wire through the two holes so that the caps held the wire against the tar paper, firmly enough to hold the weight of the cement, which we applied about a half-inch thick. We painstakingly installed many hundreds of double bottle caps in that fashion, and when we went inside the finished dome and lay down on the floor, we looked up and saw this spherical dome of black tar paper covered with shining bottle caps. It was like lying down in a planetarium. We lay there a long time contemplating the bottle caps.

"In the end we were amazed that we had ended up with one solid shelter. It was a beautiful structure, and we considered it quite a major dropping. We wanted to paint the dome to match our silver Chevy, so we bought five gallons of 'Illumination,'

Bottle-cap ceiling

which was a silver asphalt roofing compound, and smeared it all over the cement. All the furniture—chairs, counters, bedsteads, bookcases—we built out of two-by-fours. We got the power company to put up a pole and run in a line. We buried the wire that ran up to the dome. We bought a refrigerator and painted it turquoise and covered it with sequins. It was beautiful.

"The plot of land was rectangular," Bernofsky continued, "running west to east, with El Moro Road along the north edge. The land rose from the road to a small hill near the back fence. We had built the shelter atop the hill and the combination of the dome and the hill looked as if someone had stuck a scoop of ice cream in one of those stumpy square cones. From the shelter, we had a clear view of Fisher's Peak and the Sangre de Cristo Mountains. Now we had a structure in the middle of the semi-arid desert that looked as if a Martian spacecraft had landed. The creation of the dome was a demonstration to ourselves and others that there is no reason why anyone should not be able to live in a shelter in our society. Our society is so overly wealthy that there is plenty around to assist people in leading satisfactory lives and fulfilling the creative drives that lie within each of them."

While working on the structure, Bernofsky and Richert often discussed what they should name their new community. For inspiration they went back to their undergraduate days when they had started dropping painted pebbles from the rooftop of the building on Massachusetts Avenue down to the sidewalk in Lawrence, Kansas. Once a dropper, always a dropper, and Drop City instinctively rolled off their tongues.

"Those were the real roots of Drop City," Bernofsky said. "The dome was our first official dropping. This was going to be Drop City, and we were going to be droppers. We felt as if we were functioning within the cosmic forces so much that we were actually influencing them."

Over the ensuing forty years, the name Drop City would baffle many writers and scholars. "Perhaps the most pervasive myths about Drop City have to do with its name," Miller said. "In the late 1960s the word *drop* had two special meanings. First, it meant ingesting LSD; *dropping acid* was the standard argot for that. Second, many hippies saw themselves as dropouts from a decaying society, the alienated who were going to build their own culture from the ground up. So anyone who heard of Drop City immediately had two associations, and the general presumption was that the name of the commune involved one or both kinds of dropping." The FBI got it partially correct: "BERNOFSKY, on being specifically questioned as to the use of the name droppers and the name Drop City," one FBI report said, "stated that the terms had been adopted not from the viewpoint of meaning that he and the members of the community were dropping out of society and desired to isolate themselves, but rather from the viewpoint of desiring to shock society by indicating that we drop things here and there, thereafter alluding to the droppings of animals in that word usage connotation."[39]

By midsummer, Bernofsky said, the droppers had "moved out of the farmhouse and into the dome. All four of us—my wife and I, Clark, and Richard. My wife and I then decided that we wanted more privacy, so we pitched a tent between the two trees, a cottonwood and a black mulberry, that grew on our property in the southwest corner of the land below the dome. It was a small wall tent. In the mornings, we'd make a fire in the woodstove of the dome and cook up some gruel, and then we headed out to scrounge and build. We only owned hand tools, and the building of the domes took a lot of precise work. During the construction period, we were always accumulating found material from around the area. We would assemble it into massive collages. We'd place them along the fence line of Drop City and paint them with buckets of oil paint that Clark had gotten at school.

Tensegrity post sculpture

"Already, we were transforming the land. We believed in Bucky's concept of tensegrity—the unseen structure of the universe that underlies everything. As droppers, we wanted to make it manifest. We had land and an endless supply of two-by-four end pieces that we were using for heat and building material, with plenty left over. We decided to drive two-by-fours into the land itself in the tensegrity pattern, a two-by-four every four to five feet, so that the entire plot of land manifested a hexagon that broke down into cubes—all based on the equilateral triangle. The tetrahedron was the basic building block. We then started mounting little sculptures on each stake.

"We figured we had constructed a major droppage. The domes themselves became collages that we could get inside of. Boyle really pissed me off. He had some nerve to name his book *Drop City*. He would never have had any idea about any of this." Once again, the image of T. C. Boyle raised its ugly head. I did not interrupt Bernofsky's narrative to inquire why a humorous novel continued to upset him.

Meanwhile, at the Corner of Haight and Ashbury

Drop City soon evolved into a microcosm that reflected other counterculture movements developing independently and simultaneously at various points across the country around 1965. It is hard to tell who influenced whom, as many of the movements remained under the media radar during their early years. At about the same time that Bernofsky and Richert were constructing their silver hemisphere, San Francisco's three-eighths-square-mile, ten-to-fifteen-block working-class neighborhood of Haight-Ashbury had begun to morph into a giant counterculture commune—of sorts.

It didn't happen overnight. Before the influx of college kids, teenyboppers, and dropouts flooded the streets of the isolated neighborhood, the area had seemed unexceptional except for the lack of any dominating ethnic group. For the most part neighbors got along, and the friendly banter and hearty greetings along the sidewalks evoked a small-town friendly atmosphere. Students from nearby San Francisco State College, attracted by cheap housing, composed a major part of the population, as did older beats who had fled North Beach after media exposure of its anything-goes atmosphere helped turn the area into a tourist trap offering topless bars and strip joints. Rent for two-floor apartments in the Haight's old Victorian- and Edwardian-style mansions dipped as low as seventy-five dollars a month, and many of the stately homes still featured leather wallpaper, expansive window seats, art nouveau stained glass, and scroll-work trim.

The Haight's own private eight-block-long Panhandle of the Golden Gate Park offered many inviting nooks and half-hidden recesses along the walkway to the De Young Museum and the Japanese Tea Garden. A short trolley ride brought residents to and from the university, which offered many nontraditional courses through its Experimental College. In the spring of 1966, the college would hire a visiting professor—an inventor and philosopher of technology referred to in a newspaper interview as Richard B. Fuller, otherwise known as Bucky. Many of the residents restored the lost flavor of the Gay Nineties by furnishing their apartments and homes with period-style furniture and appropriate accoutrements. Some even refurbished the old light fixtures and hooked them up to gas lines. The restoration efforts didn't end with the furniture and art nouveau wall decorations, either; many residents of the Haight took to wearing Edwardian-style apparel—frock coats, high-collared shirts, frilly skirts with puffed sleeves, wide ties, granny dresses, and gaudy costume jewelry—that they unearthed in goodwill clothing bins. Fashion critics would later dub the look as *Mod*.

Slowly but surely Haight-Ashbury garnered a reputation as the hip place to be in San Francisco. Interesting and unusual businesses soon joined the twenty-four-hour House of Do-Nuts at Frederick and Stanyan streets and Bob's Restaurant at the end of Haight Street. The Blue Unicorn Coffeehouse at 1927 Hayes Street acted as a new haven for beatniks. Over time the locals began referring to the newcomers as hippies—a derisive term coined by the older beats. The more respected hipsters had been young whites who unabashedly imitated cool black jazz musicians by wearing flashy clothes, inventing their own slang, and taking drugs. The older beats saw hippies as trying to be cool but not quite getting it, not quite sure about what or who they wanted to be. The Haight-area hippies, inspired by the Edwardian motif of their new neighbors, soon pushed the unique style of decoration to another level by painting the doors of the gingerbread houses in gaudy colors and hanging rainbow window shades. Many poor hippies also donned outlandish apparel as if trying to counter the reality of their poverty with extravagant display. They daily circumambulated the eighteen blocks of the Haight decked out in colored serapes, elephant Levi bell bottoms, embroidered shirts, old Army-Navy jackets, uniforms of all types, strings of beads, moccasins, leather vests, and headbands.

As had been the case among the beats, drugs soon became the stereotypical trait that distinguished the new species of nonconformists. But unlike the beats, who indulged in alcohol and the full range of drugs, hippies tended to differentiate between good dope, like LSD and marijuana, and evil drugs like heroin and speed. Nearly every hippie in the Haight sold a little grass, and many didn't know any other way of making a buck. Enterprising craftspeople manufactured dope pipes, roach clips, and dope-inspired jewelry such as mandalas and God's eyes. The psychedelic consumers also demanded black lights, strobe lights, psychedelic posters, acid music, and literature with subjects ranging from dope and spirituality to treatises on how to survive on a farm. Before long, the owners of the traditional business establishments, some of them hippies themselves, realized they could turn a profit catering to the whims and needs of the young psychedelic crowd.

As the commercial ventures around the Haight exploited the increasing population of young hip idealists, a different movement steeped in values completely opposed to capitalism

| The Diggers |

sprang to life. The Diggers modeled themselves after seventeenth-century English religious radicals who had denounced the concept of private property, insisting that those who could use land should be able to. The hippie Diggers expanded into an anarchistic clan of individualistic self-proclaimed non-intellectuals with no political ties. They denigrated posturing buffoons and insisted that no such organization as theirs even existed—except as the human race in general. The Diggers believed that money, like God, was dead. While their parents hoarded material possessions and slaved at meaningless jobs to pad their bank accounts, Diggers, like the droppers, believed young people could live off of society's surplus. They intended to create a new type of money, or wampum, that would be negotiable only within their community. The organization had no apparent leaders, nor organization for that matter. Anyone could become a Digger and take the initiative to organize an institution that fulfilled a community need.

For a while the work of the Diggers inspired the Haight community as they found ways to help the burgeoning population of young immigrants survive on the street. The Diggers rented a double garage on Page Street, which they dubbed the Free Frame of Reference, named after the large yellow-painted wooden frame the Diggers often set up to guide people into their street events. Inside the building waited boxes of free clothes, furniture, and household items. They also organized a daily portable soup kitchen at the park near the bus stop, scoring ingredients by begging trimmings of meat and wilting

vegetables from grocery stores and from the city produce
market. Two bakeries contributed day-old bread. Anonymous
donors added to the loot at times, as did some light-fingered
thieves. A group of female students from Antioch College who
shared an apartment on Clayton Street concocted the daily
meals, and Digger guys delivered the soups and stews to the
park in twenty-gallon milk cans. The Diggers made it seem as
if people in the Haight were serious about forming a new
basis for civilization.

For entertainment there wasn't much to do in the Haight at
first besides tripping on drugs and shopping. That all changed
when Chet Helms of the Family Dog staged a rock concert
with the Jefferson Airplane at the Longshoremen's Hall on
October 16, 1965, following a Vietnam Day Committee march.
Around the same time, the San Francisco Mime Troupe held its
first benefit dance in the loft of its theater. When Phil Graham,
the troupe's manager, had to turn hundreds away because of
overcrowding, he rented the larger Fillmore Auditorium for
the next benefit. That affair drew about thirty-five hundred
patrons. After that smashing success, Graham quit the troupe
and began promoting his own dances that featured many of
the Bay Area's top bands at the Fillmore. He later opened
another dance hall in New York City, dubbing it the Fillmore
East. The Merry Pranksters also began producing their acid
graduation tests in various halls around the area.

Although new at rock dances, psychedelic light shows had
been around in one form or another in the Bay Area since
1952, when Seymour Lockes, an art professor at San Francisco
State College, developed some experimental apparatus using
projectors, hollow slides, and pigments. By the late fifties
Lockes's students routinely put on light shows for groups of
beats around California, who often accompanied the shows
by banging on bongos and clanging cymbals. Eventually some

impresarios joined up with the San Francisco Mime Troupe to produce regular Sunday night light shows.

Although most of the residents of the Haight seemed apolitical, the area wasn't too far from the birthplace of the Black Panther Party in Oakland and the antiwar movement based in Berkeley. Hippies shared many of the same values as the radicals, but the two camps seldom worked together. Hippies, after all, wanted to undermine the system all together and start anew, whereas radicals wanted to take control of the reins of power. When writer Ken Kesey, the king of all dropouts, addressed one of the first major antiwar rallies in Berkeley, he told the protesters to go home and drop out of the system altogether rather than try to fight it. Although Bernofsky had lived in San Francisco during the summer of 1962, he hadn't spent much time at Haight-Ashbury and knew little of the counterculture scene that was evolving there. For the most part, Bernofsky and Richert were following their own somewhat-mutual whimsical vision.

. . . *Ronald Reagan announced that he will be a candidate for the Republican nomination to Governor of California. . . . 5.9 million students are enrolled in the nation's colleges and universities this academic year, an increase of 12.2 percent. . . . chances are that growing permissiveness about homosexuality and a hedonistic attitude toward all sex have helped "convert" many people who might have repressed their inclinations in another time or place. . . . clubmanship has become the most popular way to avoid compliance with the discrimination-banning public accommodations section of the Civil Rights Act. . . . the draft has become the most urgent problem in the lives of practically every American male between 18 and 26. . . . the Shah of Iran has launched his country headlong into what is far and away the Middle East's fastest-moving, most ambitious development program. . . . In order to engage the Viet Cong, Americans and South Vietnamese have stepped up their*

"search and clear" thrusts into Communist-held territory, using flame
throwers, gas and explosives to flush the Viet Cong from their tunnels,
leveling whole forest areas to chop snipers from the trees. . . .
(January/February 1966)[40]

"At one point I found a huge piece of corrugated steel along
the highway," Bernofsky said, during another of our sessions.

**Life down on
the Commune**

"It was an old sign, about six feet by ten feet,
and was painted orange. I decided to re-erect
the sign on the El Moro Road, and I got some
black paint to print the lettering. My original message was
supposed to read: 'Droppers Support Nuclear Devastation of
the Earth and Support LBJ's War Policy—Die. Die. Die.' Someone later pointed out to us that I had misspelled the word,
'devastation,' so that the sign actually read: 'Droppers Support
Nuclear Divastion.' The sign turned out to be a good example
of the kind of dropping we were creating—especially since I
had done it by mistake. Our hope for the sign was that people
would think the Vietnam War was the stupidest, most moronic
activity that the United States had ever gotten involved in.
With my upbringing, I had a very different perspective on the
Vietnam War. I saw the early reports of the police action as
distortions of the capitalistic press. I viewed the communists
as the ones who cared about the repressed peoples. They were
the ones with grassroots concerns."

The droppers erected other signs with similar ironic messages.
One FBI informant described a second sign with a message.
"Bomb Vietnam, Bomb Moscow, Bomb Bombay—and other
various places throughout the world." The signs were "an obvious
attempt to shock the community," said the special agent in
charge of the FBI Drop City file. The actual words of the second
sign read: "Bomb Hanoi, London, Moscow, Rome, Chicago,
Canada, New Jersey."[41]

Before the summer ended, the droppers had recruited a new member. Peggy Kagel, a striking redhead, moved in with her ten-year-old daughter. Bernofsky had first met Kagel's husband, Richard, at a summer camp in upper state New York, where both had worked as counselors. The couple was going through difficult times, and Richard chose not to join the group. "Peg Kagel was kind, intense, and brilliant," Bernofsky said. "She loved jazz music and loved animals and was very sensitive and funny. Peggy stayed at Drop City for six to seven months before reuniting with her husband." A few years after leaving Drop City, Kagel committed suicide by overdosing on drugs.

The droppers realized very soon that they could never become self-sufficient in providing their own food. "The garden was rough to get going," Bernofsky said. "I worked and dug and scratched in the shale and watered and watered and watered—but could get nothing to grow, even after using chicken shit for fertilizer. I guess we didn't let the manure cool down enough before using it. The garden was miserable. For another attempt at some level of self-sufficiency we did get a few chickens for egg production.

| Chicken Coop |

"We built a little coop, in the shape of a cosahedron. The chickens would free range during the day and often we would get fresh eggs. Then one day we noticed one of the chickens was having spasms, with its head jerking so uncontrollably it could barely get around. We brought it into the dome to nurse it back to health, and I went into town to call my biochemist brother, Carl, about it. He told me to be very careful because the chicken could have some exotic disease that might be contagious to humans. We decided to get rid of it but couldn't decide who was going to kill this chicken. I offered that we didn't have to kill it, we could bury it alive. The others said that would be

Chicken coop

too cruel, but no one had any better idea, so I dug a hole and put the chicken in the hole and covered it up. Before I knew it my companions had dug the chicken back up. It was still alive, and Clark got an axe and took the chicken and laid its head out on a stump, but only cut halfway through its neck. The chicken took off with blood spurting everywhere, and I'm thinking this diseased bird is spurting this contagious blood over everything. Clark finally grabbed it and chopped again until the chicken was beheaded. They then reburied it. The situation with the chicken was traumatic to all of us. From that day on my fellow droppers considered me some kind of monster.

"For the most part, the cosmic forces watched over us—at least up to our low standards. Whenever we ran out of money and the forces decided to temporarily go on leave, Clark and I would go looking for temporary jobs. Sometimes we would clean out chicken shit from the big barn of a neighboring farm. The barn contained thousands of cages and the droppings would accumulate until they formed a pyramid about two to three feet across at the base, under each cage. We spent days in there with shovels and a wheelbarrow. The woman who owned the chicken ranch would pay us a couple hundred bucks [Kallweit thought the sum an exaggeration] each time we did it. After getting paid, we felt secure and rich. She also let us take the soft eggs.

"We had access to two sources of free food. Once a week we approached all the wholesale food houses and supermarkets in and around Trinidad, asking for donations of food in dented cans or smashed boxes. We accepted bruised fruit and produce, moldy cheese, dated milk and cream, meat that had turned brown, or anything destined for the dumpster. Also, once a month we drove to the fairgrounds in Trinidad to collect government surplus commodities from the Las Animas County Welfare Department. The stash often included cans of chipped beef, powdered milk and eggs, flour, bulgur, lard, and beans (all

the ingredients needed to make tortillas), and peanut butter.
When we pulled up in the silver Chevy there would be pickups
full of Mexican laborers there too. They hated the chipped
beef and would trade with us for our flour. They were very
generous to us.

"We also grabbed as much peanut butter as we could get. It
was made of ground nuts and was absolutely fabulous. At home
we fought over the peanut butter. We would sit around the open
can with spoons and take turns, making sure it was shared absolutely fairly until the can was empty. One day
we assembled to eat peanut butter and found
the can already half empty. Clark was really
uptight that someone had gluttonized the peanut butter without
sharing it. Although Clark was an alternative type, and meek
and degenerate in his mind, nevertheless certain Mennonite
values of fairness encumbered his personality to a great extent.
When Clark discovered that there had been an unfair distribution of peanut butter—that someone had been sneaking—he
was extremely upset. To him, the theft represented a significant breach of trust. Moreover, it represented the first crack
of distrust in our tightly evolving communal effort. So he called
a meeting in the dome where we would hash it all out before
this behavior could spread to other areas of our lives. He was
tense, uptight, and extremely upset. The cosmic forces were
no longer flowing freely through us. We sat around the table
facing the No. 5 can of government commodity peanut butter.
It was very funny to me, but very serious to Clark.

"I have to admit, I had learned early on that Clark was an
expert in peanut butter. While we were living together in Kansas,
I tested his expertise. I got six different brands of peanut butter
and took a dollop from each jar and put it on a Saltine cracker.
I then set them before Clark, who was blindfolded and stoned.
Clark taste tested each one and identified all of them. So I
knew Clark was a peanut butter master. When the de-charging

> **Decharging over
> Peanut Butter**

session came up, I knew we were in for some serious hallucinating. We went round and round talking about the peanut
butter and everything else. Whatever was clogging our free-
flowing thoughts, we laid out on the table to discuss, argue,
and de-charge. Clark's aim was to get everyone's mind back
on track, because we all needed to concentrate if we were to
survive the winter. After about an hour and a half, no one
owned up to sneaking the extra peanut butter. I know they all
suspected me because I was the type who would do it. And
now that I think about it, maybe it was me, but I didn't admit
it at the time because I have a certain perverse pride. At the
end of the session we ate the rest of the peanut butter that
was left in the can, one tablespoon at a time."

That first summer the droppers started constructing another
dome to use as a community kitchen.

| The Kitchen Dome |

"We set it closer to the highway," Bernofsky
said, "and this time we intended to make a
true geodesic structure with a ten-sided base.
We constructed the frame with the scab end two-by-fours, but
this time we sheathed it with half-inch plywood and again
painted it with Illumination. In the original dome we had cut
out a triangle at every juncture and filled them with glass from
car windows we had gotten at the junkyard. There were three
sections of glass in every hexagonal frame. In the kitchen dome
we installed smaller triangular windows in all the elements
surrounding the iron-sewer-pipe joints. Along the base we built
hinged wooden flaps that we could open out for circulation
and light. We capped the top of the dome with an extra pentagon that sat on the dome like a hat, and which also had retract-
able flaps. With the bottom and top flaps open, the cool air
would come through the top and drop down and go out the
lower flaps providing air-conditioned breezy comfort. We also
set up a wood-burning stove in that dome for communal cooking."

Kitchen dome

A dropper, writing under the pseudonym William Voyd, later described the second dome as a "twenty-foot diameter, two-frequency geodesic. Each triangle of an icosahedron is divided into four smaller triangles, each vertex pulled out to the surface of a sphere." For the heating, he wrote: "A small heater or open flame near the center of the dome, with a heat collector and stove pipe running out of the top, causes a column of heated air to rise around the hot metal parts. This air is in turn pushed down into the dome to recirculate. Unhampered by sharp corners, the velocity of the air is increased. Though this does not increase the heat which is radiated into all parts of the dome unshielded by partitioning walls, it does increase the volume of air per minute passing over and conducting heat directly away from the heater. This heating method is further advanced by the fact that in relation to the inner volume of the dome, the outer surface is less than any other shape, thus conducting less heat away from the dome."[42]

"We also began building the theater dome during the winter of '65," Richert said. "We constructed this forty-foot-diameter dome to accommodate film and slide projection over the entire interior surface from a projection booth beneath the floor. We did not have great success with coherent projections across the entire surface, but we did stage several events involving projections, strobe-lit spinning paintings and music. Our theater predated by several years a similar project by filmmaker Stan Vanderbeek—a project for which he received considerable publicity."

The droppers purposely set the theater dome near the parking lot, hoping that visitors would be satisfied with their examination of that building and not proceed farther up the hill to interrupt the droppers as they worked. John Curl, a writer from New York and a friend of Peggy Kagel, arrived at Drop City during the construction of the theater dome. "Suddenly there was the open latticework of a large dome structure in front of me," Curl said. "It looked like a web of interconnected wheels. Somebody was all the way near the top on the other side hammering. A hundred yards away, two bright silver metallic domes, one on the top of a small hill; the other in a low area. The lower one had an A-frame attached. They looked like landed UFOs. The sun glinted off their surfaces."[43]

For the most part, the droppers kept to themselves, occasionally flitting in and out of Trinidad to beg for food or scouring the rural landscape for useful detritus. Theirs was not

Those Who Came Before

the first community to have evolved on that patch of land. Although always sparsely settled, the area had a rich history, beginning with

Theater dome

Comanche, Kiowa, Arapaho, and Cheyenne Indians who had once hunted buffalo herds in the lower Purgatoire River valley. By the time the droppers arrived, the Utes were the only Native American tribe still existing in the area, but their reservation lay in the mountains to the southwest, not far from the Anasazi ruins at Mesa Verde. The Spanish were the first Europeans to settle the area, in the 1600s, along the upper Rio Grande west of Trinidad. They named the Purgatoire River in honor of some of their compadres who died at the hands of the Indians before receiving the last rites of the Catholic Church. The French later claimed the area as part of Louisiana and by 1700 had opened it to fur trappers and traders. When Britain defeated France in 1763, France ceded the land to Spain, which then assigned it to Mexico in 1821—the same year wagons started rolling in from the United States along the Sante Fe Trail.

Trinidad, named after a Spaniard's girlfriend, was the first town to evolve in the area, where the Sante Fe Trail crossed a spur trail leading to Denver. After the Mexican War, when the United States claimed the area and opened it for settlement in 1860, the area became part of Colorado Territory, despite a promise by the U.S. government to honor Mexican land grants. El Moro formed in 1876 as a terminal town for the Denver & Rio Grande Railroad, which had extended a narrow-gauge line to mining camps along the eastern foothills. The railroad named El Moro after a castle in Havana, Cuba. Supposedly, Fisher's Peak reminded some railroad executive of the castle's Moorish-style architecture. Two thousand people eventually moved into the hundred buildings that were hastily constructed that first year, with many finding work at the coke ovens. When commercial coal mining boomed in the nearby hills in the 1870s, the broad-gauge Atchison, Topeka & Sante Fe Railroad chose to route a line through Trinidad, which effectively sealed El Moro's fate as a ghost town. Nineteenth-century recyclists quickly disman-tled El Moro's buildings and the land reverted to prairie.

Trinidad, in the meantime, remained a sleepy town throughout the twentieth century, its population peaking at six thousand
in the sixties. Throughout that decade, every two years Trinidadians elected one of two men as mayor—either the barber or the
realtor, with each running unopposed in alternating elections.
The droppers never bothered to vote or took much interest
in the social life of Trinidad. Despite the presence of a junior
college, culturally the burg remained a backwater town. Before
the arrival of the droppers the only artist in town was Arthur
Roy Mitchell, who throughout the thirties and forties painted
front covers of Western pulp magazines. When the droppers
arrived, Mitchell, now in his eighties, still taught in the art department that he had founded at Trinidad State Junior College,
but he showed little interest in meeting the new artists at Drop
City. However, other Trinidadians displayed more curiosity.

That first summer, as the first dome rose from the sage-
brush, wild rumors spread around town that the droppers
comprised a vanguard force of an imminent communist invasion. On July 24, 1965, a special agent for the FBI recorded:
"[A]dvised that community gossip of a *strictly hearsay nature*
existed to the effect that a group of *Russian Beatniks* had
moved into the El Mora area, about 5 miles east of Trinidad,
Colorado, and allegedly bought property from FNU. . . . For
about $13,000. The rumor is to the effect that from 300 to 1,000
more Russian Beatniks would arrive in the future. . . . One
of these boys was supposed to have told a County commissioner:
"Yes, we are Communists." Subsequent FBI reports included
such descriptions of Drop City as a "continuing beatnik-type
Special Committee on Un-American Activities hippie-type
community, whose residents appear to vary from 15 to 30 in
number, were described as a clannish and rather self-contained
group, but who were not known to be engaging in any subversive
type of activity or in any violations of general criminal law."[44]

The immediate neighbors stuck more or less to the rural code of keeping their noses out of other people's business and seemed to tolerate the droppers. The Andersons, who had sold Bernofsky the land, lived to the south. "They actually got a kick out of what we were doing and were very kind and understanding," Bernofsky said. A Greek family ran a goat farm to the east, and a skeptical Italian American cattle rancher lived to the north. Once the first dome went up, the townspeople in Trinidad grew curious and initiated their own not very secretive surveillance operations.

"Every evening there would be a procession of cars to see what in god's name was going on out here," Bernofsky said. "It was all very friendly. And on the weekends it was all day long. Some people were brave enough to visit with us. Once they found out we were friendly, the word spread, and more and more people wanted to meet us and talk to us to find out what we were doing. The man who ran the Dairy Joy in Trinidad told us that if we let him put up a sign on our property he would give us free ice cream. We agreed, and he erected a sign that said, 'After a Visit to Drop City, Stop at the Dairy Joy.' The man was true to his word. At the time we all wore dropper hats that looked like caftans and were covered with sequins and other shiny baubles. These made us look like clown prince droppers. Whenever we showed up at Dairy Joy with our hats on we got free ice cream.

"When they visited the commune, the visitors parked along the road opposite the El Moro schoolhouse and walked up the road in single file, never in a bunch," Bernofsky continued. "There were all kinds of diverse people—old, young, Mexican, Anglos. We would be working all the time, cutting boards, building foundations, gardening, or snipping panels of car tops. The visitors somehow felt comfortable just coming onto the land and walking through it, asking us all kinds of questions.

Dairy Joy sign

It was as if we were some kind of bizarre human beings on exhibition. They had never seen anything like us. We were out there in the open, exposed. As this interest increased, I started counting the number of visitors on the weekend, and I remember counting more than 120 people on one day. But after a while it got annoying to have to stop work to talk to them. We painted on our sign at the front gate: 'Limit: One Question per Visit Only.' At one point we considered charging an admission fee, but instead we put up a donation box. I don't ever remember finding more than seventy-five cents in it. The donation box itself was a very carefully handcrafted item. I think people just considered it another curious item to look at.

"Just about the time the sightseers started to roll in, I acquired a new movie camera—a small Kodak 16 mm that used cheap black-and-white reversal film. The film was inexpensive to develop because it didn't require much processing in the laboratory. The positive images of the developed film were also easy to edit. Every time some building or anything else interesting was going on at Drop City, I put the camera on a tripod nearby. I would film a while and work or play a while." John Curl said that Bernofsky's films were "really funny, and captured the feeling of the early place better than any words could have."[45] Bernofsky shot thousands of feet of film during a two-year period, including many faces in the steady stream of gawkers. "I especially enjoyed filming the visitors," he said.

. . . *the newly blooded American 25th Infantry Division last month found a three-level tunnel network that snaked to 15 feet below the matted jungle and stretched more than 200 yards. . . . The exquisitely contemporary hero is girl-happy, gadget-minded James Bond. . . . "I don't have no quarrel with those Viet Congs," blared the Greatest. So the Illinois Boxing Commission canceled his March 29 title bout with Ernie Terrell. . . . everywhere the diagnosis is the same: psychotic illness resulting from unauthorized, nonmedical use of the drug LSD-15. . . . First it was free speech, then filthy speech. Now it is free love. . . . All told, Red casualties have been 21,500 dead, 3,200 captured, 40,000 wounded and 5,500 defected in South Viet Nam since October. . . . To help celebrate its 100th birthday, the University of Kansas invited a sampling of intellectuals: Designer Buckminster Fuller. . . . Gradually but unmistakably we are succumbing to the arrogance of power. . . . Though most of the country is not yet "turned on," Timothy Leary told the faithful in a lecture titled "The Politics and Ethics of Ecstasy," the "psychedelic battle" is over and won, and some 1 million Americans have already had "psychedelic experiences." . . . Not only did the Supreme Court void Danny's confession: it held that every arrested American is now entitled to consult his lawyer as soon as police investigation makes him a prime suspect. . . .* (March/April 1966)[46]

The Press Takes Notice

One brilliant December day, a visitor with his own camera dangling from a strap around his neck walked up to Bernofsky and Richert and introduced himself as Monk Tyson, a reporter for the *Denver Post*. The two droppers, working on a new dome at the time, looked at each other and rolled their eyes. As droppers they equated the media with the Establishment, and without consulting each other Bernofsky and Richert enacted a major dropping at the expense of the reporter. "We fed him all kinds of unbelievable nonsense with a straight face, which he took down like gospel," Bernofsky explained. "I told him my name was Curley Bensen and that I was a hobbit from the cosmos. I said this from atop the storage dome we had built in the form of an icosahedron. Then he turned to Clark, and Clark told him his name was Clard Svensen. Clark then gestured toward Kallweit and said: 'He's Larry Lard.' We told the reporter that we depended on the cosmic forces for survival and didn't want to be gainfully employed. We wanted to build things and create a satisfactory civilization for ourselves. And then we told him my wife was known as the Drop Lady. A week later there was this big color photo of Drop City on the front page of the *Denver Post* with an accompanying headline: HOBBITS IN TRINIDAD. We had all had a good time about it—both us and the reporter— but all of a sudden Trinidad is getting major publicity."

The *Denver Post* story appeared on the day after Christmas 1965. Since the word "hippie" had not yet come into vogue, Tyson had a hard time pigeon-holing the droppers. "A group of beatnik-type persons in their early 20s have settled on a six-acre tract at the rural hamlet of El Moro near Trinidad," he wrote. "A discarded sign and a button worn by one of the members urged nuclear devastation. But in conversation they ramble about relief for tensions and indicate this can be found in their colony. They call themselves the Droppers. A spokesman, however, was vague on whether they approve or disapprove of dropping nuclear bombs. A *Denver Post* reporter was greeted at their settlement, named Drop City, by two young men, a young woman and her 15-month-old daughter. All insisted on giving fictitious names. The young woman said her name was *Mrs. Oleo Margarine*, 23, and the child was named *Melissa*. She said she had attended Bard College at Annandale-on-Hudson, N.Y., for one year. She said her husband whom she sees *once in a while*, was named *Kago Margarine*. A stocky, dark-haired 24-year-old man said he preferred to use the name of *Curley Bensen*, that he is a psychology and philosophy graduate from the University of Kansas but a native of New York. *Bensen* did most of the talking. *Clard Svensen*, 24, a slender youth, said he was from Witchita, Kan., that he graduated with art as a major from KU and did two years of graduate work at the University of Colorado. They said a 23-year-old woman called the *Drop Lady* of Brooklyn, N.Y. and *Larry Lard*, 22, of New York, who studied art two years at KU, were away on visits during the Christmas holidays. They described the *Drop Lady*, or *Drop*, as their leader. These six persons make up Drop City's population, but *Bensen* said membership totaled *about 40*, and that 50 percent of these members are *around Boulder*, Colo.

"Living quarters are in two small buildings described as *geodesic domes* made of wood and tar-impregnated wood fiber. Domes are built of what *Bensen* and *Svensen* called facets or triangles. They said the kitchen has 40 facets and another dome obviously used as a dormitory has 30 facets. Two tents, a chicken coop, a small, conical structure covered with tar paper and an outhouse are the other buildings. Another dome under construction is to be a theatre, *Bensen* said. The largest of the two tents is used for storage and the small one is used for sleeping in the summertime, *Bensen* said. . . . The kitchen dome has hot and cold water, which drains from a sink into a shallow, smelly outside trench. Fuel comes from a butane gas tank. *Bensen* talked of expansion plans among the Droppers. He said he bought the tract for $450. Asked if payment was made by a check on Chase Manhattan Bank, he became vague but later admitted he recalled that *someone* in the group might have an account at the bank. *Bensen* and *Svensen* spoke of building a sphere for entertainment and said a feature would be one or more keyboards which would provide electronic sounds, lights and smells. He said odors would be bottled and listed some of them as perfume, grease, dwarfs, sewage, liquore, body, love potions and *anything that can be bottled*. *Bensen* said Droppers put up about $30 per month to purchase $60 worth of welfare food stamps at Trinidad, five miles up the road from the colony. This provides enough food for the six members, he added. 'If we can raise that to $75 a month, that'll be enough for booze, too,' said *Bensen*."[47]

The publicity did not stop there. The wire service picked up the Drop City story, and three weeks later the following announcement appeared in the *New Yorker* magazine's "Talk of the Town": "A group of young men and women, some of them college graduates, have settled near Trinidad, Colorado, and are attempting to get in touch with dwarfs and trolls. 'We lost contact with dwarfs, wizards, and the tree people thousands of years ago,' their spokesman, a psychology and philosophy major from the University of Kansas, has explained, and he has also expressed the conviction that the dwarfs are 'concerned' over the threat of nuclear destruction."[48] Around the same time, an editor at the tabloid *National Insider* commissioned Bernofsky to write an exposé on the hobbits from another planet who lived at the commune. The publication offered seventy-five dollars for the piece, Bernofsky said. "We collaborated on it and mailed it in. To our astonishment, the editors didn't change a single word. The front page headline read: 'The Heretics: Work Kills the Human Spirit—Why Not Quit Today?'"

Bernofsky, for one, had conflicting reactions to the sudden media attention. "The media feeds off each other big time," he said. "Eat. Spit. Eat. Spit. And they can't eat enough. Stories in several other newspapers brought in PR—and before we turned around we found our notoriety was growing. Why? Because there was so much disgust in the country over the endless war news that many people were hoping and looking for something else. Drop City represented something positive that was happening in the region. People began offering us encouragement; they supported us and gave us authentic feedback. Some would even send us small checks in the mail. I think it was because we offered an on-the-ground alternative to so much of the horror that was going on over in Vietnam."

In April 1966 another stranger walked into Drop City, this time to inspect rather than gawk at the domes.

| Steve Baer, |
| Zome Builder |

The man, who lived outside Albuquerque, New Mexico, had been driving home from Colorado Springs.

"He was an intense-looking individual, plainly dressed like a working man just off a job," Bernofsky said. "He told us that he was interested in—and astonished by—what we had achieved. He'd been watching our progress for quite some time, and he was very interested in doing it himself—not starting a commune, but building domes. He asked us for permission to build a triple-fused rhombo-icoso-dodecahedron dome on our land. We more or less said, 'Sure—where do you want to put it?' He explained each dome would have a thirty-foot diameter. 'This could be your community center,' he said. 'If you let me put it up I will pay for all the materials. In return, it will allow me to do certain experiments to see if it's structurally sound.' We said 'O.K.,' little knowing that he would enslave us as his personal laborers. And enslave us and drive us he successfully did."

This man was Mr. Steve Baer, a trained engineer, architect, and inventor who had been educated in Switzerland. "Steve was an individual who detested dope smoking hippies," Bernofsky continued. "Little did he know that we would turn him into the most famous hippie of the decade. He invented many funda-mental apparatus for solar energy that could be easily constructed by grassroots people, and he ran many experiments in Drop City." In his free time, Baer read recondite mathematical papers and also studied the work of English architect Keith Crichlow. "Steve hated Bucky Fuller and characterized his work as German archi-tecture," Kallweit said. "But he loved Bucky's idiotic poetry."

In his own writings and interviews, Baer argued that geodesic domes—with their circular floors, multiple edges and joints, and different edge lengths—had limitations as far as offering comfortable living quarters. He found them fairly complicated to construct, and that tinkering with their shape upset their structural integrity. Having become fascinated with the poly-hedrons, Baer had already begun working on a new system with which he could build a vast array of shapes with a much smaller inventory of parts. A few years after building some experimental domes at Drop City, Baer went on to incorporate a business called Zomeworks. He also collaborated with Steve Durkee to design the central complex of the Lama Founda-tion, located near San Cristobal, New Mexico.

"Steve Baer is essentially an inventor," Bernofsky said. "He invents technologies. This is different from being a slave to technologies. So he is able to stand back and see them and not be inundated by them, or obsessed with them. He could invent them. And he wanted to demonstrate his theories at Drop City."

Baer was also a philosopher in his own right. In the dropper tradition, he wanted to free people's minds—especially those of architects—from modern conventions. "Architects and engi-neers had hamstrung themselves with a paucity of shapes to which we have in the past confined ourselves because of our technology-industry-education-economy," Baer said. "There are no dramatic disclosures here, those have already been made to all of us when as children we first drew polygons, patterns and messes of straight and squiggly lines. At anyone's finger tips lie many more solutions to the architectural geometric problems of enclosing areas and volumes than a life time of study of geometric regularities and systems offer[s]. But we have sensible reasons for not breaking out into the huge freedom of irregular shapes—once done we would no longer have the aid of our machines, tools and simple formulae. Our first move can be to explore the territory we have confined ourselves to, it is far bigger than we think. Eventually we must, aided by different kinds of tools and methods drawn from as yet unrelated branches of our sciences, go forward so that we find ourselves back with the man who works with branches, reeds and mud and who needn't worry about the angle a saw blade was set at years ago in a mill in another town."[49]

By the time Baer arrived at Drop City he had discovered a unique building material that fitted perfectly with the dropper vision of recycling—the tops of junked cars. The next time he visited the commune, Baer handed double-bit axes to the droppers and told them to climb into his truck. During the next few days they harvested car tops from various junkyards across northern New Mexico and southern Colorado. "The car tops consisted of either 16-gauge or 18-gauge steel and were padded with insulation, which would fall out as we cut them. Steve knew the price of recycled steel and would figure out how much each top was worth to the junkyard owner by weight. The owners loved it because no one ever wanted the tops. For them it was a bonanza. In one day we would transform a junkyard from a field full of cars to one of ghostly autos with no tops," Bernofsky said.

"The advantage of using an axe is that it's cheap and after

> **Recycling Car Tops**

some practice it can become a real pleasure to chop the top out of a car," Baer said in his *Dome Cookbook.* "Chop along the sides first then the front and back. Throw open the doors—one foot on an open door and one foot on the car is a good stance for chopping the sides. On cars with missing back glasses be careful of standing on the shelf in back of the rear seat—some of these have gaps spanned only by cardboard and its easy to step through—old Fords are made this way. Don't swing the axe hard once you have a slot going. Cut swinging the head almost parallel to the top. If you hit flat, as you would a log you'll only smash the metal in. You have to first go after tops with a good deal of ambition, it takes a while before even the best get the hang of it." At the time, sedan tops measured between forty-five and fifty-three inches wide and between fifty and seventy inches long, while a station wagon surrendered a top as long as eight feet. A scalped van or minibus yielded even more. "With practice you can chop off five or six tops in an hour," Baer continued. "With cars packed tightly together you can work even faster because you don't have to drop to the ground. But some junkyard owners can't stand the sight of scalped cars and refuse to allow you access. The best people to work with are the men who haul the bodies to a railhead or a smelter, they don't care what you take."[50]

| A Car Top Zome |
The first structure Baer designed for Drop City was the cartop zome, which became a prototype for his fledgling business—Zomeworks, Inc. "After collecting a trailer full of car tops, he drove us back to his workshop in Corrales, New Mexico, where he demonstrated how to cut the tops into precisely measured metal sheets with electric snippers," Bernofsky said. "Instead of equilateral triangles, Steve formed the parts into Isoceles triangles. Then he showed us how to bend the edges at right angles so that we could later bolt the flanges together. After we had cut all the pieces we marked them, and then hauled them back to Drop City. I set up my camera to record the construction in a time-lapse film. It was a simple chore to assemble

Cartop zome

the panels onto an oval foundation of railroad ties. We would assemble a few panels and I would click off a few frames. Sometimes I would get involved in the work and forget, then holler: 'Wait! Wait!' And I'd take a few more shots. I ended up with two minutes' worth of time-lapse film. It wasn't a smooth-flowing standard time-lapse film like you see of sunsets or the tide coming in. But it was really cool. The materials for the structure cost about fifteen dollars and it took two and a half days from starting construction to the time we moved in."

The steel skin had no internal supports, frame, or bracing other than integral folds in the metal. While the droppers dubbed the structure the Car Top Dome, architects have referred to it as an asymmetrical zonahedron. Baer simply called it a zome—a term he borrowed from Steve Durkee.

"Durkee and I were talking about these structures and agreed that they really were not domes because they are not symmetric," Baer said. "Stretching the zones of a zonahedra makes it asymmetrical. Durkee said: 'They are zomes.' I was excited by this word—it sounds right. The word doesn't change any buildings but I kept waking up that night with the word going through my head. The next day at work Durkee and I kept saying things like—'Well, almost time to go zome.' . . . I have sometimes been shy about using the word because it sounds to myself as if I were advertising something. It may be that inventing the word is more important to something's use than the form itself."[51] Multicolored geometric patterns, painted by Richert and Kallweit who had moved into the cartop dome, soon graced the interior ceiling. "Being surrounded by all these abstractions inside this oddly shaped room felt like being in a world where colors took crystalline forms and hurtled in every direction through mental space," Curl said.[52]

. . . *The explosive population surge that added some 40 million citizens to the U.S. in the 15 years after V-J day has subsided and may well continue to decline. . . . Last week two Yale University researchers reported the discovery of a "morning-after" pill that can prevent pregnancy. . . . "Haitians," Papa Doc Duvalier says quietly, "have a destiny to suffer." . . . A survey by social scientists found that most Americans still share a visceral instinct that the U.S. should not withdraw. However, said Western Pollster Don Muchmore, "there is a complete lack of belief that we can win. . . . Local draft boards are digging deeper into their files, searching for 23-, 22-, and 21-year-olds. . . . the sporadic, five-year-old guerrilla rebellion of Iraq's stubborn 1.5 million Kurdish tribesmen flares up again. . . . there are some 60 million regular riders and annual new-bike sales have doubled to 5 million in the last twelve years. Now the cyclists are demanding rights of way of their own. . . . Last week Ronald Reagan walked off with an astonishingly large victory in California's*

Republican gubernatorial primary. . . . New York police estimate that
110 cars are abandoned every night, and the figures are proportionately
high for other cities in a nation that wears out 6 million cars a year. . . .
(May/June 1966)[53]

The Triple-dome Complex

For Drop City, Baer envisioned a grand structure that even Bucky Fuller hadn't designed yet—a triple-fused rhombo-icoso-dodecahedron. At first Baer planned a cozy livable building, with sections of the triangles, squares, and pentangles measuring four feet along the edges. Kallweit thought he had a better idea: "'Why not expand to eight feet on the side?' I said, thinking this would sort of be a modest twofold increase. But in actuality, by going to eight feet on the side we created a monster." Under the new specifications, each of the three interlocking domes stretched out over a thirty-four-foot diameter. The entire structure was built out of junk materials, with the car tops used as the panels for the separate sections. With the latticework frame in place, Richert and Kallweit carefully orchestrated the placement of the panels by color so that the patterns on the three bubbles emerged as stars, squares, and cubes. While the droppers focused on the artistic aspects, Baer carefully noted the engineering changes in the structure as it rose from the ground.

"The growth of a dome panel by panel is a marvel," he said, "watching it take its shape and strength is something at once very strange and very familiar, as if you were watching the growth of a life form from another planet, unusual because of its foreignness, familiar because it seems alive. But this process if it ends on the addition of the last panel in a rock solid dome does not reveal what was necessary and what was unnecessary in the construction of the panels or the manner in which they are connected. If rigidity were to come before the addition of the last panel it may show that you have overbuilt—but this is an unlikely occurrence."[54]

When the droppers climbed atop each of the three domes, the structures trembled. The southwest dome seemed especially unstable, wiggling and shaking and unable to hold its shape. "When we added braces in the top square it instantly changed the wiggle to a mere tremble," Baer said.[55] "The tremble later disappeared when we nailed down the outside overlapping flanges." The crew also had trouble getting the second-to-last pentagon in place. Frustrated, they took a break. In the meantime, a gusty wind picked up, slightly shaking the building. The next morning the pentagon dropped right into place. Baer's three intersecting rhombo-icoso-dodecahedrons joined together very neatly—an advantage over geodesic domes, which could not be joined to each other with any geometric grace. The resultant interior, while spatially unified, offered three distinct lobes, as well as an open loft over their common intersection. But Kallweit found it "too large, too much work, too many problems; and too hard to heat."

By now, well familiar with winter on the high desert plain, the droppers made a foray into the countryside to search for insulation for their new dome. They first stopped at a plant in Pueblo, Colorado, and asked to see the president of the firm. "I made a speech to the guy that went something like this," Bernofsky said. "We are building a new civilization in Trinidad. We need your help wherever it's possible. We are trying to invent new ways of existence and to use the waste of the society. We are doing our best to live as well as we can for our own existence from hand to mouth, and wherever people can help us, we ask that they participate in this great venture. Could you please help us with some broken bats of insulation? To our astonishment, the man led us out the back of the building to a giant pile of insulation rolls with ripped packaging. The man told us to take all we wanted. This man was generous; he was wonderful; he was great. And we went out there and found beautiful, perfect insulation. So we built sides on Steve's truck and loaded it up with this great bonanza."[56] The droppers dubbed the triple-dome the Complex, and the seventy-five-foot-long structure soon became the center of dropper activity.

"We constructed an open loft equipped with a desk, work table, and sewing area," Bernofsky said. "Beneath the loft we built a bathroom with a flush toilet and a storage closet for winter clothing and seldom-used articles. A separate room housed the bathtub. Three steps down from the main area stood the kitchen with two stoves standing back-to-back in the center, divided by spice and herb shelves. Drop Lady painted the stoves blue and drew two large gaping mouths on the doors of the refrigerators. To store grains and other foodstuffs, we constructed large pull-out bins. We ate together at two long multi-colored tables in the kitchen. In another area there were three recycled couches, plus a rocking chair made from a large cable spool. The Complex also housed the woodworking and welding shops. We decorated the walls with our paintings, as well as messages, letters, photographs, and drawings. Later, we added a patio just outside the front entrance."

The droppers soon realized that the flush toilet used too much water, so they eventually reverted to outhouses. "The ideal outhouse is a fly-proof hole," wrote Bill Voyd. "From this ideal several simple structurally pleasing outhouses have been designed and built; one of the most aesthetically pleasing of these is not enclosed but consists of a hole in the ground with a lid, surrounded by brush."[57]

Baer also designed a solar heating system for the tar-paper-and-chicken-wire dome that the droppers had constructed on the hill. "It was the prototype for Baer's flat plate collector passive heating system," Richert said. "It collected so much heat on a cold winter day that at night we had to open the windows to keep from overheating. We believe this to be the first modern-day solar-heated house in Colorado. Despite all the talk in the hippie community about alternative energy, the solar heater at Drop City seems to have been the only system installed at any commune."

While Baer freely traded his designs for the opportunity to realize his visions, his relationship with the droppers was never strictly that of architect to client. "Baer learned from Drop City, tempering his pristine polyhedral geometries with the salvage ethic and funk aesthetic of the droppers' building methods and social needs," said writer William Chaitkin.[58] Baer and his wife, Holly, also offered more than diagrams and models to the community. "Although they wouldn't classify themselves as hippies, they shared many aspects of the dropper vision and provided much inspiration," Bernofsky said—and at times they also shared financial support. Baer eventually earned the dropper name Luke Cool.

"The domes Steve designed were a wonderful expansion for us," Bernofsky continued. "We felt as if we were taking part in architectural and engineering advancement. We were parts of his experiments. Not only that, but Steve loved us, and we loved him. As it turned out he was almost as insane as we were. Now, as I look back on it, I think we actually were saner than he was at the time."

Stephen Baer never became an official dropper. He realized that too many aspects of communal living would obstruct the path leading toward his goals. "I decided I was a person who got a lot of satisfaction playing with technology," he said, "and communes weren't ready yet for sophisticated applications. If I wanted to accomplish anything, I realized it meant going back into the system and making enough money to buy the materials. All this talk about a self-contained counterculture— can you imagine us freaks trying to manufacture plastic, pipe, and glass?"[59]

One by one more domes blossomed on the site as new settlers constructed homes for themselves. By the end of the

| Opinions of Drop City Architecture |

building phase, ten structures stood on the barren site of sparse grass and prickly pear, forming an intimate community of homes all within a stone's throw of one another. "I loved Drop City immediately," said Richard Fairfield. "No hassle finding it; it was compact—all the buildings in a small, neatly arranged complex, and those domes—beautiful domes are somehow much more lovely than the loveliest of suburban mansions." Drop City also inspired the poetic side of writer William Hedgepeth. "Drop City is a half-forbidding netherworld where idealistic troglodytes lurk and live in fields of giant candy-colored toadstools. Suddenly, there are the shapes. Angular, unearthly, demented, like gawky igloos in a kaleidoscope; and here and there hunch muted distant figures back and forth between them. Stroboscopic flits of summer lightning from a passing storm tremble on the skyline up along the crests of hills. Then, gradually, the daytime darkness lifts, and there glow the domes brightly in the bare air. Yellow blue green red pink purple: brazen things just lying up there, coldly geodesic, looming on the little rise way out here in southern Colorado wasteland where no one sees or comprehends or cares. Maybe somehow all the rest of America hasn't even yet been born."[60]

It was during the construction of the Complex that the legend of the golden car top first sprouted. Bernofsky wasn't the only dropper who circulated the tale about chopping off the top of a brand new Cadillac. It turned out that there was yet another version of how the golden car top was pilfered. Peter Douthit, aka Peter Rabbit, wrote that the incident happened in a motel lot in Taos, not in Walsenburg as Bernofsky placed it. "Charlie DiJulio and Bernofsky both raised their axes together," Douthit said. "Baer nodded his head and both tools came down as one. THUNK! Two perfect cuts. They waited a few minutes to see if

DiJulio's Pit

the noise had awakened anyone. All was quiet. They went back to work, making sure every chop was as efficient and silent as possible. Inside of ten minutes the gold Cadillac was topless and the Wop and Luke were back on the road grinning to themselves in the dark cab of the pickup. 'A good night's work,' said the Wop. 'I'm only sorry about one thing,' said Luke laughing. 'I'm only sorry that I can't be there in the morning to see that mother's face when he discovers that his shitmobile turned convertible overnight.'"[61]

DiJulio's Pit

The population at Drop City continued to expand that second summer, even after Peggy Kagel left to reunite with her husband. John Curl, Charlie and Carol DiJulio and their young daughter joined the Bernofskys, Richert, and Kallweit. Charlie DiJulio was born in Philadelphia and had grown up in Fort Worth, where his father designed golf clubs for Ben Hogan. The young artist earned a BFA in painting from Texas Christian University and then enrolled in a graduate degree program at the University of Colorado in Boulder. The Wadmans and other friends continued to commute on weekends from Boulder. "It was an exciting time," Bernofsky said, "with so much creative energy and joy. I looked forward to each day. We were able to turn our backs on all the negative bullshit swirling about the world and concentrate on making stuff. We shared a sense of innocence and optimism. Clark was usually the first up in the morning and would start a bowl of gruel on the stove. Clark would also be the first out the door, his creative juices flowing, and his endless energy inspiring the others to hurry their morning routines. I remember stepping out into the cold windy morning, and there's Clark already out in the daybreak atop a dome in a freezing wind using a wrench. That was an inspiration to get out and work with him."

Douthit observed the same evanescent strain in Richert. "Clark used the place and people to whip up his creative energies," he said. "He translated almost everything into a visual or written expression—good stuff, good thinking, and very much his own strange kind of place. He took excitement out of every incident and visitor at Drop City. He used everybody really well and always set himself up as a foil for people to use."[62] On a personal level, Richert saw the main function of Drop City as providing a setting where artists could engage in creative projects. "This was probably more important to me than the politics or communalism," he said.

| Dropper Art Projects | Many of the commune's art projects originated from the collection of detritus that the droppers scavenged from alleyways, roadsides, |

and dumps. "We considered our junk yard as a major focus of

our attention," Bernofsky said. "The Drop City junkyard was the junkyard of all junkyards." A Drop City newsletter chortled: "There is enough waste here to feed and house ten thousand artists. Enough junk to work into a thousand, thousand works of art. To the townspeople in Trinidad, five miles away, we are scrounging bums, garbage pickers. They are right. Perhaps the most beautiful creation in all Drop City is our junk pile. The garbage of the garbage pickers. . . . We are sort of advanced junkmen taking advantage of advanced obsolescence."

The dropper artistic endeavors also strengthened the sense of community, Bernofsky said. "We built this great long sculpture along the fence line, and then we painted it all up. It was this great, wonderful, joyous, physical thing that we were building outside, high up where you could see it from the road. And just building that together, and melding as a group—so that here was a group with one idea—this integrated us. We were starting really to form up as an organism. For another outdoor installation, we lined up, in regimental fashion, a dozen discarded toilet bowls we had found in a field and painted them. Richard [Kallweit] also made a piece that involved hundreds of side mirrors that Baer had salvaged from junkyards. He built a beautiful sculpture. It was a six-foot piece of telephone pole with side view mirrors attached all around the pole—bristling out of the pole. His idea was to set it out in the sun and get all the mirrors reflecting down to one point and cook something. But it didn't do shit. You could hold your hand in the spot and not feel a thing."

Painting seemed the most popular form of artistic expression at Drop City. "Richert and Kallweit created canvasses of all abstract patterns and geometric shapes, molecular or crystalline, in brilliant acrylic colors," Curl wrote. "They seemed to deal in a mental physics with feelings, and [that] seemed to extend beyond the canvasses. Both artists worked in similar, but noticeable different styles. Richert's works were powerful, full of ideas,

The *Ultimate Painting*

replete with dynamic harmonies and discords, while Kallweit's were flatter and more decorative, but also rich in line and color." The two often critiqued each other's work but didn't seem very competitive. Curl also noted that Drop Lady "had a pretty good painter's hand."[63] Dropper paintings soon decorated the walls and ceilings of the domes and often appeared directly on pieces of furniture and electric utilities. The greatest of all dropper creations had to be the *Ultimate Painting*.

Ultimate Painting

"For the backing of the painting, Clark cut a circle out of three-quarter inch plywood with a sabre saw," Bernofsky said. "Each of us then took turns painting a separate portion of the wooden canvas— even those of us who had no talent. Clark then mounted the

painting onto an electric motor to spin it. Then, we set up a
strobe light that froze a different image every microsecond as
the painting revolved." At various times the droppers offered
to sell the *Ultimate Painting* for between fifty and eighty thousand dollars. The price never lowered but always increased.
"We exhibited the piece at a few local galleries before entering
it in the Engineering, Art & Technology exhibit sponsored by
the Brooklyn Art Museum and the Museum of Modern Art in
New York," Richert said. "The EAT exhibit was the brainchild
of painter Robert Rauschenberg and engineer Billy Kluver.
The artistic pioneers intended to showcase experimental work
that synthesized art and technology. To enhance the presentation we built a twenty-foot-circumference Baer-inspired ploar
zonahedron to house the *Ultimate Painting*. We painted the
pieces of the dome in a Day-Glo spectrum, then draped it
with nylon, and installed a halo of black lights overhead. Inside,
the strobe light continually froze the spinning images of the
painting." At the time the predominant art style in Manhattan
was minimalism and the beginning of Pop Art. "Our idea of a
total environment was foreign," Kallweit said. "They thought
we were from California." Richert reported that the *Ultimate*
"turned out to be a popular exhibit, the dome was overpacked
at all times by museum goers."

Curiously, the *Ultimate* never made it back to Drop City, and
no dropper knows its ultimate fate. Kallweit said, "After the
show was over, the droppers told me: 'Richard, you're from
this part of the country. Take care of the show.' 'O.K.,' I said.
So there I was. No money. No job. No place to stay. And a
show I had to take care of. Eventually, I got some work at the
museum demonstrating some of the pieces at the show, lived
on the streets of Manhattan, and got a job in a restaurant . . .
but what about the painting? I sold the black lights. I met an
artist there who had a studio in Bucks County, Pennsylvania. I

said to him: 'I'll give you the dome for a green house, if you take the painting and ship it to us.' 'O.K.,' he says. That's the last I saw of the painting."

Other spinning paintings took shape over the years. Burt Wadman, the honorary dropper who lived in Boulder, created a fractal drawing that he dubbed the *Wadman Sphere.* "Conceived shortly before the inception of Drop City, the drawing depicted a small but highly detailed square drawing," Richert said. "It was the first fractal that I had ever seen. We took the square pattern, projected it onto a circle and then spherized it geodesically onto a spinning disc. Our design preempted the fractals of Benoit Mandelbrot, the mathematician who coined the term in the eighties. Mandelbrot once boasted that several artists had used his ideas about fractals, but theirs were not as good as his. Wadman's fractal predated Mandelbrot's by several years— as did our spin painting—and in my opinion is one of the best I've seen."

The interest of Richert and Kallweit in different types of structure led to the production of a number of geometrically innovative posters. The pair eventually landed contracts with a New York poster company, The Third Eye, to reproduce and distribute the work internationally. "Several of our poster designs were early fractals that also apparently predated Mandelbrot," Richert said. "One piece, which was never published, utilized a tiling pattern now known as the Penrose tessellation, named after mathematician Roger Penrose. However, I call it the Richert/ Penrose tessellation, since I was working with it several years before Penrose 'discovered' it in 1973. The posters we designed at Drop City never sold well, but my contact with The Third Eye eventually led to a job. In 1968, as the psychedelic poster business boomed, I temporarily left Drop City and moved to New York City to become the art director for The Third Eye. At that time I still considered myself a resident of Drop City, and I signed my posters: Clard Svensen, Drop City." Gardner observed that "the paintings and psychedelic 'Droppings' were then among the most original being created at that time."[64]

| The Being Bag |

In 1967 a magazine quoted the Drop City newsletter as trumpeting that members had finished "many paintings, two novels, two volumes of poetry, two movies, children's books and other books."[65] Peter Douthit, aka Peter Rabbit, did eventually publish a novel, but the most significant literary achievement by the droppers was a collaborative production of the hippie nation's first alternative underground comic book. "We needed some income," Bernofsky said, "and I thought, 'why not distribute some of the gleam, happiness, and thoughts that had arisen in Drop City through some kind of comedy?' I wrote a couple of innocuous chapters for a comic book that carried some of the real misflavor of Drop City, while Clark, along with a little help from Richard Kallweit, came up with some amazing, innovative, and appealing illustrations. They were so creative and funny that I asked Charlie DiJulio, who lived in Boulder at the time, if he could silk-screen them, thinking that if Charlie cut silk screens we could print them off and sell the comic for five bucks a shot and have an income. And the production would be a dropping—and a collaborative offering.

"Charlie wholeheartedly jumped into the project and we first liberated some supplies from the art department of the University of Colorado. We considered the theft as part of the dropping, and we believed the excess material would only have been wasted by people with ridiculous projects that had no connection with the world. For us, it was the detritus of the Art Department. Charlie took charge of the production operation while I acted as the gofer. We strung a clothesline through Charlie's attic, and every time we hung up a page we thought it was like printing money. After two days, we took down the dried prints, and then we held a binding party back at the commune. The comic book represents one of the high achievements of Drop City."

The first episode of *The Being Bag* related the adventures of The Baron, Cleveland Trootsearch, and Ratsy Eatsit. The three characters, looking suspiciously like caricatures of Bernofsky, Richert, and Kallweit embark on a journey through a fantastic landscape to liberate the world's consciousness. In 2004 Kallweit still had Bernofsky's original handwritten notes. The introduction to Chapter IV read: "Life is not necessarily that pleasant evolutionary urge of creation, essential to the survival of the Human Race, [that] falls asunder under the weeping burden of ceaselessly quivering demand. For you and for me this is a reality of all our waking sleep. . . . Trootsearch: 'We no longer can withstand the onslaught of these chains of being, Ratsy'; Ratsy: 'Hear, Trootsearch, let's munch this last windy bit of salad.' . . . As Ratsy and Cleaveland vainly struggle over lunch a note is laundered from a nearby orb. . . . 'Your suffering is nought unless ye use the accumulated rage and guilt not to hate but to entertain and thereby force the hand of the Coming One.' . . . Skiing amongst the gilded realms of Divide, groping valiantly within the smothering knots of the chains of being, they confront the deguised [*sic*] reality of the Yo-Yo Buddha. . . . Buddha: 'Here are your chopsticks boys. Wield them as you will whilst I yo-yo.' . . . With humble rage, Ratsy and Cleveland accept the weapons and feed upon the outraged chains of being. . . . Ratsy: 'Here, Trootsearch, lets munch this last bit of windy salad.' Trootsearch: 'Yes, Ratsy. Now are we on the edge of an as yet unheard of, new and Major Break Through.' . . . Sheathing the weapons, Eatsit and Trootsearch, glowing from contact with the yo-yo and their victorious release, plummet downward toward the moulding city of Major Breakthrough"— the chapter ends.

Throughout the comic, The Baron delivers the ultimate answer with a mysterious phrase, "Tat ti tit," which translated from Brooklynese means "That's it."

"*The Being Bag* totaled ten pages," Bernofsky said. "We ran off fifty inaugural copies of the first issue titled *Unforgettable Dolts*, under the trademark: LuSiD Prod. We really chuckled over that word, 'prod.' We offered the comic for five bucks a shot, with an option to subscribe for three copies at eight dollars. We assumed our dream for a prosperous cottage industry at Drop City was about to become reality. We thought because it was so handmade and noncommercial that people on Haight-Ashbury would suck it up. It's hard to say if the product ever reached the shops in the Haight. We sold just three issues and got zero subscriptions. After a while we gave away the remaining comics. We never figured out how to plug into the capitalistic system and squeeze out money. We just tried selling the comic on the ground by hand." Kallweit added that "the cosmic forces were defeated by the forces of Capitalism. *The Being Bag* became the model for a lot of popular underground comics that came out in the late sixties. I think it still holds up—the drawing and writing—even after forty years."

About a year after the appearance of *The Being Bag*, the underground comic business burst onto the scene around San Francisco in 1968 when Victor Moscoso and Rick Griffin collaborated with cartoonists Robert Crumb and S. Clay Wilson on *Zap Comix*. The surreal, vulgar, and funny *Zap*, along with its erotic cousin, *Snatch*, published by Rip Off Press became an instant hit and profitable business. One store, the San Francisco Comic Book Company, prospered by selling nothing but *Comix*. But the droppers remained unfazed. "The goal to generate income from the project failed," Bernofsky said, "and we just went on to other stuff. But it was a happy time putting it together. The energy was good. We wanted to make things that hadn't been done or made before. It was the simple-minded tasks—the scrounging, the building, the food preparation, the painting, and the creation of *The Being Bag*—all done by hand in a very

"YOU MUST ENTER BETWEEN THE PLOW AND THE PLOTTED PATH ξ SHOULD
YOU LIE UNDER ITS SHADES OR SHOULD YOU NOT? OR WOULD IT BE
MY JURISDICTION TO BELIEVE THAT SO MAGNIFICENT A FOE WAS
NOT TO BE MEDDLED WITH APPEARING TO POSSESS SOME PRECOND-
ITIONED PATTERN OF ITS OWN? AND IF THE FORMER ANALOGY.. "
"BUT PARDON US, GOOD BARON" SAID TROOTHSERCH

'OY WHERE LIES THE WAY OF THE FORTRESS, FOR WE MUST TRULY
LEARN THE POTENCY OF OUR POWER LEST IT WEILD
CONTRARY TO THE POSITIVE VORTEX OF THE CREATURES. "
"WELL OVER THERE, TROOTHSERCH," SAID THE BARON.
"TAT AIN'T DIT !" SAID THE BARON.
" WELL, OVER THERE THEN !" SAID THE BARON.

The *Being Bag*

loving manner, very carefully and very slowly, that knitted us together."

. . . They espouse instead a racist philosophy that could ultimately perpetuate the very separatism against which Negroes have fought so successfully. Oddly, they are not white men but black, and their slogan is "Black Power!" . . . an eerie silence enveloped the field, punctuated only by what sounded like men kicking footballs; it was the hollow clunk of cops kicking and clubbing fallen marchers. . . . the Organization of American States voted 18 to 0 to withdraw the 8,000 OAS peace-keeping troops still in the Dominican Republic. . . . the Fugs' scatological satires have gained a steadily growing audience on the college campuses. . . . Amid a boiling bloodbath that almost unnoticed took 400,000 lives, Indonesia, the sprawling giant of Southeast Asia, has done a complete about-face. . . . Hairy feet and all, Frodo Baggins is the reluctant hero of this year's "In" book. . . . The Harris poll showed that the stepped-up bombing raids on Hanoi and Haiphong were endorsed by 5 out of every 6 Americans. . . . In an incredible, nearly soundless orgy of mutilation and murder, a single male intruder herded together and murdered, one by one, with packing-house precision, eight pretty student nurses. . . . Out of the President's earshot, a marine with a missing arm exclaimed: "You rotten fink!" . . . (July 1966)[66]

Meanwhile, about a thousand miles to the west, on a fifteen-acre plot of land outside La Honda, California, there had formed another loosely knit tribe whose shenanigans somewhat mirrored the goings-on at Drop City, even though the two tribes had no communication with one another. The West Coast group was led by Ken Kesey, a young writer with bulging neck muscles, thick wrists, Popeye-like forearms, and a prominent jaw and chin. Kesey had grown up in a pampered world designed by his highly successful postwar businessman father, a world that featured a modern low-slung suburban home on quiet Debra Lane in

Ken Kesey

Salem, Oregon, not far from the airport where his father kept his private plane. In his freshman year at the University of Oregon, Kesey ran off with his high school sweetheart, Faye, to get married. After a few failed attempts to break into the movie business, Kesey settled down into graduate school with a writing fellowship at Stanford University. The couple rented a two-room cottage on Perry Lane, nestled in a small cluster of similar bungalows shaded by an oak forest just a shank off the fairways of the Stanford golf course. To supplement his paltry fellowship, Kesey volunteered to submit to psychomimetic drug experiments at the Veterans Hospital in Menlo Park for seventy-five bucks a day. The array of drugs he ingested included LSD, psilocybin, mescaline, peyote, the super amphetamine IT-290, Ditran, and morning glory seeds. No one had as yet coined the term "psychedelic" to describe the effect of the drugs on the human brain. Kesey enjoyed the experience and began stealing some drugs to share with friends at Perry Lane. He also got a job as a night attendant at Menlo Park where he could work on his novel, *Zoo,* a story based around the bohemians who lived at San Francisco's North Beach. But his drug experiences and the work in the psychiatric ward at Menlo Park nudged him toward writing about patients in a mental ward. He composed several passages of *One Flew over the Cuckoo's Nest* while under the hallucinatory drugs LSD and peyote. He also convinced a fellow employee to give him shock treatment. Later he accurately described the aftereffects in *Cuckoo's Nest.*

After the publication of *Cuckoo's Nest* in 1961, Kesey took a sabbatical from Perry Lane and moved back to Oregon where he wrote his second novel, *Sometimes a Great Notion.* In 1963 Kesey returned to Perry Lane an acclaimed young writer. His associates now included writers Larry McMurtry, Ed McClanahan, and Bob Stone, dancer Chloe Scott, artist Roy Seburn, Carl Lehman-Haupt, Vic Lovel, Richard Alpert, and Neal Cassady, the former road-running sidekick of Jack Kerouac.

In a sense Ken Kesey seemed a reincarnation of this country's
first social rebel, a seventeenth-century colonist named Thomas

| Thomas Morton of Merry Mount |

Morton. A member of the Church of England,
Morton arrived at the Puritans' Plymouth Plantation in 1624 with an outfit that included
many indentured servants, and with the intention to establish
a fur-trading post at Mount Wollaston where Quincy, Massachusetts, now stands. When the project's leader grew impatient
with the slow profits and relocated to Virginia, Morton took
over. Morton's view of the New World differed greatly from
that of the neighboring Puritans. Rather than look upon the
wilderness as an evil depraved landscape that needed to be
tamed and civilized, Morton was intrigued by New England.
"The more I saw the more I liked it," he said. "And when I had
more seriously considered of the bewty of the place, with all
her faire endowments, I did not think in all the knowne world
it could be paralel'd."[67]

Whereas the Puritans perceived the Indians as dirty, evil
savages, Morton found the indigenous peoples to be much more
compassionate and generous than the Anglos. "The Indians,"
he said, "feede continually, and are no niggards of their vittels;
for they are willing that any one shall eate with them. . . .
That is, If you be hungry, there is meat for you, where if you
will eate you may. Such is their Humanity."[68]

It didn't take long for Morton to change the flavor of Mount
Wollaston. He first abolished the caste system of indentured
servants and gentlemen and spoke in terms of turning the
trading post into a commune. Plymouth governor William Bradford reported that Morton told his men: "We will converse, trad,
plante, and live together as equals, and suppporte and protecte
one another, or to like effecte." Bradford also accused Morton
of getting too cozy with the Indians by trading guns with
them, as well as teaching them how to make bullets, to load,
and to shoot.[69]

And there was more that got under Bradford's Puritan skin. Morton renamed the site of the Wollaston trading post to Ma-re Mount, or Merry Mount—and, for good reason. In preparation for a major party, the Merry Mounters cut down an eighty-foot pine tree, sawed off its limbs, and nailed a pair of buck's horns near the top. "We also brewed a barrel of beer and bottled it," Morton said, "to be spent, with other good cheare, for all comers of that day. Upon Mayday we brought the Maypole to the place appointed, with drums, gunnes, pistols and other fitting instruments, for that purpose; and there erected it with the help of Salvages, that came thether of purpose to see the manner of our Revels. . . . I also composed a special song which was fitting to the time and present occasion: Drinke and be merry, merry, merry boyes / Let all your delight be in the Hymens ioyes / Io to Hymen, now the day is come / About the merry Maypole take a Roome." The last stanza of the song included lines that alluded to local Indian women: "Lasses in beaver coats come away, Yee shall be welcome to us night and day."[70]

Bradford denounced the *frisking* of the Indian women and condemned the raucous party as a revival of celebrated Bacchanalian feasts. "If we had allowed Morton to stay," Bradford said, "we would not have been able to hold on to any of our servants for Morton would entertaine any, how vile soever, and all the scume of the countrie, or any discontents, would flock to him from all places, if this nest was not broken; and they should stand in more fear of their lives and goods (in short time) from this wicked and deboste crue, then from the salvages them selves."[71]

The Puritans quickly quashed the colonial dawning of the Age of Aquarius by arresting Morton and sending him back to England. Whether or not California authorities knew about the drug-induced shenanigans going on at Perry Lane, Ken Kesey's attempt at forming a new Merry Mount at that location

ended anyway when a real estate developer unleashed bulldozers to knock down the cute bungalows to make way for
modern homes. Unfazed, with the earnings from his novels
Kesey bought a home in a secluded area of La Honda, California, and invited a dozen denizens of Perry Lane to move
there with him.

Echoing Bradford's choice of terms to describe Morton's
sinful den, Kesey named his personal center of merriment The
Nest. As Tom Wolfe put it: "The lascivious, wanton, carnal folks
who joined him there to transcend all the usual earthly games
of status, sex, and money—soon dubbed themselves The
Merry Pranksters."[72] Merry Mounters might have sufficed as
well. Although the log structure at La Honda, with its French
doors, stone fireplace, and exposed beams resembled a lodge,
it wasn't big enough to accommodate everyone. Eventually many
of the pranksters pitched tents in the surrounding woods.
Kesey picked up the tab for food and other necessities for the
dozen or so bodies that continually rotated through, plus the
maintenance and gas for two or three vehicles—which all tallied
up to about twenty grand a year. For the most part, Kesey set
down his pen to experiment with other forms of media. Unlike
the droppers, he didn't have to scrounge in dumps or beg for
unused multi-media tools. With royalties from his best-selling
books he bought cutting-edge film and sound recorders, wired
the gully behind his home with a sound system, and hid microphones and speakers behind Day-Glo face masks tacked to the
trees. The microphones picked up the sounds of animals and
passers-by and broadcast them from the treetops like jungle
noises in a Tarzan film. He also began to experiment with film.

Like Thomas Morton, Kesey invited all sorts of people to
settle at The Nest. He welcomed minorities, although few
visited, and he especially prized people like Cassady who had
experienced the darker sides of life: prizefighters, dockworkers,
migrant field hands, motorcycle gangs. On the Hell's Angels'

first visit, the bikers enjoyed Kesey's drugs, didn't beat up anyone, and left The Nest still standing as they roared off. After that experience the bikers added LSD to their list of recreational drugs, which up to that point had included mostly narcotics and alcohol. They even contributed the term "bummer"— Angel slang for a bad motorcycle ride—to the psychedelic drug lexicon to define an LSD trip gone sour. As more young people flocked to the Nest, some of Kesey's pals began to look upon him as a prophet, and unlike the beats Kesey seemed ready to at least broadcast his vision across the country, if not lead the converts himself. "When you've got something like we've got," he said, "you can't just sit on it. You've got to move off of it. You can't just sit on it and possess it, you've got to move off of it and give it to other people. It only works if you bring other people into it."[73]

Kesey's world revolved around psychedelic drugs. He believed in their ability to liberate the mind and break down social barriers. One of his fantasies seemed very similar to the dome of sensuality the droppers had originally described to the reporter from the *Denver Post*, which eventually turned into the theater dome. Kesey envisioned a geodesic dome on top of a cylindrical shaft that would appear like a great mushroom. A stairway would lead people up the cylinder into a room with a foam-rubber floor. From beneath the foam, movie projectors, videotape projects, and light projectors would radiate images across the spherical ceiling. Under the influence of LSD, speed, or pot, people would submerge themselves in a contrived planet of lights and sounds—complete with images of themselves flashing and swirling above. Although he never constructed his trip dome, Kesey did follow through on other ideas to turn people on. His biographer, Tom Wolfe, described Kesey's anti-setting for dropping LSD as "unserene and lurid as the Prankster arts can make it and let your set be only what is on your . . . brain, man, and let your guide, your trusty handholding, head-swaddling guide, be a bunch of Day-Glo crazies who have as one of their mottoes: Never trust a Prankster."[74]

In 1965 Kesey developed the acid tests, geared to enhance the LSD trip with a bagful of diverse physical stimulants. The Pranksters rented public halls and decorated the walls with Day-Glo paintings. During the trips they projected film images onto the walls and played tapes of spontaneous expressions, all the while cutting into the broadcasts with live monologues. They flashed strobe lights and set up black lights to simulate a psychedelic experience as a band played acid rock. The Prankster house band first called themselves Mother McCree's Uptown Jug Stompers. Later, they changed the name to Emergency Crew, then the Warlocks. Mostly converted folkies, the band also featured former bluegrass banjoist Jerome Garcia on lead guitar and Phil Lesh on bass. The band eventually settled on the name the Grateful Dead. The ultimate Prankster acid test occurred over the fourth weekend of January 1966, at the Long-shoreman's Hall in San Francisco. Billed as the Trips Festival, the Pranksters publicized the event as a big celebration that would simulate an LSD experience, minus the LSD. Saturday night featured an acid test. The press went along with the notion that no actual LSD was involved. The Trips Festival grossed $12,500 in three days, with almost no overhead.

. . . *Ranging around the University of Texas tower's walk at will, he sent his bullets burning and rasping through the flesh and bone of those on the campus below. . . . "We're more popular than Jesus Christ now; I don't know which will go first—rock 'n' roll or Christianity," Lennon said. . . . Died: Lenny Bruce, 40, nightclub performer. . . . No previous medical phenomenon has ever quite matched the headlong U.S. rush to use the oral contraceptives now universally known as "the pills." . . . Throughout the U.S., the big cities are scarred by slums, hobbled by inadequate mass transportation, starved for sufficient finances, torn by racial strife. . . . His Dutch Reformed Church preaches apartheid, tells him that black men are fit only to be "hewers of wood and drawers of water," and assures him that God is on his side. . . . when U.S. forces in Viet Nam climbed above the 300,000-man mark, there were no full-page ads, no teach-ins, no placard-studded demonstrations to mark the milestone. . . . Down the streets they rampaged, roughing up Chinese in foreign dress, ordering shopkeepers to stop selling books except those that reflect Mao's thinking and to rid themselves of imported articles or luxury items. . . . "Black men," cried the speaker, must unite to overthrow their white "oppressors," becoming "like panthers—smiling, cunning, scientific, striking by night and sparing no one!" . . . Of all the opponents of any federal legislation to control firearms, none has been more persistent— or more effective—than the National Rifle Association. . . . only 50 percent of the American public now endorses the President v. 83 percent in February 1964. . . . a cluster of whites armed with ax handles, lead pipes and chains pounced on the 150 Negro youngsters who showed up to go to school. . . .* (August/September 1966)[75]

| Enter Peter Rabbit |

Around the time Ken Kesey first planned his acid tests, the droppers also took to the road to proselytize their brand of counterculture. Like the San Francisco movement, the droppers' main attraction featured a psychedelic light show and loud music. "Politically, the droppers followed closely behind Ken Kesey's Merry Pranksters in developing techniques of transforming American culture through visceral entertainment experiences," said Gardner. "They traveled far and wide with their message and their show."[76]

In the spring of 1966 the droppers staged an extravaganza called "Armageddon: The Doomsday Gig," in Dallas, Texas. One visitor who checked out the scene was an earthy, well-weathered, rough-hewn thirty-year-old named Peter Douthit. A native of Pennsylvania, Douthit stood six foot four inches tall. His life had not been very happy or satisfying up to that point. One of his earliest childhood memories was of sliding off a toilet seat in an outhouse and splashing into the pool of waste below.

When he reached draft age, he did everything he could to avoid the service. "I told them I was a faggot," Douthit said, "I told them I was a conscientious objector, I told them I was a dope monster, I told them I had heart trouble and lung trouble and was crippled and psychotic. They marked a big red X on my chest, called me The Patriot and sent me to the base hospital."[77]

After successfully dodging the draft, Douthit aspired to be a poet and ended up moving back home. When his father ordered him to change out of his Levi-heavy style of clothing and to go to work for him, Douthit rebelled: "He ordered me to change my clothes. I said that I could not and would not go to work with him. He said that I must make up my mind that I had failed as a poet. He said that I must change my clothes. He said that I must go to work for him. I got angry, furious. What do you know about failures, I shouted. I am proud of my failures!"[78]

After leaving home, for a number of years Douthit wrote copy and book reviews for a Fort Worth newspaper and put in a stint at an ad agency. "The ad agency was O.K. for a while," he wrote. "I smoked a lot of pot and listened to the radio and read and wrote a lot. It took 15 to 20 minutes a day to write whatever copy I had to write. I was also getting into cameras, running around the parks and out into the country, freaking out, looking at everything through lenses." Eventually Douthit quit the ad job and became a milkman—one who gave away all his goods. "It was all really good till the milk company started hitting on me to hit on the people for bread for the stuff," Douthit said. "None of those poor people had any bread and besides the milk company had debt insurance."[79]

It was about this time that Douthit met the droppers through Charlie DiJulio, a few days before the Doomsday Gig. DiJulio had once been an art student in Houston and had bought dope from Douthit. "I was really happy to meet Clark Richert," Douthit said. "He was full of things totally new to us, things we needed to learn. We learned. I pretended I knew a lot to keep

him going. We learned and learned the things Richert had to
teach because he had spent a hard winter, a year living in Drop
City, the model of all the southwest communities to come. Learning things that are hard to learn, things like building your own
environment, using your energies to build new institutions instead
of beating your head against the wall of outdated forms."[80]

**Armageddon:
The Doomsday Gig**

In the days leading up to the psychedelic
Doomsday Gig, Douthit helped the droppers
print posters and mail out invitations. The
publicity pulled in a motley crew to witness a major dropping.
"Got a bunch of very strange people to come together in that
place," Douthit noted, "long-haired freaks, fetishists, drunks,
a motorscooter—it was motorscooter art—and a rock band,
Fast Eddie and the Electronic Japs. The Electronic Japs were
the Wop [DiJulio] and a crippled drummer and the rest of us
banging, wailing and screaming. We had painted cardboard
and garbage by the truckload to fill the place . . . and da-glo
and blacklite and all the paint we could get hold of. . . .
Painted up everything so beautiful and fuck it up and started
all over again so beautiful . . . eyezaps everywhere. . . . The
Electric Japs were wailing and some chick started doing a far-
out dance. It was Flippen dancing at people, very aggressive,
at them. . . . Dropper films and slides were flickering all
over the painted walls and Grover tried to read the Drunken
Doomsday Address, throwing the finished pages at people
while they shouted at him . . . and it all fell into an incredible
unintelligible jumble of every person in the room telling some
truth about himself."[81]

Douthit converted to dropperism on the spot and decided
to move to Drop City. He also convinced his girlfriend, who took
the dropper name Poly Ester, and her daughter, Kathy, to go
with him to Colorado. "When we got back to the house in

Fort Worth we started gathering together all our shit," Douthit said. "[W]e rented a trailer and threw or gave away what we could and hooked up the trailer to that dropper car with one guy riding the motorscooter."[82] Curl described Douthit as being "well over six feet, with a bulbous nose, a big mouth that talked a mile a minute in an expressive face that took up most of his head, and a bad cowlick that stood straight up in back. . . . His girlfriend was as skinny as a noodle, kept twisting her hair around one finger, and trying to get her freckled ten year old daughter to sit still. Poly seemed very nervous. She'd start a thought, veer off suddenly in different directions, contradict herself a few times, all in one sprawling sentence. She was smart in an offcenter way."[83]

After the dropper road show returned to Colorado, Charlie DiJulio also decided to move onto the commune, bringing with him his wife, Carol, and two daughters—Christina, about six months old, and Elizabeth, age four. DiJulio assumed the dropper moniker Arterisio. "Charlie was dark, moody and depressed, but not evil or manipulative," Bernofsky said. "A guy bursting with talent." Curl saw DiJulio as a complex individual. "Although there was a craziness in . . . [him], there was also something endearing about him. He had a good self-contained spirit, and really loved his daughters. But his paintings were filled with exploding black pigments, guns, hurt, sad women, and body parts."[84]

Curl himself had returned to Drop City around that time after a six-month hiatus in San Francisco, where he had gone to make some money to buy materials to build his dome. He brought along his girlfriend, Jill. Curl, who assumed the dropper name Ishmael, spoke with a heavy New York accent. He had graduated from the City College of New York, traveled through-out Europe, and taught school for a while. He arrived at the commune with one completed novel manuscript under his arm, plus several short stories. "His writing style was somewhere between Nelson Algren and Hubert Selby Jr.," Douthit said. "A good writer who knew the city best and had a good eye mostly focused on the grotesque." Jill chose the name Patsy Cake Quickly. "She was short and nervous with a pursed mouth," Douthit continued. "Her gestures and movements were a weird kind of delicate. Inclined to be plump, she made the best of it. Her big tits always caught your eye and she had lovely long dark hair. She was cleaner and neater in her dress than any of the other droppers and was a pretty good careful cook."[85] Bernofsky described Jill as "an intensely neurotic Jewish American Princess. She scrutinized and analyzed everything to the very final iota of an atom—and brilliantly so."

The Main Match: Bernofsky versus Douthit

Almost from the first moment that Bernofsky and Douthit met, the two strong personalities chafed against each other. Some droppers noted that they didn't get along because they were so much alike. No doubt both were bullshitters, but they seemed to come at it from different angles. "Peter Douthit is always lying," Curl said. "He's always telling stories. He makes things up and swears they're true. . . . Bernofsky does it as a joke, or to cool everybody out. Douthit does it to make himself a hero."[86] Bernofsky made no bones about his disregard for Douthit. "I found Douthit a manipulative bully, and hated his racist remarks and swaggering air," he said. "He was about ten years older than us and had experience in the underground. He was already a depraved drug-crazed cynic. He also brought guns to Drop City and hunted rabbits. He parroted everything the droppers tried to teach him—only coming from his mouth it was hypocritical bullshit."

About a week after the new families moved in, Douthit got into a shoving match with DiJulio. No angel himself, DiJulio had his own problem with maintaining his temper. When DiJulio warned Douthit to stop ordering him around, Douthit replied,

"I'm going to have to take you out to the woodshed." When
the two started shoving each other, Douthit's false teeth fell
out, and then all hell broke loose. As the action grew more
violent, DiJulio pushed Douthit into a wall, shattering the Sheetrock. The fighters escaped from the kitchen when Drop Lady
started whacking them with a two-by-four. "I waited to see if
either of them would fix the wall," Bernofsky continued. "And
I waited and waited. I felt as if our sacred space, that we had
so lovingly erected, had been violated."

Curl had been on a sojourn in San Francisco at the time of
the fight. "When I returned to Drop City I found the air was
thick with tension," he said. "I felt shell-shocked. I had expected
the same high spirits I'd found here, or thought I'd found here
in the spring, only a few months ago." After the fight Douthit
stopped eating with the other droppers for a while, Curl said,
"and the hole in the wall of the kitchen dome was never fixed
and remained a symbol and a reminder."[87]

Peter Rabbit Hole Despite the tension Bernofsky pitched in with
the other droppers to build Douthit's dome—
a twenty-three-foot-diameter two-frequency
geodesic with five pentagonal windows and a pentagonal sky-
light, with a little extended triangle A-frame tacked on the back
for guests. "After moving in, Douthit dedicated most of his time
to his writing," Bernofsky said. "While we were busting our asses
working on the other domes, Peter was in his little dome taking
notes for his novel on Drop City." Curl also didn't appreciate
Douthit's personality or attitude, and Kallweit seemed ambiva-
lent—but Richert didn't want to run him off because he didn't
want Drop City to turn into an elitist club. Richert understood
human nature. If tension didn't originate from Douthit, it would
originate from another source. "When there was just you and
me," Richert told Bernofsky, "we saw each other as the enemy
sometimes. Remember? If we didn't have Douthit, we'd be at

The Rabbit Hole

each other's throats again."[88] In the end the other droppers agreed to individually ask Douthit to voluntarily leave for the good of the group. He agreed, in principle, but continued to hole up in his dome, complaining that he didn't have enough money to go anywhere.

A Civilization without Laws

From the inception of Drop City, the core of founding droppers had decided they would make no rules, nor devise any standards by which to judge anyone who wished to join the community. In sociological parlance, Drop City had no "cross-boundary control" over its members or visitors. The droppers welcomed all comers with open arms and offered them full use of the community's resources. Newcomers could also bail out whenever they wished. "We really believed the cosmic forces would take care of us," Bernofsky said. "We never drew up a charter or anything. The only legal paper we had was the land deed— which was in my name. The newcomers would show up and we would all pitch in and build separate domes for them. During the construction phase we set up a big wall tent for the families to inhabit. We had people showing up and making a commitment and contributing energy to develop the community. We really believed the cosmic forces would take care of us. From the start, I had always intended to add other names to the deed as the commune developed into a solid community. I hoped over time that families would sprout within the domes and our new civilization would become permanent. But, after the first year, several rumblings arose in the newcomers about the deed. They wanted their names on the deed since they thought they had made a life commitment to Drop City. They didn't feel comfortable with me being the exclusive landowner. I didn't really care about the ownership of the land, but I was concerned that others wanted shared ownership. 'Here comes the first rising of selfish interests,' I thought. But because of my faith in the cosmic forces I thought it was a little quirk that we would get over. In the cosmic realm my owning the land meant nothing.

"After Douthit, DiJulio, and Curl had moved in, Richert pressed me to sign over the land to a non-profit corporation, appointing all the current droppers as members of a board of directors. The board, in turn, would elect outsiders—mostly friends who didn't live at Drop City—to act as officers. I was torn between my trepidation of handing over the property to them and of being Mr. Cool and making it all-inclusive. And Mr. Cool won out. 'Fine, let's put your names on the title,' I said. So, we turned Drop City into a nonprofit corporation." Bernofsky wrote up a new deed that surrendered the five acres of property to Drop City, Inc., with a stipulation that the land was to be "forever free and open to all people." Then, at the last moment, Douthit and Poly Ester, even though they had announced they

would be leaving, demanded that they be included on the board
of directors. When Bernofsky heard this, he hesitated, but then
he surrendered to the cosmic forces. "Eventually, I accepted the
fact that Douthit would be around for the long run, and I signed
over the deed to Drop City, Inc."

*. . . at least 750,000 men will be required to permit the allies to seal off
the South's sievelike borders. . . . annual record sales in the past decade
have grown from $250 million to $650 million. . . . More than 60 percent
of the new generating capacity ordered by utility companies so far in 1966
will be nuclear. . . . In his house outside Los Angeles, he has installed a
Teletype-like machine that is wired into a central computer, which Foy
must share with up to 350 other users. . . . making it a federal felony
to knowingly destroy or mutilate a draft card. . . . engineers have
demonstrated a miniature version of a new battery that promises to put
the company in the electric-car business within the next ten years. . . .
Today, just over one in five Negro families earns more than $7,000 a
year, a figure that puts them firmly in the middle class. . . . gasoline
sales are up nearly 4 percent. . . . "There are almost no men left."
Unemployment is down to 3.8 percent. . . . the girl is Twiggy, the
Cockney Kid, and she's suddenly the hottest model in London. . . . the
GOP scored solid gains at every level. . . . Arab terrorists had been
averaging three raids a month inside Israel, blowing up a house here,
a bridge or water pipeline there. . . . may carry U.S. astronauts to the
moon as early as 1968. . . .* (October/November 1966)[89]

| **Conrad Beissel** | The droppers might not have realized it, but they had come to a crossroads. The persona-lity clashes developing within the community |

would eventually affect the direction of their enterprise. History
eventually repeats itself, and Bernofsky, the spiritual leader of
Drop City, might have benefited from studying the story of an
eighteenth-century commune named the Ephrata Cloister. Like
the droppers, the denizens of Ephrata welcomed all newcomers

and diligently constructed shelters for them. More important, they approached art as a lifestyle—albeit their artistic pursuits had a religious foundation. At one point Ephrata developed into the largest artists' colony in American history, but just as things seemed to be going smoothly, personality conflicts between two major players almost brought Ephrata crashing down. Studying the early commune in light of Drop City offers interesting insight not only into the myriad of obstacles that intentional communities face but also into how little and how much we human beings have changed throughout the centuries.

The Ephrata Cloister's founder, Conrad Beissel, was born in 1691 in an area of southern Germany known as the Palatinate. Orphaned at an early age Beissel first became a fiddler and a baker during a time of almost continuous warfare and social upheaval in northern Europe. In fact, political and social institutions had degenerated so badly that people began to anticipate the approach of the end of the world. Consequently, many turned away from stiff and severe church doctrine toward pietism, a type of spirituality that focused on each individual's spiritual development. Eventually some pietists grouped together to form the Church of the Brethren, otherwise known as the Dunkers for their preference of adult baptism by triple immersion. Conrad Beissel eventually joined this church. Like the Mennonites, the Brethren tried to emulate Christ's doctrines of love, nonresistance, and nonconformity as set forth in the Sermon on the Mount. They not only refused to physically defend themselves or their property but also would not swear oaths, would not indulge in lawsuits, and avoided all things political. They became generous to a fault. But what does leading a good life ever get you in this world? State officials and leaders of the established churches condemned these exemplary traits as heresy. They continually harassed and persecuted the Brethren and eventually forced them to emigrate out of Europe.

The Brethren eventually settled in Pennsylvania among communities of other non-resisters such as the Quakers and the Mennonites. Beissel made the sea voyage to Pennsylvania when he was twenty-nine. He apprenticed himself to a weaver, but he soon left to join a small group of pietists at a hermitage in the woods near Conestoga. Historians refer to this period of the world as an age of enlightenment, when an expanding sense of rationalism and scientific curiosity sparked technical, social, and political change. In short, people began to reassess their connection to the world. But Beissel wasn't interested in material objects or in his role in a changing society. He was searching for spiritual answers, not scientific ones. Rather than participate in society he desired to escape the entrapment of worldly things and the tensions of human activities. Like Bernofsky, Beissel believed civilization to be misguided, morally corrupt, and harmful to human creativity. His vision was to create the perfect environment in which to worship and glorify God—something, he felt, that contemporary religious sects could not provide. It turned

The Ephrata Cloister

out that other Brethren shared a similar desire. And other radical spiritualists soon gravitated to the Conestoga area to be near Beissel.

The former fiddler had a natural knack for preaching and could quote the Bible from memory. His charismatic personality especially moved female pietists, and the women sought him out whenever they could break away from household chores to bring him gifts of food and clothing. Beissel graciously accepted the gifts and then distributed them to the poor. But neither the place, the time, nor the situation felt quite right to the visionary, and in 1732 Beissel packed his rucksack and hiked eight miles north from the Conestoga area into a wilderness fed by a stream known as Cocalico, or the "den of snakes," about fifteen miles north of the present-day city of

Lancaster. When they discovered their spiritual leader had deserted them, many of Beissel's admirers pulled up stakes and followed. Beissel dubbed the new community Ephrata, which was an alternative biblical name for Bethlehem. To help reach spiritual perfection, he suggested that his followers practice celibacy. He called the men the Solitary Brethren, and the women Solitary Sisters. Others who wished to associate with Beissel but who still wanted to raise families became known as Householders and established farms around the cloister.

In the beginning, the members of the new commune neglected personal religious pursuits in order to help newcomers build their twenty-by-twenty-five-feet cabins. Like the droppers, everyone helped in the construction, and members did not have to pay for the shelter. They abandoned the concept of personal possessions and adapted an austere style of clothing made of unbleached linen or wool. The men and women held all things in common—but only amongst their own sex. They worked communally on all agricultural and milling operations, and each sex ate at a different table, family style. When nonbelievers condemned them for working in the fields on Sunday and other uncommon practices, the communers responded with love, setting up a school for indigent settlers and distributing pumpernickel bread baked in a communal oven free of charge. Like Drop City, the cloister had virtually no structured government of its own, yet it continued to expand; and like the droppers, most individuals of the congregation welcomed adversity and thrived in self-inflicted poverty. They surrendered family names and, like the droppers, adopted new ones. Beissel assumed the name Friedsam Gottrecht, which may be liberally translated from German as *the seed of peace in the righteousness of God*. By 1740, twelve years after Beissel had escaped to the den of snakes to be alone, the cloister's population numbered about thirty-five Brothers and nearly an equal number of Sisters. About forty families of Householders lived in the surrounding area, bringing the total population of the cloister close to two hundred people. The solitary cabins soon proved inadequate for worship and business meetings, so over the years Beissel's followers constructed a half dozen imposing community buildings.

The rituals that developed at Ephrata, it seems, might have rivaled the psychedelic happenings of the droppers and those of the Merry Pranksters. By 1735 Beissel had developed the *Nachtmetten*, or "night watch" meetings—a special initiation held for the celibate solitaires at midnight, the hour of judgment. No one could pray, sing hymns, or worship at the *Nachtmetten* without first letting bygones be bygones among their fellows. As a ghostly procession proceeded through the dark, other individual Brothers and Sisters who had dispersed throughout the grounds sang eerie-sounding polyphonic hymns.

The secret mystical society of the Zion Brotherhood, it seems, was even more bizarre. The Brotherhood's initiation rite involved two brutal procedures. To restore the votary to a state of original physical innocence, the neophyte subsisted on herb broths, hard biscuit, and rainwater while isolated in a hut or shelter in the forest for forty days. It may sound like an extreme Outward Bound initiation, but the story gets even more interesting. At some point the masters withdrew several ounces of blood from the initiate and gave him a secret elixir to drink. They repeated the process again and then administered a hallucinogen, which they referred to as the *materia prima*. The drug allegedly caused loss of speech and memory and sent the novitiate into a delirious fever during which he shed both hair and flakes of skin. Next followed an intercourse between the votary and the archangels, which allegedly concluded in complete moral and spiritual purification. The whole process of meditation, prayer, ritual, and communion behind locked doors lasted forty days. Some initiates allegedly suffered nervous breakdowns and moments of psychosis.

The Nation's First Artists' Colony

With the expansion of the Ephrata Cloister, its members began to express their spirituality as much through art as through prayer and meditation. Three main forms of expression developed: poetry, music, and decorative calligraphy called *fraktur*. *Fraktur* could also refer to a type of print, but in many Pennsylvania German schoolrooms during the eighteenth century, students illustrated short religious or inspirational sayings by decorating individual letters with likenesses of birds, flowers, and patterns of intricate lines. They preferred bright colors, though seldom brilliant. The Ephratians formalized this folk art, raising it to a plane of perfection. They illustrated the borders of the pages of their own hymnals with wildly imaginative, psychedelic drawings that featured a profusion of sun wheels, rosettes, six-petaled stars or blossoms, curious foliage forms, and florets. Illustrating pages of books with *fraktur* represented only part of the art produced at Ephrata. Historians suggest that the writers of the commune penned more poetry than all the poets in the other colonies combined. Beissel himself allegedly wrote a thousand poems and put them to music. Unfortunately, few modern American readers have studied the work, because Beissel and his followers wrote in German. By 1745 the Ephrata press regularly printed original hymnals, as music quickly became the principal unifying element within the community—especially after the Sisterhood founded a singing school.

The school allowed only women to sing at first, but later male bass voices participated also. The original hymns typically featured five-part, and later four-, six-, and eight-part harmonies. A soprano carried the air or melody, accompanied by an alto and a female tenor; two men sang the upper and lower bass parts. Beissel further divided the women into three choirs. The singers always dressed in white, even when practicing, and sat in alternate spots around the table during the Love Feast so that they could take turns singing antiphonally. Singing-class sessions generally lasted four hours, often ending with the *Nachtmetten* procession.

But in Ephrata, singing encompassed more than the lungs and vocal chords—the heart was probably the most important instrument. Attaining purity involved physical as well as spiritual exercise. Singers avoided eating milk, cheese, butter, eggs, beans, and honey, settling for wheat and buckwheat breads, carrots, radishes, and other tuberous vegetables. They drank only water. While suppressing all carnal thoughts and desires, they sang with lips barely parted and heads directed upward. Beissel strictly forbade any vocal flourishes or showy display. The overall effect created was of an organ-like serenity. Beissel's contemporaries likened his music to the Aeolian harp harmonized. "It had little or no melody; but consisted of simple, long notes, combined in the richest harmony," said Jacob Duche, a visitor to the cloister. "It is impossible to describe . . . my feelings upon this occasion. The performers sat with their heads reclined, their countenances solemn and dejected, their faces pale and emaciated from their manner of living, their clothing exceedingly white and quite picturesque, and their music such as thrilled to the very soul. I almost began to think myself in the world of the spirits, and that the objects before me were ethereal. In short, the impression this scene made upon my mind continued strong for many days, and I believe, will never be wholly obliterated."[90] Because of the demanding spiritual preparations and the total denial of self needed to perform the music accurately, modern chorales have never been able to replicate the sounds that once echoed across Ephrata.

Under Beissel's leadership, membership in the cloister continued to expand and the output of art, poetry, and music increased. But Beissel wanted more time to spend writing his own poetry and doctrinal works, so in 1740 he stepped aside as prior and appointed Israel Eckerling to take his place. Eckerling, also known as Prior Onesimus, decided to lead the commune into the modern age—even though the modern age hadn't yet arrived. To achieve this Eckerling first turned the commune into a corporation that exploited its volunteer workers and then went about tampering with the deed to the land. He first reorganized the Solitary Brothers into the Zionist Brothers and petitioned the proprietors of the land grant to put the property under his name in trust for the Zionitic Brotherhood. With this accomplished, he began running the cloister as if it were his personal fiefdom. He ordered the Zionist Brothers to reduce their sleeping hours to six a day—from ten in the evening to midnight, and from one in the morning to five in the morning.

Now run by virtual slave labor, the commune resembled a veritable industrial and market-oriented corporation under extreme pressure to produce. Eckerling swept aside Beissel's philosophy that a life of intentional poverty was the only way to holiness. He intensified livestock and agricultural production. He oversaw construction of a paper mill that eventually supplied a large share of the writing and printing paper used in Pennsylvania, as well the only high-grade cardboard in the colonies. A tannery turned out superb leathers for the commune's extensive shoemaking enterprise and bookbinderies. The fulling mill prepared materials for the weaving of various textiles; a sawmill processed lumber for a large regional market; the oil mill transformed flax seed into oils that were converted into the printers' ink used throughout the colony. The cloister's own teams of horses and wagons delivered the goods around the colony of Pennsylvania. In time Eckerling won over the allegiance of Prioress Maria Eicher to ensure that the Sisters followed a harsh puritanical work ethic as well—completely eradicating the former voluntary character of the commune.

Eckerling also proved a shrewd businessman, ordering that flour be stored until it was in demand across the colony and then selling it at high prices, for example. In the meantime

Beissel watched from the wings, not meddling, but waiting for the right time to knock Eckerling from his high horse. Israel, aka Prior Onisemus, Eckerling's downfall began when he tried to lure the Householders away from their private farms onto the commune by promising them their own living quarters. He schemed to take hold of their economic resources and land once they moved in. However, Eckerling overlooked one important matter. He did not welcome the Householder children onto the commune, nor did he provide means for the care of any minors. When family ties proved too strong for many concerned parents, Beissel finally stepped in and advised the Householders to return to their old way of life. Some scholars believe that Beissel had simply been giving Eckerling enough rope to hang himself. To regain control Beissel convinced Prioress Maria Eicher that Eckerling wanted to take control of her order as well. Following Beissel's suggestion, the prioress reorganized and reoriented the Sisterhood, changing its image from that of a cold celestial virginity to one of warm devotion and love. The Spiritual Virgins soon became known as the Roses of Saron.

In an attempt to curb the rebellion, Eckerling pronounced dark prophecies and judgments about Ephrata. But few listened to him. Both the Sisters and Brothers burned his voluminous writings in separate bonfires, and a week later, Eckerling left the commune. Once again under Beissel's influence, Ephrata reverted to the path of spiritualism and art. He shut down the mills and sold the horses and wagons. Eventually, arsonists set fire to some of the mills, and people uprooted the fruit trees. In a way Ephrata turned its back on progress, to flow against the tide that was dragging American society across the ever-expanding frontier, where people shed their old tradition of agricultural and community cooperation to assume a character of rugged individualism and self-motivated free enterprise. By the late 1770s Americans were avidly reading and following the principles set forth by Ben Franklin in his *Way to Wealth*. And most never looked back.

But then no newcomers joined the cloister, and Ephrata, because of its celibate ways, slumped into a slow spiral toward nonexistence. Beissel died on July 6, 1768. By 1810 only eight aging Sisters lingered at the cloister. Four years later, Pennsylvania's General Assembly incorporated the Society of Seventh Day Baptists of Ephrata and assigned trustees to administer the lands and buildings of the commune. Small numbers of descendants from the families continue to support congregations in several places in Pennsylvania, under the name of Seventh Day German Baptist Brethren.[91]

In many ways, Drop City mirrored Ephrata with its self-inflicted poverty, the incorporation of art into life, the loving construction of homes, the assumed names, the open-door policy for newcomers, the use of hallucinatory drugs, its community band, the sharing of resources. Of course, in many other ways it never remotely resembled the cloister. The anarchistic droppers formed no sectarian institutions, no formal lifestyle rules, and they joyfully indulged in sex. But one thing that never changes from decade to decade, century to century, or millennium to millennium, is the struggle between human beings to convince others to follow their vision of the world. Although anarchy seemingly reigned on its social surface, Drop City had a very strong spiritual and idealistic leader in the form of Eugene Victor Debs Bernofsky, who led by quiet example as he attempted to establish his new civilization.

Richert, the co-founder, had a more confined vision for the community, and his dream of creating an artists' community already seemed to have taken shape. Now, a new dropper wanted to infuse a different vision into the mix. Peter Rabbit Douthit hoped to put Drop City on the cultural map of America. Like

Eugene Bernofsky

Israel Eckerling, Douthit wanted success in the good old American sense—becoming famous and making money. The question became Which vision would the community ultimately embrace?

. . . Thirty-one months after the President proclaimed the coming of the Great Society in his memorable Ann Arbor, Mich. speech, its impact has been disappointingly slight. . . . "women are becoming sexually more assertive and demanding, and men are more indifferent and lethargic." . . . between $9 billion and $10 billion in additional funds will be needed to finance the Viet Nam war in fiscal 1967. That doubles the Viet Nam tab. . . . But the numbers, far from indicating discrimination, actually add to the evidence that the Negro has found in the armed forces the fair and opportunity-full society. . . . "Why do you call me Clay?" he screamed. "You know my right name is Muhammad Ali." . . . Mao's Great Proletarian Cultural Revolution, aimed at "purifying" Chinese Communism, erupted into strife and stridency so bitter that it produced widespread chaos. . . . the U.S. was selectively applying a new strategy: a purposeful policy of scorched earth. . . . thousands of deaths each year in cities all over the world can be linked to air pollution. . . . (December 1966–January 1967)[92]

"One day, while I ran some errands around Trinidad," Bernofsky said, "a local minister offered to donate a used mimeo-

| The Dropper Newsletter |

graph machine to Drop City. Contrary to typical dropper ethics I hesitated to accept the handout. Lately, we had begun discussing the idea of publishing a newsletter and sending it out to friends and family, and maybe to some other communes that we heard had organized around the country. I didn't mind the idea of keeping friends and families up to date with our shenanigans, but I thought we had already gotten too much publicity. Any more might attract freeloaders, druggies, or teenagers. But, in the end, I just couldn't resist free junk, so I lugged the machine back to Drop City, neglecting to ask the minister for

directions on how to use it. But, that didn't matter. It turned
out that Douthit knew all about mimeograph machines. As soon
as he moved in, he let it be known that, because he had published some poems and because he had contacts with underground newspapers, he would start a Drop City newsletter and
sell subscriptions to provide us with income, fame, and glory."

In typical dropper fashion, the congregation decided to
write the newsletter without deciding anything about editorial
control: what should go in it, and how it should be told. "Ordi-
narily we didn't make decisions by voting," Curl said. "We usually
just talked things through until either everybody was satisfied
or we'd reached a stalemate. Nobody was ever forced to do
anything; nobody had things shoved down their throat. There
was rarely total agreement about anything; but nothing was
considered decided until everybody was at least agreeable to it.
That was easy to achieve when nobody was adamantly opposed
to some proposal. But it usually took only one person resolutely against something to prevent it from happening. Unless
somebody else was just as resolutely determined to do it anyway. Force of personality was often the deciding factor. . . .
Decisions were always up for renegotiation. There really were
no rules. At least no fixed rules. Well, maybe a few, like the
rule that nobody could declare himself or herself boss."[93]

The droppers remained blissfully unaware of Albertson's
research on the processes that had led to the failure of communes
in the past—and the dangers of publishing self-promotional
pamphlets too soon. With no formal decision or announcement
made, individual droppers began to work on the newsletter.
All agreed to submit some kind of prose, poetry, or drawing
for publication. Douthit, the self-proclaimed professional PR
guy, apparently restrained himself from trying to dominate the
project. "His assertive nature was constantly trying to jump
out," Curl said, "but before it sprawled all over everybody, he'd
rein it back in, leaving room for the other droppers."[94] The

newsletter was "the first project since the hole-in-the-wall incident on which we all participated," Bernofsky added. "We worked late into the evenings in the kitchen dome. Whenever I looked up from my work I stared right into the ragged dark hole of the despoiled Sheetrock."

Douthit composed the unofficial-official dropper editorial policy, which appeared at the head on the masthead of the first newsletter: "No selectivity is exercised by the editors. The Drop City Newsletter is an expression of the individual viewpoints of the residents of Drop City and/or non-resident contributors. Nothing contained in this newsletter is necessarily the viewpoint of Drop City or its residents. The content of the Drop City Newsletter is in no way limited. We welcome contributions of any kind—news, lies, truths, drawings, literature, pornography, nonsense, ultimate realities, ads, MONEY, MONEY, MONEY."nn

Not all the droppers liked what was happening with it, Curl said, "but we hung with it. The two most popular titles for the newsletter were *Peace* and *Send Us All Your Money*. The money business was supposed to be a joke, but in retrospect, I didn't think it very funny."95 The droppers submitted a variety of projects. Bernofsky wrote *A Choice Sampling of Curly Bensen's Lexicon Ultimate*, including *Paranoia*—a zany virus; *Cosmic Forces*—the total ultimate director of progress and survival; *Money*—the obsolete system of survival and achievement; *Scrounge*—the manner in which progress is obtained; *Chowtime*—the spiritual dilemma for daily attainment; *DropCity*—to sponsor and create the avant-garde of civilization, utilizing all the remnants, at least of art, science, technology, etc; and *Dropping*—an elaborate put-on.

Richert contributed nine commandments: Dont be uptight Dont put people on Dont try to make people tense Dont hurt others Dont hurt yourself Dont be afraid Dont make anybody afraid Dont try to be a super hero Dont try to make others into super heroes. The painter also wrote a *Proposal to American Lawmakers*, in which he urged politicians to support experimental test tube societies like Drop City and exempt them from the laws of this country. "A lot of different structures could be tried to see how they stand up," Richert said, "and to see if any are of any worth." Drop Lady drew a crude map of Drop City and an overhead drawing of the new Complex. DiJulio wrote about a demon that a physicist named Maxwell used to explain certain subatomic movements; Poly Ester offered a steamy excerpt from a novel in progress. Curl composed a rant: "We at Drop City have reconciled the Dionysian in us. We harbor no illusions. 100 years ahead of our time, we are BUMS NOW. The only spirituality left to western man is total sensuality, so we have constant orgasm."

In an ad section, the droppers offered to sell the *Ultimate Painting* for fifty thousand dollars, and ten nudie pics of Curley Bensen for five bucks. They also requested donations of sound and camera equipment, as well as financial donations. Douthit's submissions caused some controversy. He proposed running a cartoon, drawn by a friend, that caricatured LBJ with a penis for a nose and jowls that looked like testicles. Some of the droppers protested because they were planning to send copies to their families. Douthit's other offerings were *Semi-Official Dropper Biographies*: "CURLY BENSEN [Bernofsky], with a lust for the sea, was born from the hawse hole of a Norwegian freighter. Her name was Ma Bensen. DROP LADY was rescued and raised by the pigeons living under the Tri-Borough Bridge. CLARD SVENSEN [Richert] grins and shuffles his feet a lot. It has been opined that he is a moron or suffers from a congenital birth defect, but we know better. He sez that the above was written by Rabbit, who is obviously jealous. LARRY LARD [Kallweit] owes it all to his beauty. He often expresses concern over his impending crucifixion. PETER RABBIT [Douthit] often mutters about sneezes, flowerpots, Mr. Mac Gregor, Flopsy,

Mopsy and Cottontail. POLY ESTER is linear and elastic. Whoop— Whoop—Whoop. ALTERESIO [DiJulio] is a gangster from Naples who rubs garlic on his dum-dum. CRAYOLA [Carol DiJulio] was rescued from living in the pasture and eating grass. I never dreamed, she has been known to say. ISHMAEL [Curl] has a vertically striped face, red purple and gold. He doesn't have $500, do you have $500? QUICKLY [Patti] is fast, we think. LUKE COOL [Baer] has the quickest six-gun in Oklahoma. He's got eleven notches on his iron, not counting injuns, messikins and niggers.

When Steve Baer read a draft of the newsletter, he thought Douthit's depiction of him branded him a racist. Douthit shrugged it off. "Where I come from everybody talks like that," he said. "At least us poor white trailercamp trash. It don't mean nothing. It ain't racist. I like everybody." Douthit refused to retract any of his submissions and pointed to the editorial policy to back him up. The other droppers didn't know what to do. "We reached a stalemate," Curl said. No one wanted to be the one to trash the whole project over it, so one by one the rest of us finally relented. We printed several hundred copies and sent them out."[96] But the newsletters barely made it out of the Trinidad post office.

When the postmaster saw the caricature of LBJ, he considered filing federal charges. The local postal carrier broke the news to the droppers that his boss had classified the drawing as obscene. A few days later the postmaster paid the droppers a visit. The FBI later questioned him about the meeting: "Post Office (XXXX), Denver, Colorado, advised that his agency conducted a preliminary investigation regarding a newsletter which was being published in the first part of 1967 by the hippie group at Drop City, Colorado, which is near Trinidad, Colorado. He stated this newsletter was considered by the Post Office Department as being obscene and contained very filthy language. (XXXX) contacted GENE BENOFSKY, who was the leader of the hippie group at Drop City. . . . He stated they were living in complete filth, were quite poverty stricken, and claimed to be dropouts from society. (XXXX) stated that BERNOFSKY told him the Drop City newsletter was a group project and no one in particular was responsible for its publication. He stated that after considerable argument with various members of the group, they claimed they had a right to publish such a newsletter and to say anything in it that they desired, and he finally advised them that if they continued to publish this newsletter, he would present it to the United States Attorney at Denver and have the case handled by the Department of Justice. (XXXX) stated that after his visit to Drop City, which was in about May, 1967, they ceased publication of the newsletter and the Post Office case was closed."[97]

Before the droppers received word that the case had been dropped, they plotted to fight for their rights to free speech. "We quickly planned to contact every lawyer we knew and defend our rights," Curl said. "We took the postmaster's reaction as a compliment, and started plotting the next newsletter as an exposé of the repressive system."[98] When the local carrier honked again the next day, he told the droppers that the postmaster had relented and that LBJ, dick nose and all, was in the mail. Bernofsky said, "He also warned us to clean up our act."

The postmaster's report to the FBI was flawed. More newsletters would emerge from Drop City. Before long Douthit had appropriated the mimeograph machine to churn out publicity about the commune. "It is impossible to define Drop City," he wrote in one flyer. "It fell out a window in Kansas three years ago with a mattress and a balloon full of water and landed in a goat pasture near Trinadad [sic], Colorado." In the same newsletter Douthit glorified creative scrounging and bragged that no dropper was employed or had a steady income. "Things come to us," he said. "We are not responsible for what and where we are, we have only taken our place in space and light and time. We are only people who want love, food, warmth. We have no integrity. We borrow, copy, steal . . . all ideas and things. We use everything. We take things, we make things, we give things. Drop City pivots on a sublime paradox, opposing forces exist side by side in joy and harmony. A psychedelic community? Chemically, no. We consider drugs unnecessary. By [sic] etymologically, perhaps. We are alive. We dance the Joy-dance. We listen to the eternal rhythm. Our feet move to unity, a balanced step of beauty and strength. Creation is joy, Joy is love. Life, love, joy energy are one. We are all one. Can you hear the music? Come dance with us."[99]

Douthit distributed his propaganda to underground newspapers and glossy magazines across the country. Always hungry for a new story, the media nibbled on the bait—especially as long-haired pot-smoking flower children were seemingly springing out of the woodwork in cities across the country. The world was about to anoint the new counterculture participants as hippies, and Douthit had jockeyed Drop City into contention for immediate fame and glory. Although some droppers welcomed the exposure, others feared it could eventually undermine the community.

A subtle rift began to appear in the self-contained new civilization. "Douthit's writing was like pabulum," Bernofsky said. "He's mouthing this hyper exaggerated nonsense. He's chanting. . . . I don't know if Douthit ever brought a nickel or dime to us. He was a writer who saw a good story and used us. In reality, he was going to ride our belief, faith, and idealism to reach his own narrow and selfish goals of fame and wealth. He completely altered the direction of Drop City. I thought the strength of our positive idealism would bring Peter over in the end, but I was mistaken." The specter of Israel Eckerling, aka Prior Onesimus, had arisen from its three-hundred-year-old grave.

. . . Died. Lieut. Colonel Virgil I. "Gus" Grissom, 40, Lieut. Colonel
Edward H. White, 36, and Lieut. Commander Roger B.Chaffee, 31; in
an explosion while testing their Apollo spacecraft. . . . the U.S. and its
allies achieved a stupendous rate of fire: 1.7 million artillery and mortar
rounds and 100 million small-arms bullets per month. . . . Chiang
Ching, the wife of Chairman Mao Tse-tung is now the deputy director of
the Cultural Revolution's subcommittee and the sole adviser to the People's
liberation Army purge group. . . . Some 14.5 million young under 17
live in families too poor to feed and house them adequately. More than
3.5 million poor children who need medical help do not receive it and
nearly two-thirds of all poor children have never visited a dentist. . . .
For the first time, a large audience has tuned in on experimental film and
is beginning to believe what a far-out few have been saying for years: the
movies are entering an era of innovation that attempts to change the
language of film and reeducate the human eye. . . . Generalissimo
Francisco Franco, 74, late last year introduced a new constitution that
is intended to give Spain at least a semblance of parliamentary democracy.
. . . Psychedelic central for the U.S. right now is a half-mile stretch along
San Francisco's Haight Street. . . . (February 1967) [100]

A second story about Drop City, which appeared in the *Denver Post* in 1967, mentioned that "the droppers don't take drugs and they work diligently on imaginative projects and art works." As far as newspapers were concerned,

Dope

Bernofsky said "it didn't make any sense to tell them the truth about drugs because we would have gotten busted. There were times we thought the feds were coming down on us, and people would take off to hide their stash in the walls of their domes. But on the other hand, no, we didn't wake up in the morning and start smoking pot first thing. It was a way to recreate for us. There were certain activities I liked to engage in while being stoned—like playing chess. At Drop City we didn't want the hype to get out that we smoked dope. We didn't want a bunch of people lying around taking drugs and experiencing eternal insights. We were outside every day with our tools making things. There wasn't any place for heavy drugs. When Leary pronounced his dictum about dropping acid and dropping out, unfortunately people assumed Drop City meant dropping acid. People would read his idiotic dictum and they would come to Drop City to drop drugs. We were on the migratory route to San Francisco for East Coasters, and people would stop in and wander around stoned and lost while we built stuff and wondered what the hell was going on with them. We encouraged them to wander off to Haight-Ashbury." Douthit reported that "the only thou-shalt-not rule at Drop City that everybody was serious about was never buying or selling dope."[101]

Even FBI informants denied that dropper associates used any type of drugs or liquor or were involved in any criminal activity. However, Douthit painted a different picture in his novel, which he published after he had left the commune. After reading the book *Drop City*, reviewer Joseph Nicholson concluded that "Consciousness-expanding drugs are at the heart of the Drop City story. The dropper's daily intake reads like a spilled bowl of vegetable soup—T's and P's and L's and D's and S's and M's galore, plus grass, hash, speed, etc. The result is a macho perception of life at its simplest—the deer, trees, sky, and mountains. At the other end, we have the drug adventures, some hilarious, some revealing, some frightening. To go with the flow, yet maintain control was the objective." Richert admitted that "the droppers were pro-LSD, but we were not all heavy users."[102]

In general, heavy drug use has turned out to be the Achilles heel of the hippie movement. The specter of drugs taken long ago now hinders many baby boomers from wholeheartedly embracing or endorsing that most significant era of their lives. Young people, including famous rock stars, died from overdoses in the sixties, made poor decisions while high, and wasted a lot of time sitting around staring into space. Many middle-aged baby boomers feel foolish today when they look back upon such moments, while rumors of past drug use continue to embarrass many modern-day politicians and threaten the careers of many successful professionals. On the other hand, dope experimentation opened the minds of some to new concepts and belief systems they might never otherwise have breached in their lifetimes. Still, many boomers now condemn drug use while others have excused or rationalized it. As time has passed, the majority of hippie boomers turned their backs on dope to indulge in more conventional drugs such as alcohol, caffeine, nicotine, and Zoloft. During the sixties the media obsessed on reporting drug use among young people, insinuating that drugs were the be-all and end-all of hippie culture—so, there's no good reason why I shouldn't continue that tradition in this book with a short digression that recaps the early hippie drug culture.

It's hard to say just how much dope the droppers inhaled or swallowed, but there's no question drugs played some role in the dynamics of the community—and in the hippie movement

Grass

in general. As the number of visitors to Drop City steadily increased, the droppers would have had a large variety of drugs to choose from—ranging from heroin to LSD. All were fairly easy to acquire at the time. Like most hippies, the droppers differentiated between good dope and bad drugs. Unlike the beats, they avoided depressants and addictive substances such as amphetamines, methedrine, barbiturates, the opiates, and cocaine. They took to heart the warnings from the singer of the rock group Mothers of Invention. "Speed is going to mess up your heart, mess up your liver, your kidneys, rot out your mind," Frank Zappa said. "In general, this drug will make you just like your mother and father."[103] The droppers believed that drugs functioned as a crutch to get one through another day of drudgery, while dope, on the other hand, invigorated the partaker and offered a way out of the intellectual and spiritual morass of the times.

Grass was by far the most popular and easy-to-purchase form of dope. The more erudite smokers called it by various foreign names: *Khif* or *hashish* (from the Middle East), *bhang* or *ganja* (from India), *ma* (from China), *maconha* or *djama* (from South America). The proletariat referred to it as *pot, grass, boo, mary-jane,* and *tea.* People smoked it in joints, baked it into brownies, or brewed it into a tea, which they called *pot likker.* Formerly the drug of working-class blacks and Latinos, marijuana had become fashionable on college campuses by 1966. The market grew so lucrative that many hippies by-passed hardcore criminal dealers to smuggle grass themselves directly from Mexico. These laid-back dealers became popular figures in the community, often socializing and holding taste tests with their customers before closing a deal. Although many hippies sold just enough to underwrite their own stash, the more capitalistically oriented found themselves making money hand over fist.

By 1966 an ounce of grass—called a lid—sold for between eight and ten dollars on the West Coast. A lid produced up to forty hand-rolled joints. Keys, or kilograms, fetched between fifty and seventy-five dollars. Many college students would purchase a key, divide it into about twenty lids, and sell them to friends and classmates, doubling their initial investment. Those in the know sought Mexican Acapulco Gold for the highest of highs. Hippies loved to smoke marijuana because it often produced feelings of euphoria and exaltation by slowing down the judgment of time, distance, vision, and hearing. On the other hand, grass sometimes produced episodes of paranoia. Much to the consternation of older beats such as Ginsberg, who smoked the drug for heightened spiritual and physical awareness, many hippies perceived pot as a healthy alternative to alcohol. In 1960 only 4 percent of youth aged between eighteen and twenty-five admitted to trying marijuana. By the

early seventies, that figure had jumped to almost 50 percent
of teens and young adults. Sixty percent of college students
reported using the drug, with the percentage much higher at
some universities.[104] Medical experts during the sixties claimed
that smoking the pungent-smelling weed did not result in
addiction, and many advocates of pot believed that the drug
would eventually be legalized.

**Lucy in the Sky
with Diamonds**

But pot wasn't the only so-called beneficial
dope on the underground market. Chemists
at the Sandoz Pharmaceuticals labs, a Swiss
company, had inadvertently developed the drug LSD in 1938
by mixing lysergic acid (derived from ergot, a parasitic fungus
that grows on rye) and volatile diethylamine (used in vulcani-
zing rubber). They then froze the concoction. LSD was an
intermediate leading to the synthesis of ergonovine and ergo-
tamine, compounds used to treat migraine headaches and to
contract the uterus after childbirth. In 1943 Dr. Albert Hoffman
accidentally took the first LSD trip while working with the
compound in the lab. He reported becoming restless and dizzy.
Laboratory equipment, as well as the bodies of his co-workers,
seemed to change shape, becoming a bit wavy, or moving. In a
dreamlike state Hoffman returned home, drew the curtains
of his bedroom, and lay down. He felt a little drunk as his
imagination took off. With eyes shut Hoffman saw brilliant,
fluid, surging colors. The out-of-body experience gradually wore
off after about two hours. Sandoz marketed the interesting new
drug under the trade name of Delysid. Under clinical observations, like those Ken Kesey participated in, scientists eventually
got the inside dope on the drug. LSD takes from thirty to forty-
five minutes to affect the brain. A trip, on a dose of 150 to 250
micrograms, typically lasts about twelve hours. A tripper never
loses consciousness and often remembers everything he imagines
or experiences. Besides the intense and beautiful colors that

Dr. Hoffman observed, acid heads often reported seeing a rainbow effect around white lights. Or they saw things like geometric forms or figures or other images that they knew didn't really exist—what scientists refer to as pseudohallucination.

Another common phenomenon occurred when one sensory experience was transformed to another, such as feeling music vibrate through the body, or seeing musical notes fly through the air. Thoughts moved much more rapidly than usual, and a person tripping on LSD could experience diametrically opposed phenomena simultaneously, such as feeling both heavy and light. An LSD trip also increased the ability to focus, so that one might suddenly become fixated on the significance of a burning candle. The past, present, and future frequently got mixed up. Also, strange bodily sensations sometimes occurred: a hand might seem to become disconnected from the body or the blood might be heard coursing through the body. But most important for personal development, LSD dissolved the ego, unlocked repressed feelings, and enabled the user to feel at one with the world. Stimulated by LSD, the nervous system became overloaded with sensations that the brain could not sort out. Sometimes this led to good trips, sometimes bad. Joy could soon devolve into intense anxiety, panic, and paranoia, which lasted indefinitely. This phenomenon was called freaking out. It often featured erratic behavior and could occur after dropping acid in an unfamiliar place or during a stressful situation. "I went on a horror trip . . . every time I got high," said Allen Ginsberg, "when the first doubt came that I might not see *Eternity* . . . or the fear came that I might get eaten alive by *God*, then the trip immediately turned into a hell."[105] Thorazine was one of a number of preparations that could dissipate a bad trip. A more common approach was for friends to talk down the alarmed tripper.

In early 1966 a thirty-five-year-old medical student in Brooklyn confessed to police that he'd been on a three-day acid trip when he committed a murder. Soon after that, Sandoz Pharmaceuticals announced it would no longer sell LSD, and the U.S. Attorney General demanded laws to control the drug even in the absence of any studies showing it to be dangerous.

Augustus Owsley Stanley III

As a bill to outlaw the psychedelic filtered through the California state senate, a California-based chemist with the Brahmin-sounding name Augustus Owsley Stanley III began producing LSD in his private lab. A grandson of a U.S. senator from Kentucky, Owsley was thirty-two years old when state narcotics agents raided his laboratory in Berkeley in February 1965. Although agents found all the apparatus and elements to make speed, they did not find any completely synthesized methedrine, so Owsley wiggled off the hook. After retrieving his equipment from the state, he set up a secret lab at a country hideaway. Under the name Bear Research Group, Owsley ordered enough raw materials to make a million and half doses of LSD. And he wasn't the only entrepreneur in town.

By 1967 local drug dealers estimated four or five LSD labs operated in the San Francisco Bay Area, making it the LSD-producing capital of the world. In the wholesale LSD business the basic unit of manufacture was the gram, or .035 of an ounce. On the streets, this paltry amount of pure LSD sold for around two thousand dollars. With a full dose constituting 250 micrograms (a "mike" being one-millionth of a gram), a gram often translated into four thousand acid doses. And twenty thousand doses still weighed less than an ounce.

Owsley produced his first batches of LSD in a powder form and stuffed it into gelatin capsules. The process, overseen by distributors, often turned into LSD parties. Participants, paid with tablets, absorbed the drug through the skin or licked it off their fingertips. Another manufacturing process involved dissolving powdered LSD in vodka, coloring it with vegetable dye, and using eye droppers to drip it onto Vitamin C tablets or sugar cubes, which easily absorbed the substance. By December 1965 Owlsey was also selling LSD in liquid form. Dealers transported the blue-tinted liquid in carefully washed containers of the similarly colored detergent Wisk.

Later, Owsley bought a pill press and began marketing the first LSD tablets. Acid heads dubbed the short, slightly irregular cylinders "barrels." By August 1966 Owsley was producing real pharmaceutical tablets known as flats. The 250-milligram flats, slightly bigger than saccharine, could be split in two along a hairline crack on one side. Owsley soon colored each batch of tablets a different color: blue dots, green flats, white, purple, and orange. Owsley regulated his distribution to keep the price at around two bucks for one flat, retail. His agents often passed out free samples, and Owsley personally distributed LSD to all the musicians he knew.

The chemist allegedly amassed a fortune before Congress declared the drug illegal on October 6, 1966, but he didn't shut down his enterprise. In fact Owsley began developing new drugs. By 1967 he had released onto the streets a concoction called STP—apparently named after the gasoline additive. STP produced a seventy-two-hour trip during which users swore they experienced the blinding white light of hallucinatory omniscience, the be-all and end-all of the drug experience. But word soon spread that STP caused many bad trips—with no escape route. Thorazine didn't work, and even the best of friends couldn't be expected to talk someone down for three days straight. About the best doctors could offer were tranquilizers and a long session of observation until the STP wore off. Underground chemists also marketed shorter-lived mind benders at the time: DMT (dimethyltryptamine) and DET (diethyltryptamine) produced only a forty-five-minute trip. Cactus-derived mescaline or psilocybin could also induce a warm high, as did psilocybin, peyote, and morning glory seeds.

There were also the hard-core, highly addictive, evil drugs like speed (methedrine) and heroin, which produced no spiritual insight and only made the user high and (especially in the case of speed freaks) often unpredictable and violent. Addicts of speed and heroin acted in completely opposite ways. While a wired heroin addict could calmly sit about, anxiety-free, a pumped-up speed freak would pace in an agitated, disturbed manner, often hallucinating. But as the methedrine wore off, the addict would drift into a state of exhaustion and sometimes fall asleep. In contrast, when heroin wore off, the addict often became agitated, suffered from cramps, and incessantly moved about.

"How much of this hippie pharmacopoeia reached Drop City is hard to ascertain," Miller said, "but it is a fair guess that virtually all of the droppers had enough experience with marijuana to understand the notion of chemical alteration of consciousness."[106] Bernofsky never thought much of LSD after experimenting with the drug a couple of times, but he understood why many young Americans might have wanted to get turned on back in the sixties—and he empathized with them. "The reason for so many hallucinatory incapacitating drugs going around at that time was the war in Vietnam. More and more drugs were being pumped into cities to keep people down. If you keep people addicted to dope, they'll never get involved in government. We tended to stay away from the hard drugs. To counter all the awful stuff going on with our government at the time, we did our best to imagine that there were entities beyond that reality—the cosmic forces—that could help us overcome the depressive environment we were living in. I had a positive idealistic feeling in faith, hope, and life itself. I felt there was basic essential goodness in people. I felt having a positive outlook would help us achieve good things. If we were negative, depressed, and hopeless—the way LBJ wanted us to be—then we would do nothing except get high."

. . . The draft may not be used to stifle dissent. . . . Japan's busy automakers bumped Britain out of its No. 3 spot, moved in behind the U.S. and Germany in world car and truck production. . . . Bobby urged the Administration to declare a bombing halt on the chance that Hanoi would then consent to peace talks. . . . The youngest draft-age men, starting with 19-year-olds, will be taken first, reversing present priorities under which 26-year-olds are the first to go. . . . Beatle George Harrison, decided to fill the blank between nose and lip with a splendid Pancho Villa brush. . . . To keep the state moving ahead and at the same time in the black, Reagan proposed a budget of $5 billion and called for $946 million in increased taxes. . . . The 7,000 mind-blown residents of San Francisco's "Psychedelphia" demand a zero-hour day and free freak-outs for all. . . . Every day, somewhere in New York City's public school system, at least one teacher is shoved or struck by recalcitrant students. . . . American deaths are averaging 150 per week v. 96 a week during 1966. Sad as those figures are, they are dwarfed by the enormous bloodletting that has been inflicted on the Communists. . . . (March 1967)[107]

Free Love

Drop City also evolved on the cusp of the free love generation, a period when the public's interest in sex exploded out of the bedroom and morphed into a public fixation. In 1965 sociologists claimed that only 20 or 30 percent of women in college had lost their virginity by the time they graduated. Among those, "only 2 percent to 3 percent could be considered promiscuous after engaging in intercourse with no thought of committing themselves to a durable attachment to their partner."[108] In the beginning, the Drop City love life resembled middle-class America, although sex outside marriage did occur among the singles living there. "People coupled up and there was a mutual respect toward the various relationships," Bernofsky said. "If there was any sleeping around or trading partners I didn't know about it. And it didn't go on as far as I could tell."

In the early stages of the commune, times could be tough on the single men, who often outnumbered available women. Richert became lovers with Peggy Kagel who lived at the commune for a short while after she separated from her husband. After Kagel left, Richert put a tongue-in-cheek advertisement in the inaugural Drop City newsletter, searching for the *ultimate chick*. "In response to Richert's ad, a letter arrived from a woman in Cincinnati, an artist named Jalal, who was searching for a new home," Curl said. "I assumed that Clark would pick up on her, since he had advertised, but either he got cold feet or something put him off, probably her kid. It was Richard Kallweit who responded. After exchanging a few letters, she arrived with her eight-year-old son, Snoop, and they squeezed into the cartop dome. To everybody's surprise Richard actually hit it off with his mail-order bride."[109]

Richert eventually found true love in Trinidad with Suzie, a long-haired blonde who had recently graduated from high school. "Suzie came from humble origins, having grown up in a trailer," Bernofsky said. "She was fascinated with hippies and wanted to get away from her miserable life at home. Despite a seven-year age difference between them, the couple established a sound relationship and Suzie eventually gave birth to two children." Over the winter of 1966–1967, while Drop City was at its most industrious, the commune sustained a half dozen couples, some legally married and with children. "I think everyone had a mate," Bernofsky said. "It was kind of a straightforward middle-class deal. The sexual politics were pretty conservative and strait-laced. We talked about how we wanted to keep that part of our lives simple. Not to get involved in fiery cross relationships. We disciplined ourselves so that it didn't go on. We were mostly college graduates and had a little maturity, and we realized how complicated and difficult life would be with any partner trading. That was one of the disciplines we had that helped us in our achievements on the land. There were no difficult interrelationships."

Peggy Kagel, it seems, viewed things differently when she explained the commune's sexual politics to Curl: "We call it the evil black snake. It just tears everybody apart. Gene and Clark claim they're trying to break down their egos, and part of that is not being possessive about women. I'm not going to tell you who did what with who, or who would barely talk to who for weeks. But I didn't see too many egos broken down."[110]

During the first two years of the commune's existence, the sexual politics at Drop City seemed to conform to that of the general public. The men performed men's work, such as building the domes; the women did women's work, such as the cooking and cleaning. Curl's girlfriend, Patsy Quickly, would complain to him about the division of labor. "How come just the women have to cook?" she asked. "I thought Drop City was trying to be different."[111] In his list of former droppers that I might contact, Bernofsky included the name of Carol DiJulio, whom Curl described as "a dropper with the imagination of a secretary." I had high hopes that the divorced mother of two would be able to present a female perspective of the community, but like Drop Lady, she bluntly refused to get involved in the project. About the only information I could cajole out of Carol DeJulio was: "The commune was a man's thing."

From Dymaxion Award to Foodstamps

In one of his newsletters Peter Douthit crowed: "Buckminster Fuller gave us his 1966 Dymaxion Award for poetically economic structural achievements. We hope to buy more land, build more Drop Cities all over the world, the universe. Free and open way stations for every and anyone." The fact is, at least according to Bernofsky, that there was no formal award, and interestingly enough, the Dymaxion Award has never been heard of since. "During our second winter at Drop City, we were having a hard time making ends meet," Bernofsky said. "So I wrote to Fuller describing our architectural achievements and our financial distress. Bucky wrote back that he loved our innovative use of materials. He also enclosed a check for five hundred dollars as a gift and drew the check up as the Dymaxion Award, so he could write it off as a tax deduction. Douthit often mentioned the so-called award in his PR to attract attention to us. Needless to say, even the droppers couldn't stretch five hundred dollars very far. Getting more and more involved in our building and art projects, we felt less inclined to leave the commune for outside work."

When the Welfare Department switched from government commodities to food stamps, the droppers immediately took advantage of that program, Bernofsky said. "We were the very first food stamp recipients in Colorado—maybe even in the country. We went straight from commodities to food stamps. We thought the program was great. Instead of getting commodities handed to us, we could now go to the store. In essence, the commodities program had been privatized. I was glad that the federal government had finally recognized they needed to feed the droppers. It was another indication that the cosmic forces smiled upon us. We were overjoyed. The only thing I didn't like was that we had to buy commercial peanut butter. We sure missed the natural peanut butter we had gotten in the big commodity cans."

The government initiated the federal assistance program to help the needy by printing food stamps in two denominations. A two-dollar stamp was blue on white, and the fifty-cent stamp was orange on white. "The currency featured weird 1930 social realist prints on them; they're a lot like monopoly money," Douthit said. The program aided farmers by buying surplus food and giving it away to people who made less than ninety dollars a month. For families each member had to earn below the same monthly threshold. The droppers, even after their congregation swelled to twenty persons, pulled in about seventy-five dollars a month as a group—all of which arrived in the form of a child-support check made out to Poly Ester. Recipients could only use food stamps to buy domestic foodstuffs, but that regulation it seems was ignored in Colorado. "In this part of the country," Douthit said, "you can buy anything your heart desires with them: guns, chainsaws, books, cars, gas, dope—you name it. I'm sure there are more food stamps than dollars in circulation in northern New Mexico and southern Colorado."[112]

But the manna from heaven didn't last very long. "After a while, they tried to cut us off," Douthit said, "but Bernofsky and I went down and hollered and screamed until they gave them back to us. The hassle was on. The next month they cut us off again and no amount of hollering or screaming would change their minds. Bernofsky and I hung around the welfare office ranting and raving for days."[113]

When the media got wind of the story, television crews and newspaper reporters from Denver, Trinidad, and Pueblo swooped in for interviews. "We told them it was all free and peace and love and brotherhood and the tribe and all that shit," Douthit said. "They put it in the papers and us on T.V. and all that shit. The A.C.L.U. got all excited and picked up the droppers' case. A couple of halfway-hip lawyers flew down from Denver and laid a very heavy trip on the welfare department who immediately passed the buck to the state welfare department. So they passed the buck to the Department of Agriculture."[114]

FBI files report the names of the attorneys as Elmer Lee Hamby and Peter Ney of the Civil Liberties Union, Denver, Colorado. In early September 1967 the state released its final decision on Drop City to the press. "The Colorado Welfare Department announced today it has discontinued granting food stamps to residents of Drop City, a self styled artist community six miles northeast of Trinidad," an article in the *Pueblo Chieftain* said. "Charline J. Birkins, welfare director, said a recent review disclosed that Drop City residents do not meet eligibility for food stamps. 'The purpose of the food stamp program,'

Miss Birkins said, 'is to raise levels of nutrition among low-income families. Primarily, it is to provide food for those who are unable to earn sufficient income to eat adequately. Residents of Drop City, however, are low income by choice. Most of the adult residents there are university graduates and are able to work.' She said the Drop City certification originally was based on four separate households living together as one family, but that subsequently the group has incorporated and is not a legal family or household under the program. The U.S. Department of Agriculture, the welfare director said, requires verification of income for food stamp certification and she added this has been difficult to obtain for Drop City. A report from the Las Animas Welfare Department, Miss Birkins said, shows the residents of Drop City Inc. declared a total income of $150—which is from a court order for support and a monthly contribution from a friend. The report says the residents solicit funds through a news letter and have collection boxes on the grounds, but no income has been reported from these sources. The state welfare director also said the composition of the household varies and anyone with the same philosophy is able to move in or out at any time making it impossible for the county to determine eligibility. In August 1967 Drop City residents paid $70 to receive $82 in bonus for a total of $152 in food stamps for 12 adults and 13 children." Adding to the futility of attempting to verify the facts about Drop City, the reader will recognize the discrepancies between Douthit's figures and those of the Welfare Department.

Few local residents seemed to sympathize with the droppers' predicament, and some expressed their disgust in letters to the editor of the *Chieftain*. "I often wonder if those hippies have ever considered what would happen if everyone in our country decided to follow their idea of an idealistic society," wrote Dale C. Lehfeldt. "Who, then, would support them or us? Either we would return to the Stone Age or all would have to get back to work." Somehow or other the droppers kept limping along.

Dropper fame spread as newspaper reporters and television crews from Denver, Pueblo, Colorado Springs, Boulder, and Trinidad continued to churn out stories about the commune. Some articles painted the droppers in a good light as hard-working and productive artists while others panned them as loafers and miscreants. The wire services picked up some of the stories, which then ran in papers up and down the Rocky Mountain front, but their reputation as an underground cultural center remained regional. That soon began to change, however.

Expanding Infamy

The commune's newsletters had generated a wave of interest in Drop City beyond Douthit's wildest dreams. First to request an article was *Inner Space: The Magazine of the Psychedelic Community*. Initially, the droppers hesitated to respond, not wanting to be associated too strongly with drug use, but in the end Curl took on the project. "I didn't have any problem with the group editing my writing," Curl said. "The article came out in the same issue as a report on the First Human Be-In in Golden Gate Park, San Francisco, a prelude to the upcoming Summer of Love [January 1967]."[115]

Then one day the shit hit the fan—at least from Bernofsky's point of view. While working on the triple-fused dome, the undeclared leader of Drop City (at least before Douthit's arrival) watched a shiny red Toyota drive through the commune gate and onto the property. Bernofsky took particular interest because most tourists showed enough respect to park along the road. "Two casually dressed, neat looking men emerged from the sedan," he said. "A necklace of cameras dangled from the shoulders of one. When I saw those cameras I thought, here comes trouble. The two men introduced themselves as reporters from *Time* magazine and said they were looking for Peter Rabbit. 'You'll find him in that dome,' I said. The reporters entered the dome but quickly reappeared with Douthit, who proceeded to lead them around the community like a drum major. When the reporters stopped to interview me, they explained that *Time* was preparing a cover story on hippies and planned to focus a spotlight on Drop City. I refused to be interviewed and retreated to my dome while the reporters spent the rest of the afternoon holed up with Douthit.

"The appearance of *Time* magazine signified to me that we had lost our direction for the development of Drop City. Now, everything that I despised about fame was happening to us. There was too much glory too soon. Our substance wasn't rooted deep enough to withstand the attention. Drop City was being sucked up by big-time commercial media, and the community began to wither. It came about because of the myopic greed of some individuals seeking self-aggrandizement. In the end their true colors showed through. They were nothing but posturing buffoons who were able to manipulate the community for their own ends. They wanted to become the Allen Ginsbergs of the hippie movement. For me, that was elemental bullshit."

Rumors of the visit by the *Time* reporters soon flashed through the surrounding community, and overnight the droppers became "important local celebrities," Curl said. "A few days later, the mayor of Trinidad, the guy who ran the barber shop, came out to Drop City. He turned out to be a pretty regular guy and invited us to build a float and participate in the upcoming annual Independence Day Parade, of which he was to be the grand marshal."[116] But the droppers were planning their own extravagant celebration as part of an effort to secure national recognition.

| The Joy Festival |

Douthit may have gotten the idea for promoting the Joy Festival from the Human Be-In, which had been staged in San Francisco in January 1967. The promoters of that extravaganza described it as an attempt to bring the tribes of hippies and political radicals together. Early on the morning of January 14, poets Allen Ginsberg and Gary Snyder and a few others had performed the rite known as pradadshina, or circumambulation, around the Polo Field in Golden Gate Park. Later Owsley's agents handed out samples of his latest batch of LSD, White Lightning, as the Hell's Angels took up posts to guard the sound system. On stage Ginsberg chanted a mantra of the hashish-smoking god of yoga, Shiva. He was followed by Timothy Leary who exhorted the crowd of twenty thousand to "turn on, tune in, drop out." As Jerry Rubin and other radicals talked politics throughout the day, participants seemed to listen with only one ear as they continually moved about in slow motion. Bands such as Quicksilver Messenger Service, Grateful Dead, Loading Zone, Sir Douglas Quintet, and Jefferson Airplane rotated across the stage throughout the day. The press pronounced the event profoundly mysterious with its Hindu, Buddhist, and American Indian trappings. "The be-in had the air of an immense shared secret," said *Rolling Stone* writer Charles Perry.[117]

Six months later, in June 1967, a short article in the counter-culture magazine *Avatar* announced that "Peter Rabbit of Drop City sends us word that the Droppers are celebrating joy with festivities June 9, 10, and 11. The newsletter/poster he sent announces *Poetry—Painting—Music—Beans—Feds—Lite Shows—Dropping—Dance—Films.* They expect two thousand, including American Indians and invite hippies to bring tents, sleeping bags, and food to the *Drop In.*" Douthit intended to hold the extravaganza in the Complex and the theater dome, both of which were under construction at the time. But not every dropper backed the idea. "We had started arguing over it right from the beginning," Bernofsky said. "I was against it for one reason. At that time no essence or soul had been built into the community that could withstand anything like the Joy Festival."

Sociologists would have agreed with Bernofsky's analysis. The droppers never attempted to program individual behavior, require newcomers to go through an initiation, or to convert; nor did Drop City present any power structures or authority figure to inspire an individual to surrender to the group's subtle and ambiguous institutions. The main dropper institution was a work ethic—or better yet, a creativity ethic, which they pursued both communally and individually. Another institution that they stridently protected—one that went hand in hand with creativity—was individual intellectual freedom. Mixing creativity and freedom transformed into dropper art. All was based on the ideals of brotherly love and the rejection of capitalistic materialism. Those individuals astute enough to understand the subtle often ambiguous institutions of Drop City pitched in to help build domes, tend chickens, and dig latrines as they simultaneously indulged in personal artistic pursuits. Those who continued to focus on themselves sometimes faltered in their commitment to the community, finding it difficult to abandon the American ideals of the self-made man or woman—despite their apparent voluntary acceptance of poverty. When individual rhythm coincided with the communal heartbeat, Drop City grew stronger. When self-interest persisted in a dropper, the bedrock of the community began to crack. Not everyone could suppress their egos as well as Bernofsky, Richert, and Kallweit had done during the early stages of Drop City—especially Peter Rabbit Douthit.

Bernofsky believed that Douthit's constant proselytizing of Drop City to the outside world initiated a process that would eventually undermine the community. "It didn't help any that the self-confessed con man was putting his own spin on the commune's intentions and institutions," Bernofsky said. "Rabbit wanted recognition beyond Drop City. He wanted fame and glory. Douthit eventually pushed the Joy Festival proposal to a vote. Drop Lady, Carol DiJulio, Jill, and I voted against the idea, but the others supported it overwhelmingly. I stood up to Douthit and lost. Clark stood with him. Without Clark's support I

couldn't withstand it." Led by Douthit the backers of the festival
sent out another newsletter further defining the festival.

With Douthit churning out reams of publicity about the
upcoming Joy Festival, Bernofsky began to withdraw. "Peter told
us it was going to be a turning point element for alternative
humanity. From the Joy Festival we would gloriously advance
into a new future for everyone. He was writing people all over
the world and all over the U.S. He worked on the hype all
winter long. The big name artists and rockers were supposedly
coming—also, the dregs, psychopaths, and buffoons."

. . . *Russia and the East European Communist regimes have begun to*
abandon "command" economics. . . . The figures brought to 8,560 the
number of Americans fallen on the battlefields of Viet Nam since 1961,
compared with 187,000 Communists killed. . . . The kick is known
to hippies as "electrical bananas" or "mellow yellow." . . . if the pill
can defuse the population explosion, it will go far toward eliminating
hunger, want and ignorance. Of the 39 million American women capable
of motherhood, seven million have already taken the pills. . . . The
avowed aim of the "Spring Mobilization to End the War in Viet Nam"
was to demonstrate to President Johnson and the world the depth of
feeling in the U.S. against the conflict. The end result—aside from probably
delighting Hanoi's Ho Chi Minh—was to demonstrate that Americans in
the springtime like to have fun. . . . To salvage Lake Erie, the U.S.
Government has embarked on a $3.9 billion program of pollution control.
. . . (April 1967) [118]

Months before the opening day of the great event, the population of Drop City began to swell. A trickle of visitors soon
became a stream, then a flood. Many travelers from the East
Coast dropped in for a short stay as they headed to San Francisco to put flowers in their hair and partake in a summer of
love at Haight-Ashbury or to attend the Monterey Pop Festival.
But others hung around, at least temporarily, to participate in

the Joy Festival. Life soon grew chaotic. Disorder invaded the new kitchen in the triple-dome Complex. Every morning long lines backed up at the bathroom doors; the more industrious newcomers went to work digging latrines. The social strains caused the original droppers to declare their first regulatory statute.

"We finally held a meeting," Curl said, "and decided that there had to be a population limit, which we set at thirty-five, even though there were already over fifty people at Drop City. Beyond that limit, there would be a three-day maximum for guests sleeping in the Complex (that wouldn't apply to the Festival). If anybody was going to stay longer than that, they had to be asked to do it, at least by one person. The loophole was that the population limit wouldn't apply to anyone who came in as a lover of a dropper. We didn't really believe that any rule could prevent love. Since that was the way most new people connected, it meant that almost everybody was excluded from the so-called rule. Everybody would briefly couple, then break up and each would take a new partner. The rule made for a lot more brief casual fucking." Many of the new arrivals had already assumed dropper-style aliases: Feather Tom, Silly Michelle, Little Joe, Gypsy David, Baby Michael Bipple, Moron Normal, Jasper Button, John the Hair, Mother, Danu, Riceman Bill, Trees, Boston John, Aurora, Zowie, Meher Charlie, Big Bill, Mantis, Kentucky Jeethro, Pabla. "The list went on and on," Curl said. "Each had a story, each was coming from somewhere and going somewhere."[119]

But other droppers decided they wanted to head in an opposite direction. The overwhelming influx particularly troubled Carol Dijulio, who worried about the safety of her two children. At first she announced that she and the kids would take refuge with her parents in Boulder until things returned to normal after the Joy Festival. But when Charlie returned to the commune after dropping them off, he announced that the girls wouldn't return ever. Charlie himself hung around for a couple more days, and then he also deserted the commune. "He threw in his paintings, rifle, clothes, and junk," Curl said. "His last words, out the truck window . . . was, 'It sure don't take long to get hip.'"[120] DiJulio's departure benefited the newcomers by opening up some living space and a half dozen people soon partitioned off the bottom of The Pit.

Meanwhile, the original droppers went about the business of building and creating things, with many of them remaining aloof of the new settlers—with the exception of Douthit, who seemed to blossom in making new alliances. "He mostly hung out with new people," Curl said. "Usually the only time I saw Rabbit now was at meals and beating down the sun [with a drum]."[121] While the original droppers still expected Douthit to leave the commune, he soon established himself as the second center of the community as he attracted many of the recent arrivals to join him at his sunset ritual. Some of the more enterprising newcomers organized a crafts-manufacturing center to take advantage of the temporary market that the Joy Festival would create. They made wooden flutes,

The Festivities

drums, Jew's harps, earrings, and tie-dye tee shirts. The resident artists also worked diligently, finishing works in progress to hang on the walls of the theater dome.

Finally the big day arrived. "The People came, three hundred of them, from all over the country," Douthit said, "beautiful people in flowers and hand-made clothes, the chicks in soft transparent things with their bodies all hanging loose. Two freaks came in on a freight car loaded with copper ore. Their bodies, clothes and hair were a weird sandy-red color the whole time."[122] The first night's meal featured beans, rice tortillas, and guacamole that had been prepared in the kitchen in the Complex and was served around the clock. The dropper house band first took the stage, led by Meher Charlie, a jazz guitarist from Chicago who had earned his name by carrying a picture of Meher Baba on his person. Baba had been an Indian guru who hadn't spoken in twenty years since taking a vow of silence. "Meher Charlie sawed a mean guitar," Curl said, "plugged into an amplifier, and became the defacto leader of the dropper band. Anybody could be in the band. You didn't have to know the slightest thing about music. All you had to do was grab a flute, drum, harmonica, kazoo or whatever noisemaker was handy, and start blowing or banging away. It was the most amazing freeform cacophony. Everybody had a good time except people listening with a sensitive musician ear." Meher Charlie had also composed the Drop City anthem—a song with no fixed verses, only a refrain that band members chanted over and over again: "Ooo-eee baby / Ooo-ooo-eee / Doo-bop-shabam / Drop Ci-tee. There was something mournful in the sound, that made me think of regret for a lost Paradise," Curl said.[123]

To the beat of throbbing drums, people gyrated their bodies in the theater dome as strobe lights spasmodically flashed on the *Ultimate Painting*, which ceaselessly whirled on its axis. The shouted conversations melded into the cacophony. Hippies passed joints, couples disappeared into the black night outside, couples returned flushed, people bought crafts, ate food, drank beer and other intoxicants, chased butterflies. While the Amarillo Dukes from Texas roared up on their Harleys, residents of a commune in New Mexico—the Hog Farm— parked their psychedelically painted bus along the shoulder of El Moro Road.

Little varied, it seemed, during the Joy Festival weekend at Drop City, except the food and music. Macaroni and cheese filled their guts on Saturday, and the droppers served pancakes on Sunday. The blues band Conqueroo alternated with hard rock Wishbone and Rangewar. In the afternoon people gathered outside to read and listen to original poetry; Steve Baer lectured on domes and zomes. Each day at sunset, Douthit led a group in beating down the sun. In the evenings the droppers and their guests reassembled in the theater dome to watch movies by Bernofsky, DiJulio, and a grainy oral sex skin flick featuring Douthit with Poly Ester performing fellatio on him. Then the light show would erupt, accompanied by loud music, and again people would dance through the night. At some point, someone started a rumor that Bob Dylan had arrived, but no one could actually say they had seen him or talked to him. A gaggle of locals from Trinidad showed up: the Andersons who had originally owned the goat pasture, the Italian rancher who lived next door, the librarian, the barber-mayor, the mailman, the Safeway dairy guy, the egg man, and two Chicano cousins who had previously visited with their girlfriends, but who brought along their wives and kids this time. Some very strange characters also showed up. General Wastemoreland appeared dressed in an army uniform topped by a cap that bristled with missiles. A presidential candidate wandered about making preposterously funny speeches. In the meantime, the candidate's brother, just released from a mental institution, molested all the women he ran into. A group of droppers finally interrupted the candidate's speech and ordered him to take his brother away.

Meanwhile Bernofsky seethed inside his private dome. "Everything you can imagine at the height of the psychedelic period of the mid-60s happened that whole week," he said. "The noise was ceaseless. I stayed away and never came close to the dome the entire weekend. I didn't want to see it or participate in it." At dusk on the final day many of the droppers gathered in the Complex. Exhausted from lack of sleep, they didn't have much to say to each other. Beer cans, stained paper plates, whiskey bottles, puke, forgotten clothing, pools of spilt bear, and dried up splotches of macaroni and cheese and guacamole littered many of the domes and the surrounding grounds, but nobody made a move to clean up. The latrines overflowed with waste. Ensconced in the silver hemisphere atop the hill—the original Tom-Joad-chicken-wire-and-tar-paper dome—Bernofsky finally had a chance to think in the quiet of evening. He felt saddened. His vision of Drop City as a gentle nurturing home where creative people could start families and make art for art's sake—no, for life's sake—had been shattered. Drop City had suddenly garnered a new reputation: a place to pursue perpetual fun, where a person could get high, maybe get laid, and feel no pressure to take on any responsibility; a place to chill out for a while before moving on to somewhere else. He sensed the change. From that day on the commune would resemble a hobo camp, a Hooverville; community would exist only in the moment, faces would forever change, no one would set down roots. Drop City had splashed itself upon the counterculture map of America—big time.

"Everything I was naively dreaming about was lost and had been turned into a senseless, meaningless behemoth of empty smoke," Bernofsky said. "I had lost all input." The next day, Bernofsky packed his family and their possessions into an old station wagon and hit the road. The FBI noted the departure and later tracked his movements: "Current investigation at Trinidad, Colorado, resulted in information that BERNOFSKY is believed by U.S. Post Office, and welfare agencies, Trinidad, to have left area in June of 1967, for the Albuquerque, N.M., area to assist in the formation or development of Drop City, South Placitas, or Buffalo City, a beatnik-hippie type community for transients and permanents now reportedly operational and similar to Drop City, Colorado. Standard Form 35 indicates BERNOFSKY proceeded directly to Los Angeles, California, from Trinidad, Colo., and discloses no activities in New Mexico enroute and sets out June 1967 to date, residence and unemployment at San Francisco, California."[124]

Although many revelers also abandoned Drop City after the

| Death of the Hippie at the Corner of Haight-Ashbury |

Joy Festival and followed in Bernofsky's wake to San Francisco, they didn't do so for the same reasons. Bernofsky eventually settled down in a job with the U.S. Postal Service.

The others headed straight for San Francisco's Haight-Ashbury district, where an even bigger extravaganza than the Joy Festival was about to take place—an event so grand, so all encompassing, so perpetual that it transcended all handbills, itineraries, and schedules. It was to make the frolic at Drop City look like a birthday party for a ten-year-old—all thanks to the mass media, which enthusiastically publicized the event free of charge. Rather than a Joy Festival, journalists dubbed the mother of all happenings at Haight-Ashbury, "the Summer of Love."

Once high schools, colleges, and universities let out that spring of 1967, young people from across the country boarded buses, airplanes, and trains, or hitchhiked toward the recently proclaimed center of hippie counterculture. The immigrants could look forward to happenings similar to the Trips Festival and the Human Be-In, which had occurred earlier in the year. Miller compared the love-ins that summer to "19th Century Methodist camp meetings—with the same kind of fervor and the same thirst for a God who speaks through emotion and not through anagrams of doctrine." The exuberance and innocence of the counterculture soon began to cloud the media's natural pessimism, which had grown to epic proportions in recent years after covering a straight diet of war, riot, and assassination. Like the hippies, journalists wanted to believe a change for the good was coming. As they furiously scribbled down the jargon of love and peace in their notebooks, many journalists began to think that maybe the kids actually had something going. Maybe they could change the world. With counterculture gurus like the Diggers, Ginsberg, and Leary, articulating their communitarian dream and hypothesizing about feeding and housing the predicted influx of converts, the media misrepresented their fantasies as a guarantee that the community would miraculously provide loaves of bread and fish to feed all the pilgrims. All the while, writers hinted that cheap drugs and free love were readily available on every street

corner in this faraway special place where many of the laws of
the land and mores of society had been suspended.

Nothing could have been further from the truth. True, the
Haight was booming—at least commercially. Rent for storefronts
on Haight Street skyrocketed to forty thousand bucks a year.
New bands formed to provide music for the free unscheduled
and unannounced concerts regularly held in the Panhandle.
San Francisco radio station KMPX changed its format from
Top Forty to dope music, playing cuts from record albums,
often an entire album, without commercial breaks. The area
also supported an alternative newspaper—the *San Francisco
Oracle,* which didn't provide much news but offered many articles about dope and spirituality, as well as treatises on hippie
philosophy. It did, however, advise any flower children en route
to bring money, sleeping bags, camping equipment, warm
clothing, and proper identification. A hundred-pound sack of
brown rice wouldn't be such a bad idea, either.

Some neighborhood groups and individuals attempted to
prepare for the oncoming tide. The Diggers, who still provided
free food daily in the park, had set up a giant crash pad. The
Switchboard, a telephonic bulletin board, took and distributed
individual messages at all hours of the day and sometimes
steered people to a crash pad or free legal services. A group
of thirty doctors donated their time to a twenty-four-hour free
medical clinic at a corner on Haight Street, mostly concentrating
on drug-related emergencies. The Free Clinic also provided
non-medical services; the Job Co-op aimed to hook kids up
with part-time jobs; and the All Saints Church held a bread-
baking event twice a week and distributed the free loaves on
the street.

And the kids poured in. Many of them wore flowers in
their hair as advised by one-hit-wonder Scott MacKenzie in his
song that climbed the charts in May, promoting San Francisco
as the in-place to be—even though the song had actually been

written to promote the Monterey International Pop Festival. Everyday, they unloaded at the bus stop at the edge of the oblong piece of Golden Gate Park that penetrated the neighborhood. Those who arrived early in the summer, on the four o'clock bus, often found free Digger grub waiting. Just as in the cattle and mining towns of the Old West, a committee of males typically checked out and welcomed the newly arrived females. Some estimated that men outnumbered females in the Haight by as many as five to one. The ranks of the immigrants included not only the sophisticated intellectuals sincerely interested in converting to the hippie LOVE philosophy but also teenyboppers, social deviants, mentally disturbed persons, two-bit crooks, Hell's Angels, reporters, government officials, sailors looking to be laid, toughs looking to beat up flower children, delinquents looking to roll them, and parents in search of lost children. In the meantime many of the established residents beat it out of town, ending up across the Bay in Berkeley.

To exacerbate the already crowded condition on the sidewalks and streets, tourists swarmed to the neighborhood, making fun of the long-haired men, gawking at the flopping breasts on the braless women, and deriding the colorful clothes and odd paraphernalia sold in the shops. For a while the Gray Line bus company offered voyeurs a sheltered ride along the already traffic-jammed thoroughfare but soon canceled the sightseeing tours when hippies began holding up mirrors in front of the bus windows to reflect the passengers' faces.

The Summer of Love officially began at 4:30 on the morning of June 21 with a thousand people celebrating on Twin Peaks, the highest point in San Francisco, to welcome the sunrise. At that time the honest kids searching for something better in life still outnumbered the outcasts, and the mood remained pleasant. George Harrison played a guitar and sang some Beatle songs in the park before hoofing it up Haight Street. Timothy Leary and Allen Ginsberg also made the scene, and Phil Graham steadily produced shows at the Filmore West auditorium. As the summer proceeded, the rising tide of newcomers turned into a flood. By the end of the summer of 1967, an estimated seventy-five thousand people had lived in the Haight-Ashbury psychedelic community, not to mention the other thousands from the Bay Area who frequently hung out in the neighborhood. Many of the more level-headed youth quickly tired of living in overcrowded filthy pads and, disappointed, headed out seeking hippie Nirvana in other places like Mendocino, the Santa Cruz Mountains, and communes—like Drop City.

Gradually, the frightening people began to outnumber the nice ones, and the Haight took on a new look. Drab, ill-fitting, mismatched hand-me-down apparel soon replaced brightly colored exotic outfits on the street. The Health Department closed down the Diggers' free barracks and those who couldn't find room on a floor of makeshift flophouses for fifty cents a night slept in the park, atop tenement roofs, or walked the streets all night. The free Digger feeds petered out, leaving the All Saints loaves of bread as the only dependable free food in town. More than ever, dope supported the underpinnings to the Haight's economy. Small-time crooks soon intruded on the easy-going friendly dope-dealing scene, delivering lousy drugs or simply robbing their customers outright. More and more undercover narcotics agents infiltrated the system, trying to work their way up to the big fish. Then, midway through the summer, the supply of marijuana on the streets dried up, after drug smugglers murdered two border guards on the banks of the Rio Grande.

As the government momentarily clamped down on smuggling, the price for grass spiraled upward, and pot disappeared from the San Francisco scene. LSD remained readily available, but few people took daily trips. With no grass available, the majority of hippies abandoned dope for hard drugs—especially speed—almost overnight. The change to hard drugs didn't end there, as many speed freaks (20 percent by some estimates) started shooting heroin to calm down after a speed run. By August the mood of Haight and Ashbury streets had changed from hope and love to paranoia, and after police discovered two brutal murders, eventually to fear. Those who had spawned the public image and psyche of the hippie—folks like the Diggers, Leary, Ginsberg, the Pranksters, acid-rock musicians, artists, and the early inhabitants of the Haight—now witnessed their dreams of a fraternal, peace-loving, all-inclusive, sharing community turn into an urban nightmare replete with human exploitation, greed, and avarice on a scale of that found in New York City's Time Square. The Diggers, who had stopped trying to feed the hordes by midsummer, now claimed that country living at a commune was the ideal life. The Job Co-op and the Free Clinic closed their doors. Along Haight Street, store managers complained of shoplifting and a decrease in customers.

On October 6, 1967, the inhabitants of the Haight gathered at dawn in Buena Vista Park, a little hillside park at the end of the neighborhood, for a funeral. A trumpeter played taps as the mourners held candles aloft. A small bonfire consumed copies of daily newspapers and the *Berkeley Barb*. Pallbearers carried a cardboard casket containing several shorn beards, strings of beads, and some pot. About eighty participants followed the procession down Haight Street under a banner that read: "Death of Hippie Freebie, i.e., Birth of the Free Man." The procession ended at the door of the Psychedelic Shop. That afternoon the police began picking up any young man who couldn't produce a draft card, presuming he was either a draft evader or a minor. They also began to send runaway kids back to their families. The international scene of Haight-Ashbury quickly faded. Without the vibrant hippies the Haight devolved into urban desolation. It is said that the junkies who remained survived by capturing and eating the neighborhood cats.

"Drop City's experiences that year almost exactly paralleled those of the Haight-Ashbury district," said Gardner. "The invitation to love and joy soon turned into a snake pit. In San Francisco, the countercultural vanguard proclaimed the 'death of hippie' that fall and then moved out. The Droppers moved out, too, though in their case (if not the Haight's as well), self-advertisement shared much of the blame."[125]

. . . Columbia has become the nation's first major university to grant recognition to the Student Homophile League, which argues that homosexuals are "unjustly, inhumanly and savagely discriminated against." . . . Vast reclamation projects have turned swamps into bean, corn and sugar-cane fields, which partly block the natural flow of the Everglades "river." . . . The alienated student realizes that the use of "pot" mortifies his parents and enrages authorities. . . . Often inchoate and inconsistent, instinctively self-serving yet naturally altruistic, the Negro fighting man is both savage in combat and gentle in his regard for the Vietnamese. . . . While the number of people in the U.S. has gone up 30 percent since 1950, solid waste—largely as a result of the ever-increasing use of throwaway packages and containers—has gone up a full 60 percent, to 160 million tons a year. . . . Four Santa Barbara college students lost most of their reading vision by looking straight at the sun. Under LSD they could do this for three or four minutes. Explained one boy: "I was holding a religious conversation with the sun." . . . [This was later exposed as a hoax.] (May 1967)[126]

Time Magazine Article

About two weeks after the Joy Festival at Drop City, *Time* released its hippie issue. Even though the six-page spread included a small color photograph of a half dozen droppers perched atop the triple-fused dome, the article didn't exactly "shine the spotlight on the commune" as the reporters had promised. The legend under the photo read: "Drop City near Trinidad, Colo., the creation of University of Colorado dropouts, who believe that geodesic domes are the shape of the future, occupy nine of them hammered together from old auto roofs." The single sentence devoted to the commune in the text only slightly exceeded the caption: "At 'Drop City,' near Trinidad, Colo., 20 hippie dropouts from the Middle West live in nine gaudy geodesic domes, built from old auto tops (20 cents apiece at nearby junkyards), and attempt a hand-to-mouth independent life."[127]

Another two columns of the piece explained more about the rural commune, "[t]he major new development in the hippie world, some 30 of which now exist from Canada through the U.S. to Mexico where nature-loving hippie tribesmen can escape the commercialization of the city and attempt to build a society outside of society."[128] Instead of Drop City, the magazine focused a spotlight on Morning Star, a thirty-one-acre ranch located outside Sebastopol, California, where about fifty hippies lived on the banks of the Russian River. The accompanying photo taken at Morning Star featured a nude woman, Pam Read, who would later ironically lament that her parents couldn't brag about her appearance in a national magazine because she was "stark raving naked."[129] No doubt, Read's naked buttocks generated more interest in communal living than the shot of the droppers lazing on their domes. Drop City had garnered some recognition, but not fame. Peter Douthit must have wondered if he hadn't chosen the wrong commune to join.

To what extent Drop City itself inspired other young Americans to turn to communal living is up to debate, but there is no doubt a movement of like-minded groups isolating themselves from mainstream society rapidly increased. Estimates vary, but some said that more than two thousand communal groups formed between 1965 and 1970. A December 1970 *New York Times* survey estimated that at least two thousand communes existed in thirty-four states. Other sociologists placed the figure at three thousand for the country.[130]

"Communes in general tested broader, more flexible forms of the family and ways of raising children," author Robert Houriet said. "They started freer, more creative schools and developed home industries that retained the integrity of individual crafts-manship. They established churches, ashrams and lay orders, revived old religions, and created entirely new ones. Above all, they infused their rediscovered awareness of immanent divinity into every action of daily life, seeking rituals and traditions with which to pass on to their children the timeless vision. . . . They intended to become a model for the counterculture of the future, when capitalism would be replaced by a brotherhood of love and men would strive to attain cosmic consciousness."[131]

Just as in the heyday of American communes during the nineteenth century, young people during the sixties formed or joined communes for various reasons. Some gathered together in religious communities across the country—based on both Eastern and Western traditions. Hare Krishna became the largest organization proselytizing an Eastern religion and by 1970 was sponsoring fifty centers around the world, with three thousand converts who often lived in dormitories divided by sex. In U.S. cities such as San Francisco, Boston, Buffalo, Seattle, Columbus, Pittsburgh, and New York, the orange-robed con-verts with shaved heads often chanted and solicited donations on street corners.

Christian Jesus Freaks would also congregate together during the seventies, often renting storefronts as places of worship. The largest of the West Coast Jesus Freak organizations, the World Christian Liberation Front in Berkeley, published its own newspaper, *Right On*, which translated portions of the Gospel into modern idiom. Jesus Freaks distributed the tracts at peace rallies, rock concerts, and in front of pornographic movie houses.

Some Jesus Freaks liquidated their private assets to pool their resources. According to Houriet, "many of them took to heart the message that Jesus is a real force in the world and stayed living with their brothers and sisters in the communal houses that spread over the West Coast: the House of David in Seattle; the House of the Risen Son, in Eugene, Oregon; The Jesus Christ Light & Power Company, Los Angeles. Following the communes, many had begun to move to the country: to Antioch Farm outside Mendocino, California; to Emmanuel Farm, near Sumas, Washington."[132]

The only commonality about sixties communes was that no two communes were exactly alike. The secular, sixteen-acre High Ridge Farm in Oregon featured two acres of gardens, a greenhouse, a main house, an A-frame, and a central building that contained the kitchen, dining room, and kids' dormitory. The only schedule determined who would cook for each meal, otherwise folks randomly helped out with planting, harvesting, and routine chores—such as making yogurt. The farm's monthly budget varied from $250 to $400 per month, which the fifteen or twenty members earned through child welfare checks, selling produce, odd jobs, and landscaping. Ken Kesey also moved his tribe of Merry Pranksters to the Northwest after tiring of continual legal harassment and drug arrests in California. He bought an eighty-acre dairy farm outside Springfield, Oregon, and by 1969 sixty Merry Pranksters received their mail there. But the daily dramas and histrionics finally got to Kesey. When his pals loaded onto a bus to drive to the upcoming rock concert at Woodstock, New York, the writer told them not to return. The few who gravitated back to the Springfield area bought their own homes.

New Mexico, despite its harsh climate and a general hostility toward hippies, quickly became a popular location for communes. Around Albuquerque intentional communities such as The Domes, Lower Farm, Sun Farm, Towapa, and Placitas took root.

Honorary dropper Steve Baer helped build some of the domes at Placitas. But the most notable commune in the Land of Enchantment was the New Buffalo commune, located north of Taos, where one of the founders purchased a hundred acres of land with his inheritance. Sharing a deep interest in Native American culture and spirituality, the founding members constructed pueblo-type buildings, the walls built with adobe blocks made of local materials. The main building featured a large oval meeting room, an adjoining kitchen, and two wings with private rooms that branched out to the sides in a motel-like pattern. Over time, a number of tepees also dotted the property. The members of New Buffalo ate mostly traditional Indian foods—corn and beans—and sometimes partook in a peyote ritual. "At first, the founders welcomed all newcomers," Houriet said, "basing their philosophy on the Rousseauian vision of the earth as it had once been: wilderness over which tribes of men freely roamed, killing no more than they could eat."[133] But the unproductive land and the limited structures could not sustain the increasing population, which at times hovered at fifty residents. After the majority of the founders left, a high rate of turnover persisted. The few remaining long-timers at New Buffalo ceased welcoming new tribal members but continued to welcome and feed guests.

On the East Coast, the Twin Oaks commune emphasized B. F. Skinner–like organization, behavioralism, and technology. Skinner's novel *Walden Two* had presented a vision of utopia in which the citizens performed agreeable work, enjoyed abundant leisure, and experienced intellectual stimulation. They lived in humble efficient homes, only worked at the jobs they enjoyed or preferred, and created their own work schedules. The community's managers and planners based all decisions on what would most benefit all the residents. "Although dyed-in-the-wool hippies disdained Twin Oaks, sociologists, students, and professionals found the commune an exceptional example of social planning and technological efficiency, an encouraging contrast to the typical commune's disorganization, instability, and insolvency," Houriet said.[134] Scholars often compared the structure at Twin Oaks to the kibbutz system in Israel.

In June 1967 the first handful of Twin Oaks members moved onto a former 123-acre tobacco farm near Louisa, Virginia, that had been purchased by a benefactor. The property featured a house and some outbuildings, tobacco, and other crops. Later that summer the members built a second building and established a cottage industry that would help support the community for decades—the manufacturing of rope hammocks which Pier One stores eventually distributed. All who lived at or visited Twin Oaks could choose from a list of jobs to fulfill their weekly work requirement, plus they could execute their tasks at any time they chose and refuse to do any task they considered unpleasant. The community took care of food, housing, clothing, medical care, and some recreational expenses of all members. Members also received a monthly allowance, which gradually increased over the years up to fifty dollars a month by 1994. New members did not turn over their personal assets, but they agreed not to use their personal wealth except for certain exceptions, such as to travel. The social and economic structure at Twin Oaks effectively dissolved gender privilege and financial advantages or disadvantages among the members and continues to do so today.

And then there was the notorious nudist-loving Morning Star commune as featured in *Time* magazine and as satirized in Boyle's novel *Drop City*. Much of Morning Star's 31.7 acres stood in the shade of second-growth redwoods, a site that had once sustained an extensive chicken farm and still featured an apple orchard. Two houses occupied the lot. Lou Gottlieb, a former bass player and comedian with the fifties' folk-pop group the Limeliters had bought the land to subdivide for the construction of upscale homes. While he procrastinated some of his friends, including Ramon Sender, moved onto the ranch. "Sender had actually visited Drop City sometime before moving to Morning Star," according to Perry. "He came back to Berkeley talking about sun worship and moving to the country. After Marin County sheriffs rousted him and his girl-friend Joan for bathing nude in the woods, he recalled Gottlieb's offer. In March, Ramon and Joan, the Jacopettis and Stewart and Lois Brand went up to have a look at the farm."[135]

Gottlieb later allowed others to join them. Most of the early residents of Morning Star studied yoga and Zen and other Eastern spiritual practices. Things started to change at the commune when the Diggers asked Gottlieb if they could start a garden at Morning Star to raise vegetables for their free lunches. After Gottlieb granted permission, a sign allegedly appeared at the Digger store in Haight-Ashbury that announced the program and guided people to the ranch. By July 1967 three hundred people frequently lined up for food outside the commune kitchen. Early on Gottlieb ordered a handful of undesirables to leave, but after the miscreants begged for mercy, he relented. From that moment on, he did nothing to stem the flood of squatters. "The reason Morning Star was a beacon," Gottlieb said, "and its main historic significance, in my opinion, is that it constituted the first attempt to live on land-access-to-which-is-denied-no-one—the legal form of which is 'waqf'—Arabic for divine ownership of immovable property. It was an attempt to solve the principal problem of communal organization, namely, who stays and who's gotta go, by letting the land choose its inhabitants thereby forming a tribe."[136]

In many ways, the naked body of Pam Read was an apt sym-bol of Morning Star, where nudity flourished. Some members removed their clothing once they stepped onto the premises of the commune and never dressed again until they left to go to town. Whenever public officials inspected or raided the commune, naked women greeted them at the parking lot. Conservative-minded neighbors deplored the exhibitionism— not to mention the sex, drug use, and squalor of the Hooverville-type shacks and lean-tos that sprung up in the forest. Narcotics officers raided Morning Star for the first time on April Fools Day 1967, but having been tipped off, the commune members had hidden their stashes. Much to the disappointment of the residents of Morning Star, the narcotics agents didn't confiscate the wine from a group of drinkers who had settled into a corner of the ranch dubbed Wino Flats. That group of antisocial men often started fights, demanded money from visitors, and stole from the community. However, the main focus of life for many of the Morning Star residents remained largely spiritual.

Many people practiced yoga and read the works of great spiritual masters. At one point, Gottlieb recruited an Eastern guru known as Father Ciranjiva to visit Morning Star. The community especially embraced Ciranjiva's Shivite use of consciousness-affecting substances. However, the marijuana and hashish aficionados of Morning Star lost interest in Ciranjiva after he got drunk for the first time and endorsed gut-rot American wine over hashish. He especially praised wine's cheapness and legality. The residents of Wino Flats, oblivious of their spiritual lives, didn't seem impressed.

In July 1967 the police arrested Gottlieb and charged him with running an organized camp in violation of state sanitation regulations. The court fights continued for years. In May 1969 Gottlieb tried to outmaneuver the authorities by deeding the land to God and volunteering to pay the taxes for the deity. A judge refused his request, and the county sent in bulldozers to knock down the numerous odd structures. Three times the residents rebuilt their shacks, and three more times the bulldozers razed them to the ground. The battle continued on and off until 1973, when the last of the residents finally abandoned Morning Star.

Death Knell for Drop City

To be sure, some good times remained for Drop City after the Joy Festival, but the place would never be the same. Drug use increased. The population ebbed and flowed, always changing as more transients flopped there. No one seemed to think of Drop City as a permanent home anymore, as a new breed of visitors descended on the commune during its later stages—mostly teenage runaways, thrill seekers, sightseers, and miscellaneous dropouts. The commune began to attract hippie tourists as well. The *Denver Chinook* reported: "People from Sweden, Norway, England, Italy, France, Persia, Kansas, Indiana, and Kentucky come to Drop City to have their pictures taken with the Hippies to show the folks back home—or to learn the Hippie Philosophy, even though there is no religion or politics or life changing philosophy at Drop City."[137] Jalal encountered tourists who pressed "their noses to the glass and say to themselves, 'aha, there she is painting psychedelic pictures,' or 'maybe we'll see someone fucking.' God, it just drives you crazy."[138] Some celebrities, according to Douthit, allegedly visited as well, including Bob Dylan, Timothy Leary, Billy Hitchcock, Richard Alpert (later Ram Dass), Jim Morrison, and Peter Fonda.

Construction projects continued. Bert Wadman, the artist and architect who had often visited Drop City on the weekends, designed and built a thirty-foot-diameter, twenty-quarter-sphere geodesic dome on his property in Boulder County before acquiring a county building permit, Richert said. "When the county ordered him to dismantle the dome, he donated it to Drop City with the stipulation that we droppers dismantle and move it. Which we willingly did. [It was o]ur largest single dome other than the theater dome, we used it to house the increasing number of transients, continuing our policy of free room and board to anybody who visited." In 1970 one writer reported that the droppers were in the midst of constructing a dome dedicated solely to holding dances. Two artists from Boulder also repainted many of the older domes in carefully planned color-coordinated patterns that lent the community a suburban touch.

With Bernofsky gone, many reporters and writers soon began referring to Douthit as the founder of Drop City. Douthit's dropper name, Peter Rabbit, became permanently connected with the commune when the Olympia Press published his novel, *Drop City*, in 1971. At least one writer, Miller, later cut him some slack: "Peter Douthit received the most attention not only because he wrote the book, but because during his two years of residence at the colony he was the tireless promoter, the greeter of visitors, the outgoing and outrageous figure whose presence dominated the scene. When visitors from communications media showed up, Douthit would come out and talk with them; fairly soon they would end up in his dome, where he could rap for hours. It wasn't hard to stick him with the tag of leader, and it was a short jump from that to founder. My guess is that Douthit rarely, if ever, claimed to have founded the place, but the visitors seem to have taken it for granted."[139] Douthit also seemed to consider himself the big cheese of the commune once the original founders dispersed. Jalal, the mail-order bride, explained that "Peter Rabbit, wanted to [be the bossman] when he lived here, but we wouldn't let him."[140]

As the steady stream of visitors continued, Richert and Kallweit witnessed the fruition of Bernofsky's oracle predicting decadence and decay. Most visitors willingly ate their food but seldom contributed money or work. They took over community space for living quarters, didn't clean up after themselves, and their waste quickly filled the latrines. Stress and anxiety levels skyrocketed at the commune, even for Douthit. "Nobody knew anybody," he said. "People would stay a month or so, get themselves a little straight and travel on. The droppers were going on the same trip over and over again: coolin' out runaways, speed freaks and smeck heads, cleaning up after them, scroungin' food for them, playing shrink and priest confessor—round and round and round." Curl also regretted the change. Describing the winter of 1968 and the spring of 1969, he observed that "for the first time I felt bored and out of it at Drop City. The early Drop City had been a storm of ideas and actions; being at its center was exciting and stimulating. Now it felt direction-less, marginal, out of the mainstream. The eye of the storm had passed and the survivors were left with the cleanup. The world had moved on."[141] A new sign eventually replaced the old Butterfly Sanctuary notice. It read: "NO PHOTOGRAPHS, VISITING HOURS WEEKENDS ONLY 8 a.m. to 8 p.m." Just about a year after the Joy Festival, an unidentified dropper—most likely Kallweit or Douthit—told a magazine editor: "We'll let anyone come for a while, but only those who contribute can stay. It has to be that way. We've learned the hard way, by letting too many come who could only take away. We're thinking of burning Drop City down. We're going to move; start out new in Canada or Virginia or on a farm near here, but this time we'll keep it a secret."[142]

Yet the restless kept coming. One dropper estimated that in its first half dozen years of existence, Drop City housed four hundred individuals for various lengths of stay. Those writers and sociologists who visited the commune during its waning years found the population ever more transient. No wonder they began to assume the wrong origin for the commune's name. "Drop City is appropriately named for it remains a place for people who need to get out of the Establishment rat race and discover an alternative route," one writer said.[143]

In the later annals of Drop City, sexual politics apparently loosened up and drug use increased. Both trends seemingly led to the tragic suicide of a young lady. "Michelle was involved in a triangle with Tom and Peggy [not Kagel]," Kallweit said. "It was causing problems so it was decided that Tom had to choose between them, so he chose Peggy. It turned out that Michelle was pregnant. Michelle had heard a rumor that children born of LSD-taking parents would be malformed, like thalidomide babies, so she aborted it. This devastated her. Her suicide note said that she had wanted to be with her daughter." Richert also reported that "one or two persons were killed either at or very near Drop City" after he had left.[144]

The original dropper practice of total dedication to art proved an ineffectual stimulant to convince new people to surrender their self-interests for the good of everyone. "For mechanisms encouraging commitment through transcendence," Gardner said, "Drop City had only the tradition established by earlier droppers, who completely disavowed such practices. The highest virtue was freedom, and when all is said and done, that is what Drop City was designed to permit."[145]

Richert remained at Drop City for about a year after the Joy Festival. That would have been spring of 1968, when he and Susie were expecting a child. "We left due to Susie's pregnancy," he said. "Her doctor told her she wasn't getting enough protein in our largely rice and bean diet. So we left temporarily, but never came back to live." Kallweit remained the longest at Drop City, staying until 1973. In 1970, when Hedgepeth visited Drop City, Kallweit was still living with Jalal in the cartop zome. Jalal described the commune at that time as "a place to do what you want to do or go through whatever changes you need to go through—if you can possibly do it in an isolated, funky place like this. We don't really have a vehicle for communicating among everybody—except recently it's been our fantastic marshmallow roasts in the evenings."[146] But Kallweit must have struggled to adapt to the character of his new colleagues.

"By 1970 Drop City was populated by the very sort of people that the original Droppers had moved out to avoid," Hedgepeth reported. "Drop City's average age was less than twenty-one, and a Dropper's education had typically ended with a high school diploma. Of all the communards I visited in 1970, these were the youngest and least experienced. But there were also a number of older Droppers who had lived in communes before and were often quite frank about using Drop City as a free ride or a rest stop. The older residents took little interest in Drop City's affairs, which were largely left to the more spirited and idealistic younger members."[147]

That same year, about forty droppers and a constant stream of visitors survived on food stamps and "a sporadic income that seldom exceeded $100 a month." Although the droppers still knew how to party, the fun "came with a certain price," Hedgepeth said. "The kitchen was filthy, and there was no soap because money was short. Hepatitis had recently swept through the commune, and still no one was motivated enough to see that soap was made available. Sleeping quarters were seriously overcrowded. The outhouse was filled to overflowing, and there was no lime to sterilize, it. In 1970 Drop City had become, if it was not from the first, a laboratory dedicated to a totally minimal existence."[148]

When Richert visited the site during the mid-seventies, after his old compatriot Kallweit had finally deserted, he discovered a motor cycle gang composed of speed freaks inhabiting the domes, which, it seems, were infested with insects. Drop Lady also returned for a visit and told Miller that her old home "reminded me of a New York City subway station, kind of, in its qualities—kind of dragged out. Too many people had walked through. Nobody had done the dishes for a long time. It was just like there was none of the nurturing going on. It was just like it was all sucked dry."[149]

By the time his book was published in 1971, Douthit had already fled Drop City and moved on to another intentional community called Libre, located in the mountains near Walsenberg, Colorado. By 1970 the residents of Libre had built seven homes in the forest on the isolated mountainside, but they refused to label the complex a commune. "We're a community,"

Douthit said at the time.[150] Robert Houriet, who visited in 1970, noted that "the domiciles included several domes that were well built and well furnished. My sensation on arriving at Libre was a dizzy fantasy of having climbed the magic mountain to the top of the world and being ushered into a chalet containing the finest distillation of the world's culture." Houriet chatted extensively with Douthit, who at that time had two wives. "Besides writing, cooking and other duties, Peter Rabbit is the community's appointed deer hunter," he reported. "When he surprises a number of deer, he *talks*—telepathically—to them, swearing to them that the flesh of the deer to be *sacrificed* will be used for Libre's constructive purposes. According to Peter, one deer will move away from the others and remain still until shot."[151]

Eventually Douthit abandoned the Libre as well and landed in Taos, New Mexico, where he remained a self-promoter into the new millennium. A 2004 Web site touting the arts around the area has a description of Douthit: "perhaps best known locally as a founding light of Drop City, Libre, Taos Poetry Circus, SOMOS, and the World Poetry Bout Association, Rabbit has been on the cutting edge of poetry and communitarian movements his whole life." Although Douthit published six books of poetry and prose, fame and fortune continued to elude him. He financed his artistic career with work as a motel desk clerk, chef, food and beverage manager, teacher, tutor, substance abuse counselor, house parent, census enumerator, organic farmer, bartender, fund raiser, horticulturist, and "whatever it takes to make a living." Douthit revisited Drop City before his book was published and didn't like what he saw. Of his dome, he said, "That beautiful open space is chopped up into funky littered little compartments, like an ant hill. Weird. None of the droppers had been there longer than seven months, except for Skismasca the Cat. There were nine droppers, all but two sleeping in one dome—the old kitchen—a wall-to-wall mattress scene. No one

Peter "Rabbit" Douthit

seemed very sure where anything was at, but they were learning

| Douthit's Epiphany |

from the very beginning. They had no historical sense of the place; hassles and scenes were repeated endlessly."[152]

In the end, it seems, Douthit learned the lessons Bernofsky had been trying to teach him. "It was the hardest lesson I've ever learned, and before I got it into my thick skull I brought a community down. Some say it was change, even necessary change; but the people aren't as high, the level of consciousness and the quality of life aren't as high as they were before the Rabbit brought down the hordes on Drop City. [Bernofsky] said, 'Trust the Cosmic Forces; they'll take good care of us.' . . . I couldn't hear a word."[153]

. . . *Egypt, having already moved some 80,000 troops into the Gaza Strip and all along its 117-mile border with Israel, announced that it would not permit Israeli ships or vessels bearing strategic materials to Israel to enter the Gulf of Aqaba. . . . U.S. planes have not only bombed Hanoi and vicinity several times recently by day and night, but regularly streak overhead on the way to other targets. . . . By the war's second day, it was clear that the Arab armies were crumpling like so many papyrus tigers. . . . the President named Thurgood Marshall, 58, great-grandson of a Maryland slave, to be the first Negro Associate Justice of the Supreme Court. . . . Muhammad Ali, otherwise known as Cassius Marcellus Clay, 25, was convicted of refusing induction into the U.S. Army. . . . Around her, bedecked with beads, boots, faded Levi's, granny dresses, stovepipe hats, bells and tambourines, 50,000 members of the turned-on generation celebrated the rites of life, liberty and the pursuit of hippiness. The seekers at Monterey had assembled not for a freak-out but for a tune-in—the first International Pop Festival. . . . (June 1967)*[154]

By 1973, after the last desperate dropper had vacated the old goat pasture, many of the original droppers on the board of trustees for Drop City had become disheartened and nervous about the dilapidated condition of the domes and the littered property. A few old droppers visited the site to nail shut the doors to the buildings and set up "No Trespassing" signs on the barbed-wire fence. Steve Baer dismantled the original cartop zome and resurrected it on the grounds of his Corrales home.

| **Bernofsky's Attempted Return Engagement** | Ironically, within a month of the abandonment of Drop City, local scavengers, having learned well from the droppers, descended |

on the domes and gutted them. Vandals also started some fires.

But Eugene Victor Debs Bernofsky wasn't about to let his vision die without dignity. In 1978, thirteen years after founding Drop City, he asked the board of directors for permission to resurrect it from the grave, by restoring the domes to their former splendor. He also wanted the deed back in his name so that he could run things as he saw fit, in case another community eventually formed there. "I wanted to come back and clean it up," Bernofsky said. "I wanted to rehabilitate the land. I wanted to get the idealistic process working again. This time there would be fewer mistakes made. The most important element of success depended on the quality of individuals—not beliefs or things like that." Ten people comprised the board and all had a vote. Much to Bernofsky's chagrin, the board rejected his request.

Years later Kallweit explained his decision: "I really hadn't thought that Gene actually was considering going back in time. I guess he really had a vision, after all. I thought he just wanted the land so he could sell it. Better to have just a myth. Too many ghosts wandering around there. Michelle, the girl who committed suicide, needed to rest. Gene hadn't seen her after she blew herself away. I think I had the deciding vote. I didn't know how others had voted. I just was conflicted. Gene never said, at least to me, what he had in mind. The town needed a rest, the neighbors needed a rest. As Steven King said, 'Time had moved on.'" Richert also seemed to lament his decision in later years. "Now I think that's probably what we should have done [allow Bernofsky to return to Drop City]," he said, "but then I didn't believe it was his property and I kind of believed it was the larger group's property and it had a different purpose. I was thinking, if he wanted his investment back we could give him the money but we couldn't give him the property back."155

Bernofsky considered the rejection another betrayal. "I was astonished. I realized then that Clark had been putting me on for some time. Even though he had disassociated himself from the land he couldn't stand the idea of my going back there and getting it going again." After the board's decision, there seemed to be no reason to any longer maintain Drop City as a parcel of land that would remain forever free. The members hired a lawyer to remove the clause and then sold the property to a local farmer. One by one the colorful domes fell to the bulldozers and Drop City eventually disappeared from the face of the Earth.

At just about this point in my research, I once again ran up against a road block in my attempts to complete the Drop City project. In spring of 2005 I contacted Richert to make arrangements to visit with him in Denver where he resided at the time. Although I didn't expect to reap as much information from him in two or three days of interviews as I had during two winters with Bernofsky, I still hoped to gather enough insight from a different perspective that would bring the quality of my manuscript up to a level approaching a definitive text. Just from the detailed emails Richert sent me, I knew Drop City had played a major role in his life, and throughout the years he had apparently mulled over its impact on himself and the rest of society. However, a few days before I was to leave on the seven-hundred-mile drive from Missoula, I canceled the trip for some reason or other. I can't remember if I'd come down with a cold or if I just couldn't afford gasoline, which had spiked in price as usual as Memorial Day approached. I emailed my apologies to Richert, and in his reply he mentioned that he hoped we might be able to meet some other time.

In the fall of that year, I felt comfortable enough with my health, resources, and my schedule to venture down the Rocky Mountain front to Denver, so I emailed Richert once again with another request to meet. When I got no response within two days, I tried again. A week passed, and still no response. I then telephoned. There was no answer, but I left a message on an answering machine. A week later, not having heard from him, I called again, but this time I left no message. I was beginning to suspect Richert had either died or had experienced a change of heart. As far as Bernofsky knew, he was still alive and kicking. Frustrated, I placed the project aside until later that winter, when I attempted to contact Richert once again, but to no avail. I finally got the hint, although I couldn't understand why he had suddenly started spurning my advances. He had seemed so passionate about his experiences at Drop City and so eager to tell his side of the story. My suspicions eventually drifted toward Drop Lady, but she denied having anything to do with Richert's withdrawal. By that time, I didn't really care. The project had been going on too long, and I was ready to move on, so I let it ride. I mentioned at the very beginning that Kallweit warned me it might be impossible to tell the real story of Drop City. And it seemed that Richert, at heart, agreed with him. Richert allegedly told Curl when they first met that "Drop City is fiction. It's happening but at the same time it's fiction. The only way anybody could possibly write the truth about this place is through fiction."[156]

When I finally gave up on the project, I slapped the title *Drop Dead, Drop City* onto my computer file. At the time I felt the phrase was an accurate expression not only of my own frustration but also of Bernofsky's. I finally conceded that maybe Drop Lady had the right idea all along. The experience had been their own; why try to immortalize the lives of the droppers—in a book few people would probably read anyway? Why should people be interested in Drop City except perhaps for nostalgic reasons? After all, the droppers had failed—as had the Diggers, the summer of love at Haight-Ashbury, and the entire hippie movement. We all had failed in the end. As Boyle and many neoconservative writers have pointed out, the sixties were little more than a decade-long embarrassment. Flower power? Back-to-the-earth movement? Anti-consumerism? Come on—get serious! Our generation's only legacy was some great music—and an even greater target for satire. Just as the droppers often demonstrated, hippies didn't even take themselves seriously, so why should anyone else take them (or us) seriously now? And what did Drop City represent—if anything but a foolish dream? After all, it eventually disintegrated as a community.

Now, I realize, I was playing right into the hands of the neoconservatives. True, my generation—especially when compared to our parents' generation—had seemingly achieved little. Our parents had organized and carried through on one of the most glorious and important engagements in world history—the conquest of fascism. My generation not only lost a war to a tiny so-called *third-world* nation, but we also ultimately chose peace as our weapon—flowers over guns, understanding over hate, equality over lineage and inheritance. Of course, by attempting to reverse a trend that began when a man first killed, raped, or stole from another man or woman, we set ourselves up for failure. A leopard, even if he chooses to, cannot erase its spots in one generation.

Ironically, Drop City came to life at a time when American community had evolved to its most advanced state of social interaction. By 1965, according to sociologist Robert D. Putnam, community groups and organizations across America stood on the threshold of a new era of unprecedented involvement and influence on society. Instead, the movement then abruptly faltered. By the time Gene Bernofsky purchased the five-acre goat pasture, the fabric of American society had already begun to unravel. Over the ensuing forty years, many Americans stopped voting, following politics, and reading the daily newspapers; they resigned from fraternal and professional organizations, and from social and civic clubs; they stopped attending PTA meetings and running for city council and public boards; they even stopped getting together to play bridge or to dance. Putnam noted that we now even bowl alone rather than in leagues. And it all started with the hippie generation. Putnam's research revealed that our elderly parents, the World War II veterans, still for the most part deal in social capital, but we baby boomers have almost completely withdrawn. Did we just give up when our dreams for a better world disintegrated before our eyes like a bad acid trip? Did the embarrassment over our failure to change the status quo cause us to turn inward, away from one another? Our embarrassment has distracted us from asking a more pertinent question: Did we really fail as miserably as we think we did?

It's easier to spot our glaring mistakes, follies, and poor judgment (the drugs, the foolish clothing, the bad hair, a general irresponsible attitude) than to recognize our successes—the advancement of civil rights for more people (though not all), an anti-war attitude that persists in a large portion of the population, a general heightened ecological awareness among all demographic groups. All these achievements could have brought us closer together rather than shame us into hiding behind the walls of our living rooms to experience life vicariously through television screens. Nothing—not low education, not full-time work, not long commutes, not poverty, nor financial distress— is more broadly associated with civic disengagement and social disconnection than society's dependence on television for entertainment, Putnam said.

After forty long years Americans are beginning to recognize and acknowledge this disconnection from each other, and we are beginning once again to think about what makes community work. Across the nation people are once again investigating intentional community, eco-villages, and co-housing. Will they learn from the past? Or, like the droppers, will they head off into the wilderness depending on the serendipitous guidance of those generally undependable cosmic forces? These new community movements can learn much from Drop City—not only from its failings but also from its many successes.

No society exists in perpetuity, of course. The great classical civilizations of Rome, Greece, and Persia eventually imploded, as did the colonial-based empires of Europe. All had their good points and their bad, and although Drop City—Bernofsky's vision of a "new civilization"—existed for only the blink of an eye when compared to many other civilizations, it did experience a splendid golden period. For two glorious years, the original droppers achieved many of their ambitions and realized many of their visions. For twenty-four months, and perhaps a year or two longer, they evaded the birthright of drudgery and conforming that postwar American society had intended for young adults. They succeeded in tuning out the persistent static of war, racial conflict, poverty, mass murders, and social strife in order to maintain optimism and hope. Life became theater as they shifted through the various roles of pauper, pioneer, philosopher, low-lifer, laborer, architect, sociologist, construction worker, latrine digger, scholar, poet, painter, writer, but most especially, artist. Although they fell short of developing a permanent alternative to mainstream American society, the droppers successfully integrated life with art, and art with life. They not only represented the aspirations and dreams of millions of other young people in this country during those trying times, they also proved that many aspects of the unwritten hippie philosophy could work successfully on a day-to-day basis.

Clark Richert

"I often describe Drop City as the best years of my life," said Richert. "It was a period of freedom and the feeling of unlimited possibilities."

Many droppers continued pursuing artistic careers after leaving the commune. Kallweit, DiJulio, and Richert established themselves as professional artists and teachers; Douthit continued publishing as a poet. Bernofsky, of course, wasn't finished leaving his mark on society either. After infiltrating middle-class America he continued to act as a one-man subversive wrecking crew against bland American culture, becoming a thorn in the side of the Establishment whenever and wherever he thought he could make a difference. During the seventies he made a name for himself in the Midwest as a producer and director of black-and-white underground films. During the same period, as he settled into a career with the postal service, he promoted union issues during a period when the majority of Americans shifted

Life after Drop City

their allegiance from labor to management and self-enterprise. His involvement in the U.S. Postal Service included the publication of a newsletter that exposed management abuses of the clerks and letter carriers.

After moving to Missoula in the eighties, Bernofsky restored films for the fledgling Wildlife Film Festival, helped Missoula Community Access Television get off the ground, and produced his environmental advocacy films. He also raised three children. Bernofsky never abandoned the ideals of the sixties, which so many other baby boomers have renounced, but he did adjust his philosophies when he saw fit.

"As for the cosmic forces," Bernofsky said, "I no longer believe in them. In fact, I've come totally around to the other side when it comes to communal living. I think that it's a batch of bullshit to try to build a society separate from the regular society, and that it really amounts to a form of arrogance, and that people are better and healthier just getting themselves a job and working in the society in which we all are."[157]

But Bernofsky neither regrets nor denounces his involvement at Drop City. "While I was there, I woke up every day excited to get to work. There was a great energy at Drop City. We were doing what we wanted to do. Everything we did was creative, from making the domes to constructing the sculptures along the fence line. That was what we lived for. We were making droppings all the time. Our first big mistake was constructing those domes. If we had just put up regular shacks, no one ever would have taken any notice of us, and who knows, maybe I'd still be living at a place called Drop City."

The Truth about the Golden Cartop

Almost as an afterthought during our last session, as I swirled the sugary dregs in my coffee mug before taking one last sip, Bernofsky set me straight on one of Drop City's most famous apocalyptic tales. "You know that story about us chopping the gold

Source of the Nile

cartop off of the Cadillac?" he asked. "It never happened. We were coming back from Colorado Springs with about one hundred tops and it was getting to be late at night. We stopped somewhere around Walsenburg. Parked outside a bar was a fancy car and we joked about chopping off the top to tease Steve Baer. He got really uptight that we were even joking about it. I probably said to him: 'Steve, go in and order some food. Me and Charlie will be right in.' But Baer was no fool. He marched us into the bar ahead of him. This is the first time I've ever told the truth about that story. I guess it's time to set the record straight."

Afterword

Just about the time I sent my manuscript off to begin the process of publication, Bernofsky announced that a professor of media at Fordham University had contacted him about making a documentary film about Drop City. In the early summer of 2007, Professor Tom McCourt and filmmaker Joan Grossman flew into Missoula to talk about the project with Bernofsky. Shortly after the film crew departed, Bernofsky and I met for coffee.

"Joan (Grossman) even got (Drop Lady) to talk about the commune on camera."

I spilled my coffee.

"What? How did she do that?"

"Well, let's just say that Joan has a lot of charm."

"Meaning . . . I don't"

"Well . . ."

Actually, I was pleased to hear the news. I always believed Drop Lady had an important story to tell, and I'm glad she's finally telling it. Plus, now I'm off the hook when the horde of media descends on Bernofsky's back door demanding interviews with his reticent wife.

To see and hear Drop Lady, and to view vintage film shot by Bernofsky during his stay at the commune, look for the documentary *Drop City*, scheduled for release in spring 2010, from Pinball Films, out of Brooklyn, New York.

Notes

1. *Time* 85 (January 1965): 1–4.
2. Unless otherwise noted, the author accumulated all the material attributed to Bernofsky during a series of interviews conducted in 2002 and 2004.
3. T. C. Boyle, *Drop City* (New York: Viking, 2003), 9.
4. Hanna from http://www.amazon.com/review; Sender from http://www.laurelrose.com.
5. *Time* 85 (February 1965): 5–9.
6. FBI report 140-17378 (New York).
7. Judy Kaplan and Linn Shapiro, ed., *Red Diapers: Growing Up in the Communist Left* (Chicago: University of Illinois Press, 1998).
8. The FBI gleaned this information from the *Handbook for Americans,* compiled by the Internal Security Subcommittee of the Senate Judiciary Committee (S. Doc. 117, April 23, 1956), 91.
9. The FBI gleaned this information from the *House Report 1311 on the CIO Political Action Committee* (Special Committee on Un-American Activities, March 29, 1944), 78.
10. *Time* 85 (March/April 1965): 9–13.
11. FBI report 140-1393 (Kansas City), 3; FBI report 140-25527 (Kansas City), 2.
12. FBI report 140-25527 (Kansas City), 2.
13. *Time* 85 (May/June 1965): 19–26.

14. Unless otherwise noted, the author collected all material attributed to Richert via a number of emails in 2004, and all material attributed to Kallweit in emails and other correspondence during 2004.

15. *Time* 86 (July 1965): 1–5.

16. Barry Miles, *Ginsberg: A Biography* (New York: Simon and Schuster, 1989), 337. Much of the information on Allen Ginsberg comes from this work.

17. Joyce Johnson, "Beat Queens: Women in Flux," in *The Rolling Stone Book of the Beats*, ed. Holly George-Warren (New York: Rolling Stone Press, 1999), 42.

18. John Tytell, "The Beat Generation and the Continuing American Revolution," in ibid., 59.

19. Information about the foreign meddling of the United States during the fifties can be found in Howard Zinn, *Postwar America, 1945–1971* (Indianapolis: Bobbs-Merrill, 1971); quote is from page 89.

20. Cab Calloway, *The New Cab Calloway's Hepster's Dictionary: Language of Jive* (New York: Cab Calloway, 1944), reprinted in Cab's autobiography, *Of Minnie the Moocher and Me* (New York: Thomas Crowell, 1976), 253; Kerouac from Miles, *Ginsberg*, 128.

21. Miles, *Ginsberg*, 128, 65.

22. Ibid., 73.

23. *Time* 86 (August 1965): 6–9.

24. Leopold Sedar Senghor, "Negritude: A Humanism of the Twentieth Century," in *Colonial Discourse and Post-Colonial Theory*, ed. Patrick Williams and Laura Chrisman (New York: Columbia University Press, 1994), 32.

25. FBI file 62-13428-7 (New York).

26. Peter Rabbit, *Drop City* (New York: Olympia Press, 1971), 19.

27. John Curl, *Memories of Drop City: The First Hippie Commune of the 1960s and the Summer of Love* (New York: iUniverse, 2007), 41.

28. *Time* 5 (February 1965): 82.

29. Hugh Gardner, *The Children of Prosperity: Thirteen Modern American Communes* (New York: St. Martin's Press, 1978), 35.

30. Timothy Miller, *The 60s Communes: Hippies and Beyond* (Syracuse, N.Y.: Syracuse University Press, 1999), 31.

31. Gardner, *Children of Prosperity*, 2.

32. Miller, *The 60s Communes*, 2.

33. *Time* 86 (September/October 1965): 10–18.

34. William Bradford, *Of Plimoth Plantation* (Boston: Wright & Potter, 1898), 162.

35. Much of the information about nineteenth-century communes in the United States comes from two sources: Ralph Albertson, *A Survey of Mutualistic Communities in America* (1936; New York: AMS Press, 1973), and Ernest S. Wooster, *Communities of the Past and Present* (New York: AMS Press, 1924).

36. The information on twentieth-century communes was garnered from Timothy Miller, *The Hippies and American Values* (Knoxville: University of Tennessee Press, 1991), 7–13.

37. All Fuller quotes in the next few paragraphs are from Buckminster Fuller, "Grand Strategy for Solving Global Problems," at http://www.buckminster.info/strategy/grandstrategy.htm.

38. *Time* 86 (November/December 1965): 19–26.

39. Timothy Miller, "Drop City: Historical Notes on the Pioneer Hippie Commune," *Syzygy* 1.1 (Winter 1992); FBI report 140-2095 (Denver), 6.

40. *Time* 87 (January/February 1966): 1–8.

41. FBI report 140-2095 (Denver), 9; Curl, *Memories of Drop City*, 90.

42. Bill Voyd, "Funk Architecture," in Paul Oliver, ed., *Shelter and Society* (New York: Praeger, 1969), 157, 5.

43. John Curl, *Memories of Drop City: Adventures in the Counterculture of the 1960s* (E-book, 2005), 32.

44. FBI report 140-2095 (Denver), 1, 2.

45. John Curl, *Memories of Drop City: Adventures in the Counterculture of the 1960s* (E-book, 2005, pages unnumbered—no longer available). Curl apparently revised this opinion in his published book, where he wrote: "Curly was always filming everything that happened with his 16 mm camera, and taking stills too. He was documenting Drop City. He'd edited some of his footage into a short, humorous, rapid-cut film that he showed over and over again." Ibid., 53.

46. *Time* 87 (March/April 1966): 9–17.

47. Monk Tyson, "Colorado's 'Drop City': Theme Is Destruction," in the *Denver Post*, December 26, 1965, 46.

48. *New Yorker*, January 22, 1966, Talk of the Town section, 21.

49. Steve Baer, *Dome Cookbook* (New Mexico: Lama Foundation, 1968), 1.

50. Ibid., 21.

51. Ibid., 24.

52. Curl, *Memories of Drop City*, 79.

53. *Time* 87 (May/June 1966): 18–25.

54. Baer, *Dome Cookbook*, 24.

55. Ibid., 25.

56. Timothy Miller's unpublished "Transcript of Interview with Eugene Victor Debs Bernofsky," Lawrence, Kansas, August 5, 1984, 36.

57. Voyd, "Funk Architecture," 163.

58. William Chaitkin, "The Commune Builders," in *Architecture Today*, ed. Charles Jencks (New York: Harry N. Abrams, 1982), 224.

59. Baer's remarks extrapolated from Robert Houriet, *Getting Back Together* (New York: Coward, McCann & Geoghegan, 1971), 216.

60. Richard Fairfield, *Communes U.S.A.: A Personal Tour* (Baltimore: Penguin, 1972), 202; William Hedgepeth, *The Alternative: Communal Life in New America* (New York: Macmillan, 1970), 153.

61. Peter Rabbit, *Drop City*, 46.

62. Ibid., 56.

63. Curl, *Memories of Drop City*, 56, 52.

64. Gardner, *Children of Prosperity*, 35.

65. Fairfield, *Communes U.S.A.*, 12.

66. *Time* 88 (July 1966): 1–5.

67. Thomas Morton, *New English Canaan* (Amsterdam: Stam, 1637), 179–80.

68. Ibid., 137.

69. Bradford, *Of Plimoth Plantation*, 289.

70. Morton, *New English Canaan*, 176–77, 279.

71. Bradford, *Of Plimoth Plantation*, 289.

72. Tom Wolfe, *The Electric Kool-Aid Acid Test* (New York: Bantam Books, 1968), 137.

73. Kesey cited in ibid., 194.

74. Ibid., 233.

75. *Time* 88 (August/September 1966): 6–14.

76. Gardner, *Children of Prosperity*, 35.

77. Peter Rabbit, *Drop City*, 8. Biographical information about Peter Douthit and his experiences with the droppers comes from this book he wrote under an assumed name.

78. Ibid., 8–9.

79. Ibid., 10, 11.

80. Ibid., 12.

81. Ibid., 13.

82. Ibid., 15.

83. Curl, *Memories of Drop City*, 39.

84. Ibid., 84.

85. Peter Rabbit, *Drop City*, 66.

86. Curl, *Memories of Drop City*, 79.

87. Ibid., 77, 109.

88. Ibid., 80.

89. *Time* 88 (October/November 1966): 14–22.

90. Jacob Duche, quoted in E. G. Alderfer, *The Ephrata Commune: An Early American Counterculture* (Pittsburgh, Pa.: University of Pittsburgh Press, 1985), 115.

91. Ibid., 189.

92. *Time* 88 (December 1966): 23–26; 89 (January 1967): 1–4.

93. Curl, *Memories of Drop City*, 108.

94. Ibid., 104.

nn. *Dropper Newsletter*, in Bernofsky's files.

95. Curl, *Memories of Drop City*, 115.

96. Ibid., 119, 120.

97. FBI report 140-2095 (Denver), 21.

98. Curl, *Memories of Drop City*, 120.

99. *Dropper Newsletter*, in Bernofsky's files.

100. *Time* 89 (February 1967): 5–8.

101. Peter Rabbit, *Drop City*, 125.

102. FBI report 140-2095 (Denver), 8; Joseph Nicholson, "Drop City," book review, *Rolling Stone* 86, July 8, 1971, 52; Richert quoted in Miller, "Drop City: Historical Notes," 26.

103. Quoted in William Dudley, ed., *The 1960s* (San Diego: Greenhaven Press, 2000), 201.

104. Figures from Miller, *Hippies and American Values*, 28.

105. Miles, *Ginsberg*, 103.

106. Miller, "Drop City: Historical Notes," 26.

107. *Time* 89 (March 1967): 9–13.

108. *Time* 85 (1965): 9–13.

109. Curl, *Memories of Drop City*, 138.

110. Ibid., 44.

111. Ibid., 85.

112. Peter Rabbit, *Drop City*, 59, 60.

113. Ibid., 60.

114. Ibid., 61.

115. Curl, *Memories of Drop City*, 138.

116. Ibid., 149.

117. Charles Perry, *The Haight-Ashbury: A History* (New York: Random House Rolling Stone Press, 1984), 130. I found much of the information on this subject in this book, which is a wonderful account of the rise and fall of the hippies in San Francisco.

118. *Time* 89 (April 1967): 14–17.

119. Curl, *Memories of Drop City*, 144.

120. Ibid., 142.

121. Ibid., 148.

122. Peter Rabbit, *Drop City*, 73.

123. Curl, *Memories of Drop City*, 147, 148.

124. FBI report 140-2095 (Kansas City).

125. Gardner, *Children of Prosperity*, 38.

126. *Time* 89 (May 1967): 18–21.

127. *Time* 90.1 (June 1967): 22.

128. Ibid.

129. Miller, *The 60s Communes*, 48.

130. Ibid., xix.

131. Houriet, *Getting Back Together*, xiv–xv.

132. Ibid., 344.

133. Ibid., 143.

134. Ibid., 279.

135. Perry, *Haight-Ashbury*, 85.

136. Miller, *The 60s Communes*, 52.

137. Paul Longest, "Drop City, Colo.," in the *Denver Chinook* 3, December 9, 1971, 46.

138. Hedgepeth, *Alternative*, 156.

139. Miller, "Drop City: Historical Notes," 27.

140. Hedgepeth, *Alternative*, 157.

141. Peter Rabbit, *Drop City*, 43.

142. Richard Fairfield, *The Modern Utopian* 2–5 (May–June 1969): 22

143. Fairfield, *Communes U.S.A.*, 207.

144. Miller, "Drop City: Historical Notes," 44.

145. Gardner, *Children of Prosperity*, 35.

146. Hedgepeth, *Alternative*, 157.

147. Hedgepeth quoted in Miller, "Drop City: Historical Notes," 33.

148. Ibid., 34.

149. Ibid.

150. Houriet, *Getting Back Together*, 223.

151. Ibid., 226.
152. Peter Rabbit, *Drop City*, 156.
153. Ibid., 147.
154. *Time* 89 (June 1967): 22–25.
155. Miller, "Drop City: Historical Notes," 35.
156. Curl, *Memories of Drop City*, 50.
157. Miller, "Transcript of Interview with Eugene Victor Debs Bernofsky," 11.

Notes on Sources

Firsthand accounts by former residents of Drop City include *Drop City* (New York: Olympia Press, 1971) by Peter Rabbit, aka Peter Douthit; and *Memories of Drop City: The First Hippie Commune of the 1960s and the Summer of Love* (New York: iUniverse, 2007), by John Curl. Steve Baer writes about his work with the droppers in *Dome Cookbook* (New Mexico: Lama Foundation, 1968). An article about Drop City's architecture, "Funk Architecture," was apparently written by a dropper under the pseudonym Bill Voyd; it appeared in *Shelter and Society* (New York: Praeger, 1969), edited by Paul Oliver.

Books by writers and sociologists who visited Drop City include William Hedgepeth, *The Alternative: Communal Life in New America* (New York: Macmillan, 1970); Hugh Gardner, *The Children of Prosperity: Thirteen Modern American Communes* (New York: St. Martin's Press, 1978); and Richard Fairfield, *Communes U.S.A.: A Personal Tour* (Baltimore: Penguin, 1972).

Two volumes by Timothy Miller proved an excellent source for a historical view of communes and the hippie movement in general. These are titled *The 60s Communes: Hippies and Beyond* (Syracuse, N.Y.: Syracuse University Press, 1999), and *The Hippies and American Values* (Knoxville: University Press of Tennessee, 1991).

Charles Perry's *The Haight-Ashbury: A History* (New York: Random House Rolling Stone Press, 1984), Nicholas von Hoffman's *We Are the People Our Parents Warned Us Against* (Chicago: Quadrangle, 1968), and Tom Wolfe's *The Electric Kool-Aid Acid Test* (New York: Bantam, 1968) were invaluable resources on the hippie movement around San Francisco in the mid-sixties. Other books on the period include Lewis Yablonsky, *The Hippie Trip* (New York: Pegasus, 1968); W. J. Rorabaugh, *Berkeley at War—The 1960s* (New York: Oxford University, 1989); and *The 1960s* (San Diego: Greenhaven Press, 2000), compiled by editor William Dudley.

There are many interesting books available about communes in the nineteenth century. Two that I used were Ralph Albertson's *A Survey of Mutualistic Communities in America* (New York: AMS Press, 1973), and Ernest S. Wooster's *Communities of the Past and Present* (New York: AMS Press, 1924). For an interesting read about the eighteenth-century Ephrata Cloister, consult E. G. Alderfer's *The Ephrata Commune: An Early American Counterculture* (Pittsburgh, Pa.: University of Pittsburgh Press, 1985).

For information about Allen Ginsberg and the Beat Generation, I consulted many of Jack Kerouac's novels, Barry Miles's *Ginsberg: A Biography* (New York: Simon and Schuster, 1989), and *The Rolling Stone Book of the Beats*, edited by Holly George-Warren (New York: Rolling Stone Press, 1999). For insight into the life of the children of communist parents, see *Red Diapers: Growing Up in the Communist Left* (Chicago: University of Illinois Press, 1998), edited by Judy Kaplan and Linn Shapiro.

Acknowledgments

Many thanks to the English and American literature faculties at Brandeis University and the University of Montana for their insight into research techniques and the understanding of literary theory—most especially to professors Jill Bergman, Arthur Edelstein, Katie Kane, Alan Levitan, and the late Phillip Rahv and Milton Hindus. I'd also like to express my thanks to the many instructors and associates who have helped me come to understand the art of writing throughout the years. These include Frank Allen, Judy Blunt, Kevin Canty, Earl Gant, Greg Hanscom, Bill Kittredge, Alan Lelchuk, Bob McGiffert, Ray Ring, Danzy Senna, Dennis Swibold, Brady Udall, Carol van Valkenburg, and Charlie Wood. Thanks to Pippa Letsky for her brilliant copyediting. A big thank you to my friend and former landlord Wayne Kruse for keeping the rent affordable during my last eight years in Missoula. And many thanks to Jo for forcing me to be creative. And a lifetime of gratitude to Mark Medvetz of the University of Montana–College of Technology for giving me the opportunity to teach writing.

Index

Abandoned cars, 105
Abortion, 58
Abstract expressionism, 38
A.C.L.U. *See* American Civil Liberties Union
Africa, 51–52
Air pollution, 147
Albertson, Ralph, 62, 148
Algren, Nelson, 132
Ali, Muhammad, 35, 95, 147, 199
ALP. *See* American Labor Party
Alpert, Richard "Ram Dass," 122, 192
Amarillo Dukes, 176
American Civil Liberties Union, 167
American Labor Party, 17, 21, 22
American Medical Association, 41
Amity Experimental Community, 63
Anabaptist, 37; Hutterite, 37;
Martyrs Mirror (book), 37;
Mennonite, 37–38, 86; Russian
Anabaptists, 37
Anasazi Indians. *See* Native
Americans
Anderson (neighbor), 56, 68, 93, 177
Antioch Farm, 187

Anti-war movement, 58, 81
Apartheid, 128
Apollo spacecraft, 154
Arab terrorists, 136
Arapaho Indians. *See* Native
Americans
Armageddon: The Doomsday Gig.
See Drop City
Atchison, Topeka & Santa Fe
Railroad, 91
Audubon (magazine), 6
Avatar (magazine), 171

Baer, Holly (wife), 109
Baer, Steve "Luke Cool," 99, 109,
111, 176, 188, 209; architectural
philosophy, 100–101; car tops,
100–102; construction strategy,
105–107; *Dome Cookbook* (book),
101; home, 102; newsletter
controversy, 151; solar heating
system, 108; view on hippie
communes, 109; Zomes,
103–104; *Zomeworks*, 102
Baez, Joan, 35

Baha'i, 63
Bard College, 97
Bear Mountain State Park, 24
Bear Research Group, 160
Beat generation, 44; evolution of
    name, 47; definition, 48
Beatles, 58; George Harrison, 181;
    John Lennon, 127
Beatniks, 43
Being Bag (comic). *See* Drop City
Beissel, Conrad, 137, 138, 139, 142
Bernofsky, Bernard (grandfather), 12
Bernofsky, Carl (brother), 14, 25,
    26, 30, 85
Bernofsky, David (father), 12, 15,
    17, 19; David's Notions and
    Trimmings store, 18
Bernofsky, Eugene Victor Debs
    "Curley Bensen," 3, 7, 8, 10, 17,
    18, 21, 35, 39, 49, 54, 63, 66, 73,
    96, 111, 145, 193; African trip,
    50–53; ancestors, 11–15; attempt
    to resurrect commune, 200; on
    Steve Baer, 109; *Being Bag*,
    117–21; bicycles, 7, 23–24;
    chicken killing, 83–85; college
    education, 31–33; departure
    from commune, 178; on Dout-
    hit, 132, 153, 172; Dymaxion
    Award, 166–67; filming, 94–95,
    103; golden car top, 4–6, 110,
    207–209; high school educa-
    tion, 27–30; Joy Festival, 171,
    173, 177; LSD, 162; newsletter
    contribution, 149; on media,
    98–99, 170; on Clark Richert,
    112; on Suzie Richert, 164;
    painting, 39–41; photography,
    25; sexual relationships, 164;
    Wall of Bureaucrat Negativity,
    11; World Wide Films, 4;
    writings, 30
Bernofsky, Maria Adele (mother), 12

Bernofsky, Mrs. "Drop Lady" (wife),
    34, 53, 97, 108, 133, 172, 196,
    202, 203; newsletter contribu-
    tion, 150
Bernofsky, Rose (grandmother),
    12, 15
Bethlehem, Israel, 139
Bicycle sales, 104
Birkins, Charline J., 167
Birth control pill, 104, 127, 173
Black Mountain College, 38
Black Panther Party. *See* Civil
    rights movement
Black power. *See* Civil rights
    movement
Blithedale Romance, The (novel), 61
Blue Unicorn Coffeehouse (San
    Francisco), 78
Bon, The (department store
    chain), 19
Bond, James, 95
Boro Park Club, 17
Borsodi, Ralph, 62
Boswell, James, 11
Boulder, Colorado, 53, 54, 97, 169
Boyle, T. C., 7, 9, 10, 34, 50, 76,
    189, 203
Bradford, Gov. William, 59, 123, 124
Brethen. *See* Church of the Brethren
Brook Farm, 60. *See also* Fourier,
    Charles
Brooklyn Art Museum. *See*
    Brooklyn
Brooklyn Doctor's Hospital. *See*
    Brooklyn
Brooklyn, N.Y., 21; Art Museum,
    115; Asylum, 26; City Market,
    17, 18; Doctor's Hospital, 9;
    Smith's Candy Store, 27
Bruce, Lenny, 127
Bummer (expression), 126
Burroughs, William, 44
Bush, Pres. George W., 11

Cage, John, 38
Calloway, Cab, 47
Casablanca, Morocco, 50, 51
Cassady, Neal, 122
Catalyst, The (coffee shop,
   Missoula, Mont.), 18, 19, 35
Catholicism, 37
Chaffee, Lieut. Com. Roger B., 154
Chaitkin, William, 109
Chase Manhattan Bank, 98
Cheney, Dick, 11
Chernovitz, Bukovina, Rumania, 13
Cheyenne Indians. *See* Native
   Americans
Church of the Brethren, 137
City College of New York, 132
Civil rights movement, 3, 16, 29,
   58, 81, 121, 128, 136, 147; Black
   Panther Party, 81, 128; black
   power, 121
"Clard Svensen." *See* Richert, Clark
Clark Fork River (Montana), 18
Clark, Sheriff James "Bull," 16f
Clubmanship, 81
Colorado State Welfare Depart-
   ment, 166–67
Colorado Territory, 91
Columbia University, 44, 184
Commanche Indians. *See* Native
   Americans
Communes, 56; seventeenth
   through nineteenth century,
   58–62; sixties, 57, 185–91;
   twentieth century, 62–63
Communism, 46, 62, 81, 92
Communist Party, 15, 17, 18, 21, 46
Conestoga, Penn., 138
Coney Island, New York, 22
Corso, Gregory, 44
Corso, Sally (wife), 44
Cosmic forces, 53, 85, 86, 199, 207
Crichlow, Keith, 100
Cross boundary control, 134

Crumb, Robert, 119
Cultural revolution (China), 128,
   147
Curl, John "Ishmael," 89, 95; background, 131–32; on Bernofsky,
   132; on DiJulio, 131; on Douthit,
   132; newsletter contribution,
   150; population control, 174;
   writing influences, 132
"Curley Benson." *See* Bernofsky,
   Eugene

Dairy Joy, 93
Dalton, Karen, 39
Days of Wine and Roses (movie), 45
Debs, Eugene Victor, 15
Decline of the West (book), 48
DeFeo, Jay, 39
DeKooning, Willem, 38
Denver Chinook (newspaper), 192
Denver Post (newspaper), 96, 126, 154
Denver & Rio Grande Railroad, 91
DET. *See* Drugs
De Young Museum, San Fran-
   cisco, 77
Diggers, 79, 179, 180, 183; Free
   Frame of Reference, 79; history
   of, 79–80; Morning Star
   Commune, 190
DiJulio, Carol (wife), 111, 131,
   171, 174; on commune life, 165
DiJulio, Charlie "Arterisio," 110,
   111, 117, 129, 131, 174, 209;
   background, 112; newsletter
   contribution, 150
DiJulio, Christina (daughter), 131
DiJulio, Elizabeth (daughter), 131
DMT. *See* Drugs
Dodecahedron, 70
Dome Cookbook (book), 101
Domes, The, 187
Dominican Republic (invasion
   of), 34, 58, 121

Douthit, Peter "Peter Rabbit," 52, 53, 117, 131, 135, 145, 165, 176, 185; as commune leader, 193; background, 128–29; depiction of Drop City, 152; food stamps, 166–67; golden car top, 110; on Jill, 132; later life, 197; Libre, 196–97; newsletter contribution, 150–51; on Richert, 112, 130; with media, 169

Draft. *See* Military draft

Drop City, 6, 8, 10, 34, 35, 36, 53, 56, 102, 197; Armageddon: The Doomsday Gig, 128–30; art projects, 74–76, 112, 113; attitude of droppers toward Douthit, 133–34; *Being Bag,* 117–21; board of trustees, 135, 199; building community, 113; car top dome, 103, 200; changes at, 174, 192, 193, 196; commodities program, 166; compared with Ephrata Cloister, 145; Complex dome, 171; de-charging session, 86–87; deciding on structure types, 63–64; decision making process, 148; *Denver Post* story, 97–98; description of property and surroundings, 73; descriptions by visitors, 110; doctrines and institutions, 134, 172; drop outs, 194; drugs, 154–55, 192; Dymaxion Award, 165–67; editorial process, 149; fence line sculpture, 113; fight between Douthit and DiJulio, 132; food sources, 85; food stamps, 98, 166–68; first dome, 68–76; golden car top, 4–6, 110, 207–209; inhabitants, 111; Joy Festival, 170, 174, 175–78, 184; junk yard, 112–13; kitchen

dome, 87–89, 97, 197–98; leaders, 145; LuSiD Prod, 119; mimeograph machine, 148; music, 176; myths surrounding name, 74; naming of, 73; newsletter, 148–53; *New Yorker* story, 98; nicknames, 96; nonprofit corporation, 135; overall achievements, 205; ownership of, 135–36; peanut butter, 86–87; Pit, 175; population, 174, 192; postal investigation, 151–52; rabbit hole, 133; sale off, 201; scrounging, 68; sex life, 163–64, 194; sexual roles, 165; signs, 93, 94, 194; solar heating system, 108; suicide, 194–95; theatre dome, 89; tourist attraction, 93–95; Ultimate Painting, 114–15, 176; vandalism, 200; Wadman dome, 192

Drop City (novel by Peter Rabbit), 196; review of, 155

Drop City (novel-T.C. Boyle), 7, 9, 50, 76, 155, 189; plot line, 8

"Drop Lady." *See* Bernofsky, Mrs.

Droppers, 40, 73, 82, 92, 96, 125, 184

Droppings, 6, 117; origins of term, 40

Drugs, 78, 126, 153; DET, 161; Ditran, 122; DMT, 161; electrical banana, 173; good dope/bad dope, 156–57; heroin, 52, 162, 183; IT-290, 122; LSD, 74, 95, 122, 126, 154–55, 158–60, 171, 182, 184; marijuana, 29, 30, 54, 126, 157–58, 182, 184; material prima, 140; mescaline, 122; morning glory seeds, 122; Panama red, 42; peyote, 122; psilocybin, 122; psychedelic, 122; speed, 126, 162, 183; STP,

161; trade, 52, 182; white light-
ning, 171
Duche, Jacob, 142
Dunkers. See Church of the Brethren
Dupont Chemical Corp., 3
Durkee, Steve, 100, 103
Dutch Reformed Church, 128
Duvalier, "Papa Doc," 104
Dylan, Bob, 177, 192
Dymaxion, 65

Eckerling, Israel "Prior Onesimus,"
142, 144, 147, 153
Egypt, 51
Egyptian-Israeli War, 199
Electric car, 136
El Moro, Colo. See Trinidad, Colo.
El Prado Museum, 52
Emergency Crew. See Grateful Dead
Engineering, Art & Technology
(EAT) exhibit, 115
Ephrata Cloister, 137–45; as art
colony, 141–42; fraktur, 141;
Householders, 140, 144;
material prima, 140; music,
141–42; Roses of Saron, 144;
Solitary Brothers, 139, 143;
Solitary Sisters, 139; Zion
Brotherhood, 140, 143
Erasmus High School, 27, 28
Everglades, 184
Experimental films, 154
Expo 67. See Montreal World Fair
Eyes in the Woods, The (novel), 27

Fainlight, Harry, 44
Fairfield, Richard, 110
Family Dog, 80
FBI, 16, 17, 21, 32, 33, 51, 74, 82,
92, 151, 155
Fifties, 46
Fillmore Auditorium, 80
Fillmore East, 80

First Dutch Reformed Church, 27
Fisher's Peak, 73, 91
Fonda, Peter, 192
Food stamps. See Drop City
Ford Motor Company, 66;
Rotunda Building, 66
Fourier, Charles, 60
Franco, Gen. Francisco, 154
Franklin, Benjamin, 145
Free Clinic. See Haight-Ashbury
district
Freedom of Information Act, 16
Free Frame of Reference. See
Diggers
Free speech movement. See Uni-
versity of California at Berkeley
"Friedsam Gottrecht." See Beissel,
Conrad
"Frodo Baggins." See Hobbits
Fuller, Richard Buckminster
"Bucky," 64, 77, 95, 100, 105;
Grand Strategy for Solving Global
Problems (lecture), 66

Gallup poll, 29
Garcia, Jerome. See Grateful Dead
Gardner, Hugh, 56, 57, 116–17,.
128, 195
Gasoline sales, 136
Gemini 4, 35
"General Wastemoreland," 177
Geodesic dome, 64, 66
German Colony of Anaheim,
California, 61
Ginsberg, Allen, 43–44, 46, 48, 49,
171, 179, 180
Go (novel), 48
Golden car top. See Bernofsky,
Eugene
Golden Gate Park, San Francisco,
77
GOP, 136
Gottlieb, Lou, 189, 190

Graham, Phil, 80, 182
Granny dresses, 58
Grapes of Wrath (novel), 63
Grateful Dead, 8, 127, 171; Jerome
  Garcia, 127; Phil Lesh, 127
Great Society, The, 147
Grisson, Lieut. Col. Virgil I. "Gus,"
  154
Guatemala, 46
Guevara, Che, 58

Habitat for Humanity, 62
Haight-Ashbury district, San Fran-
  cisco, 76, 163, 119, 173, 180,
  184; businesses, 78; "Death of
  Hippie Freebie," 183; develop-
  ment of area, 76–81; Free Clinic,
  180, 183; Job Co-op, 180, 183
Hamby, Elmer Lee, 167
Hanna, Pam, 9
Hare Krishna, 186
Harris poll, 121
Harrison, George. See Beatles
Harvard University, 64
Hawthorne, Nathaniel, 61
Heathcote Center, 63
Hedgepeth, William, 195–96
Helicon Hall, 62
Hell's Angels, 125, 171, 181
Helms, Chet, 80
Heroin. See Drugs
High Ridge Farm, 187
Hilton, Paris, 11
Hippies, 43, 44, 56, 57, 78, 81,
  100, 170
Hitchcock, Billy, 192
Hitler, 13
Hobbits, 96; "Frodo Baggins," 121
Ho Chi Minh, 173
Hogan, Ben, 112
Hog Farm, 176
Holmes, John Clellon, 48
Homosexuality, 16, 81

Houriet, Robert, 186, 189, 197
House of David, 187
House of Do-Nuts, 78
House of Risen Son, 187
House Un-American Activities
  Committee, 46
Hudson River, 25
Human Be-In, 169, 170, 179
Huncke, Herbert, 47
Hunter College, 68
Hutterites. See Anabaptist

Icosahedron, 88
Inner Space: The Magazine of the
  Psychedelic Community
  (magazine), 169
Iraq, 104

Jalal, 164, 192, 195
Japanese auto industry, 163
Japanese Tea Garden, San Fran-
  cisco, 77
Jazz Age, 45
Jefferson Airplane, 80, 171
Jesus Christ Light & Power
  Company, 187
Jesus Freaks, 186
Jews, 60
Jill "Patsy Cake Quickly," 131, 171
Job Co-op. See Haight-Ashbury
  district
John Birch Society, 21
Johnson, Joyce, 45
Johnson, Pres. Lyndon Baines, 50,
  121, 150, 151, 162, 173
Johnson, Samuel, 11
Jordan, Clarence, 62
Joy Festival. See Drop City

Kagel, Peggy "Oleo Margarine,"
  83, 89, 111, 165
Kallweit, Richard "Larry Lard," 36,
  37, 85, 105; art, 104, 105, 111,

117; artistic style, 114; background, 70; mirror pole, 113; observations on Baer, 100
Kansas City, Missouri, 40
Kaprow, Allan, 38
Kennedy, Bobby, 163
Kerista commune, 9
Kerouac, Jack, 44, 46, 47, 122
Kesey, Faye (wife), 122
Kesey, Ken, 81, 124, 187; acid tests, 127; background, 121–23; sidekicks, 122–23
King, Jr., Martin Luther. *See* Civil rights movement
Kiowa Indians. *See* Native Americans
Kluver, Billy, 115
KMPX (radio), 180
Koinonia Farm, 62
Korean War, 46
Kurds, 104

Labadists, 59
La Honda, Calif., 121, 125
Lake Erie, 50, 173
Lama Foundation, 100
LaPorte, Roger, 68
"Larry Lard." *See* Kallweit, Richard
Las Animas County Welfare Department, 85
LATWIDNO, 9
LaVigne, Robert, 44
Lawrence, Kans., 30; Massachusetts Ave., 32, 35, 38, 42, 73
LBJ. *See* Johnson, Pres. Lyndon Baines
Leary, Timothy, 95, 155, 171, 179, 181, 192
Lebanon, 46
Lehman-Haupt, Carl, 122
Lennon, John. *See* Beatles
Lesh, Phil. *See* Grateful Dead
Libre. *See* Douthit, Peter

Life of Johnson (biography), 11
Loading Zone, 171
Lockes, Seymour, 80
Lone Star Lake, 42
Loomis, Mildred, 62
Lord of the Rings, The (book), 69
Lovel, Vic, 122
Lower East Side. *See* New York City
Lower Farm, 187
LSD. *See* Drugs
"Luke Cool." *See* Baer, Steve
LuSiD Prod. *See* Drop City
Luther, Martin, 37

Mandelbrot, Benoit, 116
Manifest Destiny, 44
Ma-re Mount. *See* Merry Mount
Marijuana. *See* Drugs
Marshall, Thurgood, 199
Martyrs Mirror (book). *See* Anabaptist
Marx, Karl, 14, 20
McCarthy, Joseph, 46
McClanahan, Ed, 122
McKenzie, Scott, 180
McMurtry, Larry, 122
McNamara, Robert, 16
Medicare, 41
Meher Baba, 175
Meher Charlie, 175
Mennonite. *See* Anabaptist
Merry Mount, 124; Merry Mounters, 124, 125
Merry Pranksters, 80, 125, 127, 187
Mesa Verde. *See* Native Americans
Mexican War, 91
"Michelle," 194–95, 200
Mid-American Art Show, 40
Miles, Barry, 44, 48
Military draft, 81, 104, 129, 136, 163
Miller, Timothy, 9, 56, 57, 74, 162
Miranda rights, 95

Missoula Community Access
    Television, 207
Missoula, Mont., 3, 7, 18
Missoulian (newspaper), 7
Mitchell, Arthur Roy, 92
Mod (fashion style), 77
Modjeska, Madame, 61
Montague Junior High, 22
Montana, 38, 54
Montauk Junior High School, 21
Monterey Pop Festival, 173, 181, 199
Montgomery, Alabama, 29
Montreal World Fair, 66; Expo 67,
    66–67
Moore, Michael, 7
Mormons, 60
Morning Star commune, 9, 189–91;
    legal troubles, 191; narcotics
    raids, 191; *Time* story, 185
Morrison, Jim, 192
Morton, Thomas, 123–25
Moscoso, Victor, 119
Mount Wollaston, Mass., 123
Muchmore, Don, 104
Museum of Modern Art, New York
    City, 115

National Guardian (newspaper), 17
National Insider (newspaper), 98
National Rifle Association, 128
Native Americans, 123; Anasazi,
    91; Arapaho, 91; Cheyenne, 91;
    Comanche, 91; Kiowa, 91; Mesa
    Verde, 91
Nelson Art Gallery, 40
Nest, The, 125, 126
New Buffalo, 188
New Harmony Community of
    Equality, 60
New Mexico, 55
New York City, 15, 42; Lower East
    Side, 43–44, 49, 53
New York Times (newspaper), 185

New Yorker (magazine), 98
Ney, Peter, 167
North Beach, San Francisco,
    Calif., 77, 122
Nuclear power, 136

Okeefenokee Swamp, 4, 7
"Oleo Margarine." *See* Kagel,
    Peggy
Olompali Ranch, 9
On the Road (novel), 48
One Flew over the Cuckoo's Nest
    (novel), 122
Oral contraceptives. *See* Birth
    control pill
Organization of American States,
    121
Orlovsky, Peter, 43–44, 49
Outhouses, 108
Owen, Robert, 60; Owenite move-
    ment, 60

Panama Red. *See* Drugs
Papele, Annie (mother), 21
Papele, Fred, 21, 32, 33
Peace Corps, 51
Penn, William, 37
Pennsylvania General Assembly,
    145
Penrose, Roger, 116; Penrose
    tessellation, 116
Perry, Charles, 190
Perry Lane, San Francisco, 122, 124
"Peter Rabbit." *See* Douthit, Peter
Peyote. *See* Drugs
Philadelphia, Penn., 12, 13, 15;
    Market Street, 12
Philadelphia Mandolin Orchestra,
    12
Pietism, 137, 138
Pilgrims, 59
Placitas, 187
Plymouth Plantation, 59, 123

Polar zonahedron, 115
"Poly Ester" (Douthit's girlfriend),
130, 136, 177; newsletter
contribution, 150
Population shift in rural America, 54
Poverty statistics, 58, 154
"Prior Onesimus." See Eckerling,
Israel
Prioress Maria Eicher, 144
Psychedelic: light shows, 80–81;
posters, 116. See also Drugs
Psychedelic Shop, 183
Public School 132, New York City,
11, 24
Puerto Ricans, 43, 49
Pueblo, Colo., 4, 107, 167, 169
Pueblo Chieftain (newspaper), 167,
168
Purgatoire River, 91
Puritans, 123, 124
Putnam, Robert D., 203

Quakers. See Society of Friends
Quicksilver Messenger Service, 171

Rangewar, 176
Rauschenberg, Rother, 38
Read, Pam, 185, 190
Reagan, Gov. Ronald, 81, 104, 163
Record sales, 136
Red Belt of the Bronx, 21
"Red diaper" babies, 21
Rhombo-icoso-dodecahedron, 99,
105
Richert, Clark "Clard Svensen,"
35, 36, 53, 54, 57, 63, 66, 68, 73,
86, 89, 96, 108, 111, 117, 145,
172, 201; art, 40–41, 104; artistic
style, 114; background, 37–39;
departure from commune, 195;
influences, 38–39; newsletter
contribution, 149–50; poster
career, 116

Richert, Suzie (wife), 164
Riga, Latvia, 12
Right On (newspaper), 186
Rip Off Press, 119
RMK-BRJ, 68
Rolling Stone (magazine), 171
Rothko, Mark, 38
Rubin, Jerry, 171
Russia, 16
Russian Anabaptists. See Anabaptist
Russo-Japanese War, 13

Sandoz Pharmaceuticals, 158, 160
San Francisco Comic Book
Company, 119
San Francisco Mime Troupe, 80, 81
San Francisco Oracle (newspaper), 180
San Francisco State College, 77, 80
Sangre de Cristo Mountains,
Colo., 73
Sante Fe Trail, 91
School of Living, 62
Scott, Chloe, 122
Sebastopol, Calif., 185
Seburn, Roy, 122
Selby Jr., Hubert, 132
Selma, Alabama, 29
Sender, Ramon, 10, 190
Senghor, Leopold Sedar, 51
Sermon on the Mount (biblical text),
38, 137
Sexual revolution, 163
Shah of Iran, 81
Shakers, 60
Sinclair, Upton, 62
Sir Douglas Quintet, 171
Snake Pit, The (movie), 45
Snatch (comic book), 119
Snyder, Gary, 171
Socialism and socialists, 16, 21
Society for the Preservation of
Early American Standards, 63
Society of Friends, 37, 138

Society of Seventh Day Baptists of
    Ephrata, 145
Solid waste, 184
Sometimes a Great Notion (book), 122
SOMOS, 197
Special Committee Un-American
    Activities, 21, 92
Speed. *See* Drugs
Spring Mobilization to End the
    War in Vietnam, 173
Stanford University, 122
Stanley, Augustus Owsley III,
    160–61, 171
Staten Island Ferry Terminal, 25
Statue of Liberty, 26, 66
Steinbeck, John, 63
Stipleman, Maria Adele. *See* Ber-
    nofsky, Maria Adele
Stone, Bob, 122
STP. *See* Drugs
Student Homophile League, 184
Summer of Love, 169, 179–84
Sun Farm, 187
Szabo, 44

Taos, New Mexico, 39
Taos Poetry Circus, 197
Temple University, 12
Tensegrity, 65
Texas Christian University, 112
Third Eye, The, 116
Time (magazine), 54, 169, 170,
    184, 189
Tolstoy Farm, 63
Towapa, 187
Trembling Waters (film), 3
Trinidad, Colo., 6, 55, 85, 96, 107,
    167, 185; El Moro, 56, 91;
    history of, 89–92, 93
Trinidad State Junior College, 92
Trips Festival, 127, 179
Trump, Donald, 11
Twiggy, 136

Twin Oaks, 188–89
Tyson, Monk, 96
Tytell, John, 45

Ultimate Painting. *See* Drop City
Underground comics, 117–20
Undermining Yellowstone (film), 3
Unemployment rate, 136
United Fruit Company, 46
University of California at Berkeley,
    21, 29; free speech movement, 95
University of Colorado, Boulder,
    54, 64, 66, 112, 117, 185
University of Kansas, 6, 30, 31, 33,
    35, 38, 39, 41, 53, 95, 98
University of Oregon, 122
U.S. Dept. of Agriculture, 168

Vanderbeek, Stan, 89
Veterans Hospital, Menlo Park,
    Calif., 122
Vienna, Austria, 13
Vietnam War, 3, 29, 33, 34, 35, 38,
    41, 42, 50, 58, 68, 81–82, 95,
    104, 128, 136, 147, 154, 162,
    173, 184, 199
Volkswagen, 50
Voyd, Bill, 88, 108

Wadman, Burt, 69, 192; spinning
    painting, 116; Wadman sphere,
    116. *See also* Wadmans
Wadman, Peggy, 69. *See also*
    Wadmans
Wadmans, 112
Wall of Bureaucratic Negativity, 11
Waqf, 190
Waste water treatment, 68
Watts riots, 50
Way to Wealth (book), 145
White, Lieut. Col. Edward H., 154
Wichita, Kan., 37, 39
Wildlife Film Festival, 207

Williams, Huw, 63
Wilson, Clay, 119
Wishbone, 176
Worker, The (newspaper), 17
World Christian Liberation Front,
  186
World Poetry Bout Association,
  197
World War II, 13, 16, 44, 46
World Wide Films, 4

Yale University, 104
Yellowstone National Park, 3

Zap Comix (comic book), 9, 119
Zinn, Howard, 46
Zippers, 15
Zomes. *See* Baer, Steve
Zomeworks. *See* Baer, Steve
Zonahedron, 103
Zoo (book), 122

LaVergne, TN USA
20 January 2010
170593LV00003B/1/P